The Ascent of Britain

The Ascent of Britain

PETER WALKER

SIDGWICK & JACKSON
LONDON

First published in Great Britain in 1977
Copyright © 1977 Peter Walker

TO TESSA

ISBN 0 283 98338 8

*Printed and bound in Great Britain by
The Garden City Press Limited
Letchworth, Hertfordshire SG6 1JS
for Sidgwick and Jackson Limited
1 Tavistock Chambers, Bloomsbury Way,
London WC1A 2SG*

CONTENTS

	Acknowledgments	6
Chapter		
I	The Role of Patriotism	7
II	The Tory Tradition	14
III	Equality of Opportunity	40
IV	The Tories and the Trade Unions	50
V	A Programme for Industrial Democracy	67
VI	Government & Industry working together	85
VII	Our Inner Cities	124
VIII	Racial Harmony	147
IX	The Liberation of the Permanent Tenantry	163
X	Positive Planning	177
XI	Temporary Expedients or Permanent Solutions?	182
XII	The Ascent of Britain	202
	Index	216

ACKNOWLEDGMENTS

The author and publishers are grateful to the following for permission to use extracts from their copyright material: (pages 7, 9 and 10) Cassell and Co. for Sir Winston Churchill's *War Speeches*; (page 12) Secker and Warburg for 'The Lion and the Unicorn' from *The Collected Essays and Journalism of George Orwell*; (page 25) Allen Lane for Anthony Sampson's *Macmillan*; (pages 26 and 41) Macmillan Publishers Ltd for Harold Macmillan's *Memoirs*; (pages 36 and 37) Colonel Maxwell for Julian Amery's *Joseph Chamberlain and the Tariff Reform Campaign*; (page 38) Hamish Hamilton for A. J. P. Taylor's *Rumours of War*; (page 57) The *Daily Telegraph* for their supplement article on Edward Heath; (pages 64 and 65) The National Union of Mineworkers for a quotation from their magazine 'Miner'; (pages 148 and 149) The British Council of Churches for *The New Black Presence in Britain – a Christian Scrutiny*.

CHAPTER I

The Role of Patriotism

'I speak to you for the first time as Prime Minister in a solemn hour for the life of our country, of our empire, of our allies and, above all, of the cause of freedom.'

A S far as I can remember, these were the first words I heard spoken by a politician. They were spoken by Winston Churchill in a broadcast shortly after he became Prime Minister in 1940. I was living in a suburban house in South Harrow, an eight-year-old attending the nearby primary school, a playground footballer and an active member of the Cubs. To me the war was a matter of great excitement. It was obviously the major event being discussed by my family. My father, a factory worker at the H.M.V. factory, to which he cycled each day, was already working on production for the war. My mother was working in a small local factory making blackout blinds. My brother, four years older than myself, and attending the local grammar school, was eager to join the Navy and commented with considerable authority upon every scrap of news on the war at sea.

Instead of playing cowboys and Indians with the other boys in the street, we now played games in which we constantly defeated the Germans.

Winston Churchill's wartime speeches had a considerable effect upon my political attitudes. His was a remarkably effective broadcasting voice. The family gathered round the radio in eager anticipation of his words, knowing that they would be both courageous and encouraging.

In that first broadcast of 19 May 1940, towards the conclusion of his speech, he said:

Our task is not only to win the battle but to win the war. After this battle in France abates its force, there will come the battle for our island, for all that Britain is and all that Britain means. That will be the struggle. In the supreme emergency we will not hesitate to take every step, even the most drastic, to call forth from our people the last ounce and the last inch of effort of which they are capable. The interests of property, the hours of labour, are nothing compared with the struggle for life and honour, for right and freedom, to which we have vowed ourselves.

The first politician I had heard speaking was making a total call to patriotism, and it is a simple approach to patriotism that has motivated and affected my political attitudes in the thirty-five years since I listened as a schoolboy to those inspiring words of Winston Churchill.

In the next three years we were to spend most of our lives, apart from school, in an Anderson shelter dug out of the garden some four or five feet below the surface. It was about ten foot long and ten foot wide, with a corrugated steel roof, cement foundations, and a great deal of earth piled on top. It was far more exciting than the customary bedroom, with visits by insects constantly enlivening the scene. The fact that the four of us were together in one room, my brother and myself sleeping on two bunks above our parents, meant that we enjoyed a great deal more of each other's conversation than would otherwise have been the case.

I was fortunate in having parents who always encouraged us, and were ambitious that their children should get to a grammar school and have a good education. Throughout the war they took us every week to the public library and made sure we listened to a whole range of captivating radio programmes. I can recall very little political discussion, for there were no political divisions between us. Any critic of Winston Churchill was condemned. When Mrs Attlee visited my school in order to open a fund-raising fête for some wartime effort, I was thrilled when she spoke to me at my stall and gave me her autograph. I had no conception that she was the wife of a leading socialist. I had no idea what a socialist was!

Spending the formative years of seven to thirteen in wartime London as a member of an intensely patriotic family was bound to have lasting effects. I can remember collecting scrap metal to build Spitfires and delivering the weekly roster for the fire watchers in our street. My mother and father, both fire watchers, were issued with tin helmets and sent to training school to be trained in the disposal of incendiary bombs. An unexploded bomb fell two doors away. I met members of the Polish squadron stationed at Northolt aerodrome. The tiles were knocked off our roof by a bomb and we had shrapnel in the garden. These were the everyday excitements of being a schoolboy at such a time in such a place.

All minds were concentrated on the anxieties and hopes for victory in the war. There was little interest in pre-war politics, in spite of the fact that both my mother and father had regularly done voluntary work for the Conservative Party during election campaigns. They were forgiving towards Neville Chamberlain's policy of appeasement, believing that he had been stalling for time in order that Britain might be more prepared. They had immense admiration and devotion for Winston Churchill, which was certainly shared by their children.

I remember well the impact made upon me when, later in 1940 after France had fallen, we listened to Churchill speaking again to the nation. Already I was old enough to know of the heroes of the past, and it was tremendously exciting suddenly to hear my Prime Minister say to me over the radio,

> Therefore we must regard the next week or so as a very important period in our history. It ranks with the days when the Spanish Armada was approaching the Channel and Drake was finishing his game of bowls, and Nelson stood between us and Napoleon's Grand Army at Boulogne. What is happening now is on a far greater scale, of far more consequence to the life and future of the world and its civilisation than these brave old days of the past.

He then went on to give us confidence in our ability to resist an invasion.

> Besides this we have more than a million and a half men of the Home Guard who are just as much soldiers of the regular army as the Grenadier Guards and who are determined to fight for every inch of the ground and for every village and every street.

My father was a member of that Home Guard. My street was ready for battle.

I knew that I was at the heart of history. Churchill ended that speech with the words,

> What Hitler has done is to kindle a fire in British hearts here and all over the world which will grow long after all traces of the conflagration he has caused in London have been removed. He has lighted a fire that will burn with a steady and consuming flame until the last vestiges of Nazi tyranny have been burnt out of Europe, until the old world and the new can join hands to rebuild the temple of man's freedom and man's honour upon foundations which will not soon or easily be overthrown.

The Nazi tyranny was burnt out of Europe. We did join hands with the new world across the Atlantic. Five years later victory was ours, and I went with my mother and father to the centre of London and saw for the first time the great man himself being cheered through Parliament Square. Later we stood outside the Palace cheering the King and Queen and Winston Churchill together on the balcony. I witnessed the happiness and the joy of thousands of my ordinary fellow countrymen celebrating a victory in which they had all played their part.

It was therefore a surprise that shortly afterwards a general election was held. I was three when the previous general election had taken place. Now I was thirteen, and attending Latymer Upper School, to which I had been fortunate enough to obtain a scholarship. I was surrounded by boys of high ability, and a teaching staff that inspired. I had begun to enjoy for the first time the process of thought, and to possess a strong thirst for knowledge – debate, discussion and argument became a major new pleasure.

A general election? What did this mean? I had only known a nation that was united with but a single purpose in mind. Who were these political parties, and was it really the wish of anybody to replace Winston Churchill as Prime Minister? I questioned my parents. I discovered their allegiance to the Conservative Party and their willingness to join the local committee in canvassing and other electioneering work. I remember asking them why they were Conservatives. One distinct argument I can remember was that under the Conservatives there was a much greater diversity of choice; nationalization meant that there would be only one firm producing one product and not very efficiently at that, whereas now we could choose from a whole range of products produced by a wide range of firms.

Another of their arguments was that before the war, in the face of the growing might of Hitler, it had always been the Labour Party who had wanted to disarm. The advantages of free enterprise and the Conservative Party's desire that Britain should remain strong appeared to be the basic issues that determined their political views. For a questioning thirteen-year-old my parents' word alone was not enough; I shared the desire of most teenage children to disagree with their parents.

I went with great enthusiasm to the local political meetings. There were four candidates, Conservative, Labour, Liberal, and one from a left-wing party that fought in the 1945 election called the Commonwealth Party, led by Sir Richard Acland, and I was able therefore to hear the whole range of political arguments. Fascinated by the whole process of politics, eager to come to conclusions about my own viewpoint, I went as ever to a man to whom I owe a great deal, Mr Goodhead. Mr Goodhead was not only the most important teacher at the primary school I had attended between the ages of five and eleven, but in the evenings he also acted as the librarian of the public library which was housed in the school classrooms. I told him I wanted to read some books that would give me the viewpoints of all the political parties. The selection in this small library was narrow, and he obtained other books for me. I remember his main suggestion on the Labour Party was a large volume written by George Bernard Shaw called *An Intelligent Woman's Guide to Socialism, Capitalism, Sovietism and Fascism*. I read *Das Kapital*; I found this rather hard and difficult going, but very convincing in parts. The books representing the Conservative cause tended to be biographies of former Conservative statesmen. There was relatively little literature to support the modern Liberal Party, apart from some of the works prepared for Lloyd George in the early 1930s.

I came to the conclusion that my parents were right and I joined them in campaigning in the 1945 election. I delivered literature and leaflets to much of South Harrow. I saw to it that our own semi-detached house had more posters in its windows than any other house in the locality. I applauded the Tory candidate at meetings and joined in with the hecklers at meetings of the opponents. It was a new excitement, a new adventure, a fascinating battle of a new type, and one in which the side that I had decided to support was certain to succeed – after all it had Winston Churchill as its leader and it was inconceivable that those cheering thousands I had so recently seen in Parliament Square should do other than vote for him to continue as our Prime Minister.

Thus I quickly learned the total unpredictability of politics when a few months later (there was in 1945 a delay between the voting and the declaration of the poll due to servicemen's votes having to be collected from overseas) the Conservative Party and Churchill suffered a massive defeat.

Thirty years after the 1945 defeat of the Conservative Party there is a similarity with the current issues. There is still the battle between free enterprise and nationalization. There is still the argument as to whether we should strengthen our defence or reduce our defence expenditure. And my basic approach to politics is still based upon a recognition of the very real importance of patriotism in its most enlightened form as the basis of political progress.

If some of the issues are similar the situation is very different. Thirty years ago when I was at school being taught geography the red patches on the map were British and the few remaining colours were the rest of the world. History was taught to show us how Britain had become one of the great world powers. Now almost all of the British Empire has disappeared, we are far from being the greatest of world powers, and in place of the national pride that I witnessed on victory day there is a mood of cynicism and depression. As a nation we seem to have lost our way in those thirty years.

Some would argue that the passing of national greatness is to be welcomed. Those cosmopolitan 'friends of every country but their own' so bitterly assailed by Disraeli are happy to reinforce a mood of self-doubt and lack of confidence. They are, however, involved in a dangerous enterprise. Political thinkers of both left and right have long recognized the force of patriotism. Writing in 1940, George Orwell saw patriotism as a network of feelings and loyalties which served to preserve our identity, our sense of what we were. 'In England,' Orwell wrote, 'patriotism takes different forms in different classes, but it runs like a connecting thread through nearly all of them. Only the Europeanised intelligentsia are really immune to it.'

For a nation patriotism represents a uniquely cohesive factor, binding a nation together and giving it strength. Patriotism represents the highest unifying factor that a nation can possess on a secular level.

My own political thinking was very much affected by reading Lord Milner's definition of patriotism. According to him, patriotism meant that at home you pursued policies the object of which was to see that every person born to be a citizen of your country rejoiced in that birthright. This, he argued, meant pursuing policies of social reform that would eventually eradicate poverty and squalor.

The restoration of a national patriotism is of vital importance in its effect upon the individual. When patriotism departs, cynicism enters. The individual seems to have less desire to be creative – and it is the aggregate desire of individual citizens to be creative that brings about the advancement of a nation's resources.

Britain must readjust and face her situation realistically. Our era as a world power is finished and will never return.

CHAPTER
II

The Tory Tradition

IT was a stroke of good fortune for me that I met Leo Amery, one of our most distinguished pre-war statesmen and the father of Julian Amery, when in my early teens. I had just made a speech at the Conservative Party Conference, and he was kind enough to encourage me in my political activities.

From time to time he invited me to his home in Eaton Square. He talked to me of his experiences and I enjoyed the benefit of his very considerable political wisdom. He gave me books to read and spoke to me about the figures from the past that had made an impression on him.

He particularly urged me to read the works of Edmund Burke. There is strangely enough a considerable similarity between Burke and Leo Amery: neither of them held the highest offices of government, but both of them always had a considerable influence on their contemporary scene. In the same way that the thoughts and wisdom of Edmund Burke made an impact upon politics and philosophy for decades after his death, so too will people in the future turn to the writings and views of Leo Amery for inspiration.

Edmund Burke was the founder of modern British Conservatism. Indeed the late Richard Crossman regarded him not only as the intellectual father of the Conservative Party but as the philosopher of English political life as a whole.

Burke's central theme was an attack upon the arrogance of what he called 'private reason', the arrogance of the intellectual who believes that he can reform society without taking notice of the collective feelings of his compatriots, or the history of the society in which he lives; what he was attacking was very much like the ideology of the Marxist, socialist, or believer in extreme *laissez-faire* of our own day. For, just as in the eighteenth century men believed that the scientific discoveries of the Enlightenment enabled them to plan the future development of society, so, in our own time, the development of Marxism has led many to believe that politics can be reduced to ideology.

Burke's idea was that every man's private reasonings must be carefully checked against the evidence of the similar reasonings of others in his society, and against the particular traditions of that society. For the institutions which might well work in one society would not necessarily work if transplanted into another. Burke applied this analysis in his defence of the American colonists against George III, when he argued that it was vital to govern America according to the circumstances created by history and geography, and 'not according to abstract ideas of right, by no means according to mere general themes of government, the resort to which appears to me, in our present situation, no better than arrant trifling'.

Later Burke attacked the French Revolution precisely because the French had not adopted the empirical methods of the American colonists and had ignored the need for practical reforms through their excessive attachment to ideology. Burke compared the French Revolution with the 'Glorious Revolution' of 1688 in Britain. Why was it that the French Revolution led to bloodshed and tyranny while the English revolution led to a more practical defence of existing liberties? Burke saw that this was because the English preserved what they were not compelled to destroy; although they departed from the precedents of history they did so with great reluctance. Burke was not hostile to reform, he was by no means an unthinking reactionary, but he realized that when something new was created legitimacy for it could only be obtained by absorbing it into a national tradition which had already existed for some time. That is the principle that was neglected in the French and Russian revolutions. Those revolutions lacked men with the ability to improve and the disposition to preserve, which Burke saw as the hallmark of a great statesman. Burke did not believe there were any general laws of politics, and, as he argued in *Reflections on the Revolution in France*, 'circumstances (which for some gentlemen pass for nothing) give in reality to every political principle its distinguishing colour and discriminating effect. The circumstances are what render every civil and political scheme beneficial or noxious to mankind.' Thus it is that there is no contradiction in the Conservative supporting the American revolution but opposing the French; or in supporting state intervention in the nineteenth century while being, on the whole, opposed to it today in the twentieth century. It is all a matter, as Burke realized, of 'circumstances'.

Burke noticed the central principle of Conservatism, namely that every political system and every constitution is a balance between opposing elements, a balance between reform and preservation. Either extreme is likely to be mistaken: too rapid and too radical reform is dangerous, just as there is a danger in retaining the *status quo* after it has ceased to have any real justification. Radicals commonly underestimate the first of these dangers, and continental right-wingers the second. In his *Reflections on the Revolution in France* Burke argued that 'a state without the means of some change, is without the means of its conservation'. It is the reforming nature of British Conservatism that has saved it from the fate of many continental right-wing parties doomed to remain permanent minorities in their own countries.

In his speech on the East India Bill Burke put forward his views on reform. There are, he said, abuses in all governments, and all abuses need to be reformed, but small abuses should be left alone if they are not dangerous. It is only 'large' abuses that justify us in destroying long-held rights in order to reform them – and by a large abuse Burke meant that it 'ought to be utterly incurable in the body as it now stands constituted'. 'All this,' he said, 'had to be made as visible to me as the light of the sun, before I did strike off an atom of their charter.'

Often, of course, the statesman is faced not merely with an abuse that requires reform but with a conflict of rights. For in many political situations there is some right on both sides, and the question is how to reach a compromise. This was the problem facing the British government in dealing with the American colonists. Burke believed that intelligent political action could have secured a compromise. But instead of this the British insisted upon standing on their 'rights', thereby losing the allegiance of the Americans. The duty of the statesman, on the contrary, is not to 'aggravate but to reconcile'. In this sense, Burke realized that the *status quo* itself cannot be maintained without change. It somehow has to have change built into it. For this reason it is foolish to argue about whether Burke was really a Liberal or a Conservative. For, in order to conserve, one has to liberate; and liberation is not genuine unless it also conserves.

Government for Burke involved essentially the practical problem of how to rule equitably in the historical circumstances facing a country. Government, he argued, is 'a practical thing made for the happiness of mankind, and not to furnish it a spectacle of uniformity, to gratify the schemes of visionary politicians'.

The charge against the French revolutionaries was precisely that they did not understand the limitations of political action, and so removed the barriers to absolute power and tyranny. A statesman, according to Burke, should not see his country 'as nothing but carte blanche upon which he may scribble whatever he pleases' but 'always consider how he shall make the most of the existing materials of his country'.

In his book *The Suspecting Glance* Conor Cruise O'Brien argues that Burke was essentially a suspicious thinker – and there is a sense in which this is true. Burke realized more than most of his contemporaries that civilization rested upon an extremely thin crust and that if the barriers to absolute power were destroyed the most frightful horrors would ensue. He would have been less surprised than most of his contemporaries at the tyrannies which have marked the twentieth century, tyrannies based not upon aristocracies or monarchies but upon the power of whole peoples. He realized that democratic totalitarianism represents the worst government of all, and that is why he was so adamant about preserving the barriers to absolute rule; strong healthy local government, the checks and balances of the English constitution, the limitations of state power. In this sense Burke is the first modern political thinker. Government, in his view, should be centrally concerned with the preservation of law and order, the maintenance of property rights, and the improvement of the condition of the people.

It is, then, in his understanding of the practical nature of politics that Burke's importance to present-day Conservatives lies. His theory of balance, his awareness of the connections between tradition and reform, and his distrust of ideology all make him a founding father of Conservative thinking.

The greatest practical problem facing the politician today is how to make the best use of the assets we have as a nation. Our assets consist of the abilities of our people and the raw materials that we possess. Our future purpose must be to use these resources to the fullest extent, and by so doing to achieve a success out of all proportion to both the size of our population and the extent of our raw materials. Recent history shows how national revivals can take place: the remarkable recovery of West Germany from a position of devastation; the fast and continuous rise of Japan; the speedy recovery of France from a period of disillusionment and disorder.

National revival must be based upon economic strength. This is not to be materialistic, for only economic strength will enable Britain to eliminate the poverty that still exists in our country, and to patronize generously the arts and cultural activity, so providing a better and fuller life for all. It is only from a position of economic strength that we can make a contribution to the development of the continents of Africa and Asia, showing that as in the past we eliminated slavery and tribal warfare so in the future we will contribute equally to the elimination of poverty, hunger and disease.

Britain has a considerable potential for achieving economic success. First, we have a worldwide commercial connection, which is the result partly of our history and partly of our economic need to purchase most of our raw materials abroad. Secondly, we possess a know-how in international trade that is still probably greater than that possessed by any other nation. The basic mechanism of the City of London, although capable of improvement, is an invaluable asset to a nation seeking new commercial greatness. Thirdly, we possess a record of inventiveness which is quite remarkable for its extent and for our failure to exploit it fully.

These are some of our strengths, but we must also recognize the weaknesses and disadvantages of our present system. There is a lack of confidence in both the public and private sectors of the British economy. The private sector has recently undergone traumatic financial experiences. Industrial relationships between employer and employee are frequently the relationships of adversaries rather than partners, and while it is easy to argue for the superiority of private enterprise in theoretical terms it is quite another thing to relate these arguments to the hopes and fears of ordinary people.

For what is at issue in many people's minds is whether the framework of private enterprise favoured by Conservatives is morally legitimate. Many people would accept that free enterprise is more efficient than socialism – support for nationalization has always been small – but they are sceptical as to whether Conservatives can provide a moral justification for the form of society they favour.

As compared with both feudal and socialist societies, a free enterprise society is peculiarly vulnerable to this accusation of lacking moral legitimacy. Many companies are under suspicion for not being sufficiently concerned with the environment or with the welfare of their employees. It is not necessary to take the more extreme criticisms seriously to argue that companies must be seen to have more active social consciences if private enterprise is to be regarded as a morally legitimate as well as an efficient method of organizing economic life.

A further criticism is that a system of private enterprise creates, indeed relies upon, great inequalities of income and wealth.

Private enterprise has provided an economic system with more individual freedom than any socialist system in the world. Indeed, there exists no society which is both collective and free. The freedoms so rightly defended by Conservatives and believers in private enterprise will not be universally valued, however, unless our form of society can succeed in eliminating poverty and securing a decent standard of living for all. Freedom without bread is an empty virtue – this is the truth that the Marxists so wilfully distort to create a totalitarian system of their own. It is useless for Conservatives to preach about freedom unless they can also succeed in creating a fair society.

But what is fairness? Many socialists believe that fairness implies equality. For them society is only fairly organized if there is an equal, or nearly equal, distribution of income and wealth. But why should this be fair? A society in which incomes were equally distributed might well provide a lower average standard of living than a less equal society. In particular it may well be that the standard of living of the poor in an egalitarian society would be lower than in a society where inequalities existed. Egalitarianism then may be neither efficient nor fair.

At the opposite pole from egalitarianism, one could imagine a society whose aim was to maximize its national product at whatever cost. This too must be unsatisfactory if the cost is seen in terms of widespread poverty, no help for the disadvantaged, and unchecked industrial pollution. It still might conceivably be efficient, though even that is open to considerable doubt, but it could not for one moment be regarded as fair.

In practice what we want is an acceptable compromise between efficiency and fairness. The egalitarian sacrifices efficiency to fairness. The man who only values economic growth sacrifices fairness to efficiency. What is wanted is a middle way. We want a society that can create the wealth that alone can assist the poor and disadvantaged. Inequalities are only fair if they tend to benefit those in society who are worst off. Thus fairness and efficiency are in effect to some extent complementary virtues. A country which secures a high rate of growth is also likely to have a high rate of social mobility and therefore a greater degree of equality of opportunity. A stagnating society, on the other hand, is likely to suffer widespread resentment, particularly in industrial relations. There is what is perhaps a peculiarly British vicious circle where a low rate of growth encourages class resentment and class resentment prevents us from achieving an efficient industrial structure.

It is a remarkable fact that at a time when the workings of capitalism are being increasingly questioned in the name of fairness and equality, this type of argument is virtually never rehearsed. Lack of a positive moral defence for capitalism sometimes gives the Conservative Party the air of being a party of concessionists, as it was in Peel's day, a party always on the defensive against opponents which buys off trouble by making concessions today to avoid bigger concessions tomorrow. The central institutions of private enterprise which the Conservative Party exists to defend find themselves bereft of ideological support and half accept the case against them.

In fact there is not the slightest need for the Conservative Party to adopt this posture. It simply needs to show that the inequalities associated with a regime of economic growth are to the advantage of lower income groups, and make their standard of living higher than it would be under an egalitarian system. The record, not only in the United Kingdom but throughout the world, furnishes abundant support for this argument.

Growth demands the payment of higher salaries to industrial managers, but this is a small price to pay for the great gains in welfare which can result from economic advance; if those with managerial ability or other scarce talents which are beneficial to society are in short supply (and they are in every country in the world), and if to induce the exercise of these abilities high salaries and inequality are required, then it must be rational for society to pay those high salaries. But the test of these inequalities must be the contribution they make to the welfare of society. This justification of inequality is not then a justification of the *status quo*; indeed it implies drastic and radical reforms to secure a socially responsible capitalism in which inequalities do contribute to public welfare.

The pursuance of equality to the degree that it eliminates sources of savings and investment destroys the means of providing more and better jobs and reduces both efficiency and fairness. On the other hand, it is right that the state should see that inequality does not destroy basic rights and freedoms. Inequality of wealth would have meant considerable inequality of justice if the state had not provided legal aid services. If election expenditure had not been limited and free time provided for political broadcasts, disparities in wealth could have resulted in considerable inequality of political power. To the extent that people still live in poverty money continues to buy a lower infant mortality rate and to provide a greater chance of a long life. Without considerable state intervention in the provision of medical care this discrepancy would be far greater. There are many freedoms of the market place that we find necessary to restrict: there is general agreement, for example, that we should restrict the freedom to sell drugs or to provide medical and veterinary services unless the person concerned is appropriately qualified.

More controversial are those restrictions on free market forces designed to protect state monopolies such as the Post Office, the airlines, and the gas and electricity industries. There are also limitations of freedom that come under the general heading of consumer protection. This, too, is a controversial area, for some argue that it frees the consumer from the dangers of exploitation while others see it as undesirable intervention.

The private possession of wealth involves both the freedom of the individual to own that wealth and a restriction on the freedom of the 55 million other citizens who are deprived of access to it. Access to corporate wealth is, however, less restricted than access to state wealth. Consumers and employees have more freedom and opportunity prior to state ownership than after it.

Milton Friedman has said 'that the freeman recognises no national purpose except the consensus of the purposes for which the citizens centrally strive'. This amounts to saying that the national purpose is nothing more than an aggregate of selfish aims. The free enterprise system is frequently criticized for being a system based on self-interest. But self-interest is a greater protection of general freedom than blind obedience to a doctrine or a leader. Self-interest also tends to carry with it a desire to improve the quality of living of those that surround the individual, for it includes affection and loyalty to the family, frequently to the village or the town in which the individual lives, and to the nation as a whole. History also teaches that where there have been organized attempts to suppress self-interest, whether in the cause of religion or a political doctrine, there has always been a very considerable restriction of individual freedom and a loss of human happiness. It is also true that the rewards of free enterprise tend to be far less harmful than similar rewards that are provided in totalitarian states, where rewards tend to be a result of individual oppression or feudal privileges. Providing the free enterprise system organizes its society in such a way that the losers can still lead a decent life, the prizes for the winners, be they in the form of splendid houses, larger cars or yachts, do little harm to society as a whole.

Inequality of opportunity is difficult to define and to measure. There are a number of examples of inequality of opportunity which are clearly capable of remedy by social action. This is true of racial and sexual discrimination in jobs. Black people will frequently not attempt to take advantage of the facilities for education for managerial positions because they feel there is no hope of their becoming managers. As a result of this they accumulate fewer skills and society loses through this section of the population deciding not to develop their abilities to the full. There is little doubt that equality of employment opportunity can be a very important ingredient in economic growth.

If we are to seek efficiency and economic growth we must also recognize that we should not tolerate a tax system whereby neither rich nor poor are able to keep a significant part of any additional income that they earn. If, for the wealthy, tax rates are at such penal levels as to make early retirement attractive or to force the person concerned to move abroad where taxation is less heavy, then penal levels of taxation will be to the detriment of economic growth. All incentive is lost when government aid to the poorer sections of society takes away one pound of assistance when an extra pound is earned. Such people, caught in the 'poverty trap', have no reason to use their talents and so improve national prosperity.

For those who profess belief in equality of opportunity there must be acceptance of the urgency of helping the bottom fifth of the income scale to become part of what is generally an affluent society. Economic circumstances deprive the poor of access to decent housing, and of the mobility gained by the ownership of a car, and stop their children taking advantage of the best that education offers.

The market needs to be kept in its place, but it must also be given enough scope to accomplish the many things that it does well. It is important because of its power to limit the bureaucracy and because of its contribution to protecting our freedom against exploitation by the state. So long as it is genuinely competitive, and responds reliably to the signals transmitted between consumers and producers, it encourages experiment and innovation and provides incentive for work effort and productive contribution. Society would have immense difficulty in finding a tolerable substitute for such a system.

The conflict between equality and economic efficiency is inescapable. Because of this it could be argued that capitalism and democracy are an improbable mixture. It is, however, a mixture in which one ingredient has an important impact on the other; it enables us to put some rationality into equality and some humanity into efficiency.

Competition is to be valued, not because the free play of competitive forces leads to social welfare – it does not – but because it enables us to pursue whatever objectives society may have by allocating resources effectively. Capitalist society has already shown an immense power to evolve and meet the changing economic and social requirements of society. Originally the prime socialist criticism of a capitalist society was that it could not solve the problem of poverty, and only by a wholesale reorganization of industrial life would it be possible to provide sufficient for all. Then in the interwar years it was said by socialists that capitalism inevitably involved large-scale unemployment.

It may seem that a centrally planned society has certain advantages in allocating resources efficiently, and that such a society can relate prices more closely to marginal costs than a capitalist society. But this is to ignore the element of human fallibility. It is not enough to show that an *ideal* socialist society might in principle be able to allocate resources more efficiently; it also has to be shown that a system of free enterprise often fails to do so, and that centralized bureaucracy has in practice done better. It is a question not of ideology but of a balance of advantages.

When we move away from the statics of resource allocation and consider the dynamic aspects of an economic system – innovation and flexibility – the advantages of a system of free enterprise are very great. The ability to innovate is crucial in a world in which the problem of resource allocation itself is not static. In an advanced economy we are not asking simply how existing resources should be allocated at the lowest cost, but whether our present methods and techniques are more efficient than others which might be adopted.

A society organized on socialist lines is likely to be inherently hostile to innovation and risk-taking; hostile to a situation where future discounted costs and receipts cannot be worked out by a computer, but are at issue between alternative and untried methods and techniques. The recent partial reintroduction of the price mechanism has resulted in a considerable improvement upon previous socialist methods of resource allocation, but the will to innovate does not exist in central investment boards. Innovation, so all experiments and common sense suggest, requires a diversity of lending institutions, a diversity of means for obtaining investment. Such means are only characteristic of capitalist societies.

Another overwhelming advantage of a society organized on the principles of private enterprise is its flexibility. Socialism represents an unchanging method of organizing economic life, capitalism is remarkable by virtue of its ever-developing character. The capitalism of today is qualitatively very different from the capitalism of the early 1950s, let alone the capitalism of the interwar period. This flexibility results from the fact that capitalism adopts an *ad hoc* approach to its problems. The central characteristic of socialist thought, on the other hand, is, in Popperian terms, its wholism; it attempts to reorganize the whole structure of society to cure particular ills. A moment's glance at the chameleon-like quality of capitalism in adapting its colours to succeeding patterns puts the difference between the two systems into perspective.

Harold Macmillan in his book *The Middle Way*, published in 1938, showed that capitalism was not a fixed and unchanging method of organizing economic life, and that it was far more adaptable than even some of its more sophisticated defenders realized. He argued that Keynesian remedies and planning policies could be used to deal with unemployment, while the essential nature of capitalism and its reliance on private risk-taking could remain unchanged. Later Macmillan attempted to introduce planning measures to deal with the macro-economic problems of growth and income. Keynes and Macmillan can be regarded, therefore, as the intellectual progenitors of the reformed capitalist society in which we now live.

Lord Salisbury defined Conservatism as the belief that 'nothing matters very much and few things matter at all'. Such a definition would not embrace Harold Macmillan, who was an innovator and a creative politician. We owe to him many of the most constructive acts of British policy since the war: the first attempt to enter the Common Market, the withdrawal from Africa, the successful housing policy after 1951 which made the idea of a 'property-owning democracy' meaningful, the development of an incomes policy and a commitment to economic growth.

In his well-known biography of Macmillan, Anthony Sampson argues that he is 'a study of ambiguity'. But, in fact, Macmillan's skilful political tactics concealed a genuine strategy and commitment. Many of his ideas were developed in the 1930s and retained during the 1950s and 1960s. In the first volume of his autobiography Macmillan wrote that during the interwar years he learned 'lessons which I have never forgotten. If, in some respects, they may have left too deep an impression on my mind, the gain was greater than the loss.'

In 1925 Ramsay MacDonald invited progressive Tories to join the Labour Party, and Macmillan replied that MacDonald 'totally misunderstands the moral principles and ideals of democratic Toryism'. Macmillan's political philosophy was poles away from *laissez-faire*, but he never believed in the socialist solution of public ownership as a means to economic recovery. He sought a genuine 'middle way'.

Macmillan argued that both believers in *laissez-faire* and socialists conveyed a 'totally wrong impression of the nature of the problem with which we are faced and the methods of reasoning by which we might find their solution'. This was because they both discussed economic arguments in terms of abstract principles. According to one side, the *laissez-faire* system was theoretically perfect, a self-balancing mechanism within which unemployment was a temporary and abnormal phenomenon. According to the other, unemployment could not be cured until the socialist state arrived, that is, until the means of production, distribution and exchange had been nationalized.

Both these groups held a totally abstract view of society. In Macmillan's words, the argument 'tends to create an impression that the really important question in dispute today is whether we should strive to preserve a definite form of social organization called Capitalism or seek to overthrow it in favour of an equally definitely delineated form called Socialism'. People are then 'given the impression that Capitalism is a static, unchanging form of economic and social organization, working in accordance with preconceived rules and principles'. But this, of course, is a misleading way of looking at the problem; for 'nobody ever invented capitalist society: what we call capitalism came into existence in response to certain economic needs'. Indeed, the capitalism of the 1930s was very different from the capitalism of the nineteenth century. Capitalism is an evolving form of social and economic organization. It is not something fixed, rigid and unchanging.

By the 1930s capitalism had already incorporated into its structure nationalized industries, public utilities of various kinds, and large-scale monopolistic industries. Macmillan attempted to show Conservatives that they had already in practice abandoned the system of *laissez-faire* which they claimed to be supporting. He wanted to use the protective tariff to play a part in a much wider and more creative policy of reconstruction. Central to such a policy was 'a development or industrial commission, planning the growth of the nation's economic life and helping industries to reorganise themselves in the changed conditions'. 'My plan was that the Committee should be empowered to call into being representation of labour as well as management.' This is the first mention in Macmillan's work of the National Economic Development Council (Neddy), which he introduced in 1961 and which plays such a vital role in contemporary economic affairs.

Macmillan regarded the Labour Party's policies for dealing with unemployment as hopelessly doctrinaire; for Labour claimed that there could be no solution until all industries had been nationalized. But the millennium of a collectivized society would not come about for at least a generation; what was to happen to the unemployed in the meantime? It was the total approach to politics of socialists which so repelled Macmillan. 'The Socialist Parties,' he said

> disclaimed all responsibility for all that was wrong by repeating the parrot-cry – 'It is the fault of the system'. This was supposed to mean that there was nothing to be done except by revolutionary changes which would, paradoxically enough, have been singularly distasteful to most of those who recommended them. In theory they were 'root and branch' men; in

fact they shrank in practice from the radical doctrines which they recommended in principle.

It was precisely because of their total approach that Labour was condemned to put forward palliatives; they were incapable of constructive thought, because they could not believe that anything could be done before the millennium. No wonder their utopianism prevented them from appreciating the 'middle way'.

To Macmillan, the constructive Keynesian policies which he was advocating were far more in conformity with the philosophy of Conservatism than were the policies of the Conservative leadership. This was because his own policies represented an evolutionary rather than a doctrinaire approach to social and economic problems. There is a clear distinction to be drawn between a policy that arises naturally out of the evolutionary trends in society and a policy that is elaborated upon a basis of abstract principle. The political ideas of a nation in regard to the organization of its economic life are largely formulated out of the actual experiences of men in dealing with the problems which any given policy may claim to solve. To anyone who studied the facts of social life and economic organization it was clear that planning was accepted in practice, even if denied in theory. Large industries investing large amounts of capital planned ahead; so did government in its social and industrial policies.

> The ideal of planning is slowly but definitely gaining ground as the real nature of the problems now confronting us is revealed. It is a view which arises out of the realities of industrial and commercial life. It has found its adherents not so much among theorists as among those industrialists who see that it is in harmony with what they find it necessary to aim at in the daily conduct of their business.

Macmillan, then, was able to show that Keynesian policies did not require the acceptance of a social philosophy inconsistent with that professed by the Conservative Party. Instead it would tend to reinforce that philosophy, by creating the conditions under which an individualistic society would flourish. In this way it would be the most satisfactory defence for capitalism against the menace of those who wanted to collectivize the economy and destroy individualism. Macmillan was a radical in that he wanted to change society in accordance with the doctrines of Keynes; but he was also a Conservative in that he saw society as adaptive and flexible, not fixed and rigid.

His experiences in the 1930s greatly coloured Macmillan's policies as Prime Minister in the 1950s. When faced with a choice between *laissez-faire* and a policy of economic growth he came down unhesitatingly on the side of full employment and growth. In July 1957 he said, 'When I am told by some people, some rather academic writers, that inflation can be cured or arrested only by returning to substantial or even massive unemployment, I reject that utterly.'

In 1961 Macmillan set up the National Economic Development Council composed of minister, industrialists and trade union leaders. A clear and unambiguous commitment to a 4 per cent annual growth rate was made. Neddy was to have its own planning staff, independent of the Treasury. In 1962 Macmillan set up the National Incomes Commission, the forerunner of many similar bodies recently.

At the same time his government adopted the recommendations of the Plowden Report so as to enable public expenditure to be looked at in a global rather than a piecemeal, departmental way, as had hitherto been the case. He began the process of industrial modernization, especially in the railways under the chairmanship of Dr (now Lord) Beeching, who was appointed by Macmillan. In this way Macmillan laid the foundations of modern economic management.

In dealing with the structural problems endemic in a modern economy Macmillan found himself committed to government intervention if full employment was to be secured. His policies really did represent a middle way in that they secured the benefits of individualism without the burden of mass unemployment.

Harold Macmillan's mastery and domination of the politics of the later 1950s and early 1960s rested upon two factors. First, his ability to see beyond ideological slogans to the realities beneath; secondly, his understanding that unless capitalism could show sufficient social responsibility it could never win mass support. These beliefs place him in the very centre of the Conservative tradition, and help to explain his success in government.

Following Harold Macmillan, the moderate right has been able to appreciate the rationale of such a society much more rapidly than the left. It has been able to see that planning is compatible with capitalism more quickly than socialists have been able to see that the price mechanism is essential to efficient socialism.

This defence of the free enterprise system differs markedly from that given by Adam Smith and the classical economists, yet it is worth reminding ourselves of the essential advantages of capitalism which the classical economists, who were all political liberals, sought. The great advantage of capitalism is that it allows more freedom for the individual than a socialist system would, because under it power is more widely dispersed. A country's freedom is likely to be greater when political and economic powers are separated than when the state owns and takes decisions for a large section of industry. Socialists rightly object to monopolies and to the concentration of private industrial power, but such evils are heightened when economic and political powers are concentrated in the same hands.

Capitalism also ensures that private entrepreneurs have the freedom upon which a successful economic system depends. For economic freedom is an important part of the total freedom which a man should enjoy: the freedom to choose one's job, the shops from which one buys things, the bank in which one deposits one's money. This sort of freedom is clearly vital, and any interference with it diminishes the extent of individual choice.

Government intervention is necessary, however, not only to achieve full employment and control inflation, but also to secure wider social objectives. In a modern society the government must elaborate national goals, let industry know its target for the rate of growth, and make clear how productive capacity may be increased to make the objective feasible. Governments also have a duty to prevent the unpleasant by-products of growth such as damage to the environment, as well as very wide responsibilities in the fields of housing, education and the social services.

What is the difference, it may be asked, between this view of interventionist Conservatism and the kind of social democracy favoured by the right of the Labour Party? A few leading socialists have come to realize the vital importance of economic growth if social reform is to be achieved, that social reform must come not from soaking the rich – there are not enough of them to soak – but from the wealth obtained from economic growth. Socialism, according to these thinkers, cannot come from redistributive taxation unless there is a surplus available for redistribution, and this surplus must be provided by economic growth. There is, nonetheless, a very fundamental difference between this school of thought and interventionist Conservatism. Social democrats will the same end, economic growth, but they are unable to will the means. Encouragement of private industry goes against their ideological preconceptions.

Socialist budgets, imposing swingeing taxes and ever-increasing costs on industry at a time when the prime need is to increase industrial investment, show this very clearly. Social democrats proceed from the view that the mechanism of private enterprise is a necessary evil to be tolerated but not supported. Conservatives, on the other hand, see the system of private enterprise as a benefactor. A successful industrialist who invents a new product or satisfies an important consumer need can produce just as much benefit as a social worker. Can there be any doubt that private enterprise has been able to secure real material improvement on a vast scale for the great majority of people?

The Conservative task, however, is not just to defend capitalism, but to enhance it. Radical reforms are needed to secure a socially responsible capitalism; under such a system those inequalities which do exist must be seen to contribute to the public welfare and therefore not to be unreasonable.

Perhaps one of the biggest changes must come in endeavouring to obtain a genuine redistribution of capital. We need to return to Iain Macleod's ideal of a capital-owning democracy. The socialist concept of the redistribution of wealth is to take away from the wealthy and thereafter to have that wealth administered by the politician and the bureaucrat, supposedly on behalf of the public at large. The Conservative approach to the problem of the redistribution of wealth should be to try to redistribute wealth so that more individual people have a stake in society. This means looking objectively at our existing taxation system and asking whether it is fair and in accordance with the various contributions that are made to our industrial success. Nineteenth-century capitalism consisted largely of industrial concerns in which the proprietor and the manager were one, so that the rewards given to successful proprietors were also rewards to the managers. This is no longer the position, for in many industries the proprietor and the manager are not synonymous. Our major industrial concerns have boards of directors who rarely have more than a small stake, if any, in the company that they manage. Our taxation system should be changed so that the rewards of successful management are at least equal to the rewards of successful proprietorship.

We must also examine the nature of the wealth currently controlled by politicians and bureaucrats to see how much of it can be transferred to individuals. In the field of public housing a vast bureaucracy supervises one-third of the people of this country, who have become permanent tenants. The nationalized industries were created because of the original desire of socialists to have workers controlling industry instead of a few privileged owners. They have generated, as we can now see, less rather than more of a feeling of participation. These are spheres in which there can be a worthwhile and exciting redistribution of wealth from the politician and the bureaucrat to the individual.

It is not just the financial relationships within capitalism that need to change, but also the human relationships. The increasing complexities and technicalities of modern existence in an industrial society show up the differences in capabilities between men. This must result in a conflict with the democratic ethic of equality. It is for this reason that men feel frustrated, unhappy and unable to understand the processes that govern their lives. They feel themselves to be passive victims of change. It is vital that the structure of administration be made more comprehensible to people. They should be told in clear terms the basis for government action. So far, most capitalist governments have been unable to develop the rapport with people which is essential if their allegiance is to be obtained. There is a failure to communicate both on the part of government and of industry. This failure has perhaps resulted from the continuing feeling of superiority among those who have the power to take the big decisions. The relationship between baron and serf, continued between landowner and tenant, still sometimes exists between industrialist and worker, as is well illustrated by the nineteenth-century terms 'master' and 'men'. We are still a long way from giving individuals the opportunity of developing and applying their full abilities.

For too many the bulk of their lives is determined by the domestic environment in which they were born or by the education that was made available to them in the first quarter of their lives. For too many an early opportunity missed results in a life wasted.

In my teens, under the direction of Mr Goodhead and out of my hostility to a socialist history master at Latymer, I became a passionate student of the life and works of Disraeli, and I came to realize that relationships between rich and poor had not essentially changed since the time when he was writing.

There was hardly a page of the six volumes of Monypenny and Buckle's life of Disraeli that did not excite me. For the son of a Jewish bookseller to become Queen Victoria's Prime Minister and to be for so long the leader of the nineteenth-century Tory Party seemed in themselves achievements almost beyond belief. Discovering the romanticism, energy, vision and intellectual ability of such a man made an important impact upon my life. I recall the joy of reading his novels. When I read his first novel, *Vivian Grey*, which I did at the age of fifteen, and found out that he had written it at the age of twenty-one, I realized the considerable inadequacy of my own abilities and learning.

But the book which made most impact on my political thinking was his remarkable novel *Sybil*, particularly the conversation between Egremont and the two strangers in the ruins of the Abbey. The conversation expresses the 'One Nation' theme, a theme that has been vital to Tory Party philosophy in the years since.

The stranger, commenting upon the disappearance of the monasteries and the rise of landlords, says:

'There were yeomen then, sir: the country was not divided into two classes, masters and slaves; there was some resting-place between luxury and misery. Comfort was an English habit then, not merely an English word.

'The monks were, in short, in every district a point of refuge for all who needed succour, counsel, and protection; a body of individuals having no cares of their own, with wisdom to guide the inexperienced, with wealth to relieve the suffering, and often with power to protect the oppressed.'

'You plead their cause with feeling,' said Egremont, not unmoved.

'It is my own; they were the sons of the people, like myself.'

'I had thought rather these monasteries were the resort of the younger branches of the aristocracy,' said Egremont.

'Instead of the pension list,' replied his companion, smiling, but not with bitterness. 'Well, if we must have an aristocracy, I would rather that its younger branches should be monks and nuns than colonels without regiments, or housekeepers of royal palaces that exist only in name. Besides, see what advantage to a minister if the unendowed aristocracy were thus provided for now. He need not, like a minister in these days, entrust the conduct of public affairs to individuals notoriously incompetent, appoint to the command of expeditions generals who never saw a field, make governors of colonies out of men who never could govern themselves, or find an ambassador in a broken dandy or a blasted favourite. It is true that many of the monks and nuns were persons of noble birth. Why should they not have been? The aristocracy had their share; no more. They, like all other classes, were benefited by the monasteries: but the list of the mitred abbots, when they were suppressed, shows that the great majority of the heads of houses were of the people.'

Then comes a second stranger and the conversation is continued.

'You also lament the dissolution of these bodies,' said Egremont.

'There is so much to lament in the world in which we live,' said the younger of the strangers, 'that I can spare no pang for the past.'

'Yet you approve of the principle of their society; you prefer it, you say, to our existing life.'

'Yes; I prefer association to gregariousness.'

'That is a distinction,' said Egremont, musingly.

'It is a community of purpose that constitutes society,' continued the younger stranger; 'without that, men may be drawn into contiguity, but they still continue virtually isolated.'

'And is that their condition in cities?'

'It is their condition everywhere; but in cities that condition is aggravated. A density of population implies a severer struggle for existence, and a consequent repulsion of elements brought into too close contact. In great cities men are brought together by the desire of gain. They are not in a state of co-operation, but of isolation, as to the making of fortunes; and for all the rest they are careless of neighbours. Christianity teaches us to love our neighbour as ourself; modern society acknowledges no neighbour.'

'This is a new reign,' said Egremont, 'perhaps it is a new era.'

'I think so,' said the young stranger.

'I hope so,' said the elder one.

'Well, society may be in its infancy,' said Egremont, slightly smiling; 'but, say what you like, our Queen reigns over the greatest nation that ever existed.'

'Which nation?' asked the younger stranger, 'for she reigns over two.'

The stranger paused; Egremont was silent, but looked inquiringly.

'Yes,' resumed the younger stranger after a moment's interval. 'Two nations; between whom there is no intercourse and no sympathy; who are as ignorant of each other's habits, thoughts, and feelings, as if they were dwellers in different zones, or inhabitants of different planets; who are formed by a different breeding, are fed by a different food, are ordered by different manners, and are not governed by the same laws.'

'You speak of——' said Egremont, hesitatingly.

'THE RICH AND THE POOR.'

Nearly a century later, in spite of all the benefits of technology, we still have 'Two Nations', and it should still be the main purpose of the Tory Party to create one.

Disraeli's novels and thought pose an essential political dilemma, a dilemma not only of his own day but of ours as well. Can a Conservative political philosophy come to terms with the reality of an industrialized society, one characterized not only by rapid change and technical progress, but also by a dissolution of the very traditional ties which seem to give Conservatism its meaning? Disraeli's answer to this problem makes him the first prophet of Conservatism in an industrial society; it explains his relevance to our own times; it explains also why most contemporary Conservatives revere him as the founder of the Party in its modern form.

Disraeli was concerned to attack the liberal materialism of his day. Many nineteenth-century critics failed to notice this; they were misled by the superficial glitter of the novels to believe that they were nothing more than celebrations of aristocratic life. But, in fact, Disraeli intended to criticize the degradation of the aristocratic ideal. His heroes, although blessed with wealth and good fortune of every kind, demand something more than the conventional future of a member of the ruling class. They seek a social ideal through which they can organize their lives.

In Disraeli's view the degradation of the aristocratic ideal had led to the decline of the Conservative Party, which, from being a party of high principle, social reform and devotion to the interests of the people, had become just a party of concessionarists and place-seekers whose only aim was the spoils of office. The Conservatives were thus quite unable to combat the Liberals and radicals whose aim was to subvert traditional institutions. 'No party was national,' wrote Disraeli in 1870, 'one [the Tory Party] was exclusive and odious, and the other liberal and cosmopolitan.'

For a Conservative, the regeneration of society must come, not from analysis in terms of general and abstract principles, but from that active and vital renewal which comes from a consideration of the past. In their enthusiasm for Benthamite rationalism the Liberals made the mistake of completely ignoring the past.

In the General Preface to the Collected Edition of his novels, written in 1870, Disraeli claims:

> What has led to this confusion of public thought and this uneasiness of society is our habitual carelessness in not distinguishing between the excellence of a principle and its injurious or obsolete application. The feudal system may have worn out but its main principle, that the tenure of property should be the fulfilment of duty, is the essence of good government.

Thus Disraeli shows that the central concept of Conservatism is the concept of responsibility – the responsibility of the land in the nineteenth century, the responsibility of industry today.

Disraeli believed that positive state action was needed to alleviate the suffering caused by unplanned industrialization. He was forced to combat two different types of Conservative: first, the concessionist, typified by Peel, whose only idea of policy was to do what the other side did, but a few years later; secondly, the reactionary, who wanted to remain with a dead and lifeless past instead of using the principles of the past to reinvigorate the present.

Disraeli supported the extension of the franchise of the great Reform Bill of 1867. In his famous ministry of 1874–80 he put forward a number of important reforms to improve housing and factory conditions, and he ensured that the trade unions would be protected by law. Indeed he laid the foundations of modern society so effectively that one Labour member confessed in 1880 that 'the Conservatives had done more for the working classes in six years than the Liberals in forty years'.

At the same time Disraeli strengthened Britain's position abroad, rescuing it from the isolationism which had existed since the death of Palmerston. His brilliant coup, the purchase of the Suez Canal shares, ensured not only that Britain would have a commanding influence in the Middle East, but that the route to India would be safe from attack. Disraeli realized intuitively that there was a connection between social reform at home and strength abroad – though it was left to Joseph Chamberlain to draw the explicit connection. It was, however, Disraeli who first made the Conservative Party the party of imperialism and nationalism, a position that it has never really lost since. In his novels Disraeli provided the intellectual and imaginative foundations of modern Conservatism; in his politics he applied the insights of his novels to practical situations. The late Leo Amery was certainly right when he found in Disraeli the antidote to the other two dominant philosophies of our time: the naïve optimism of the Liberals and the hate-filled pessimism of Marx.

Joseph Chamberlain added to the Conservatism of Burke and Disraeli a specific economic content as well as allegiance to a strong foreign policy which placed Britain's interests first. His son, Austen, in an introduction to a collection of his father's speeches, wrote, 'from first to last he was a great reformer and a greater Imperialist'.

Chamberlain himself had not begun as a member of the Conservative Party. He was one of the great rebels whom the party had successfully assimilated. He was not a natural Conservative. Indeed in 1895 he wrote about the Conservatives, 'they are narrow, so apathetic, so indifferent to everything that does not touch themselves or their privileges or their fortunes. Am I to sit still in the presence of want and misery and ignorance...! Between reaction and revolution there should be a middle path if only I could find it.' This search for the 'middle way' between reaction and revolution was also a central theme of the political careers of Burke, Disraeli and Harold Macmillan.

Many of his contemporaries saw Joseph Chamberlain as the first statesman of the new democracy. A French commentator, speaking of him in 1893, said, 'he is the man of the present hour; he marks the second age of the democracy... he has displayed... that independence of the time, that touch of modernity, which makes of him the first interpreter and the sole possible regulator of the needs and passions of the democracy'.

Although Chamberlain became a member of the outer circle of the Conservative government of his day, the Conservative leaders never really accepted him. As Julian Amery has written,

> for all their imagined mutual respect and long collaboration, Salisbury was the most implacable opponent of Chamberlain's ambition... His genius was of the negative kind. He knew

that concessions sometimes had to be made, but he regarded it as the function of the Conservative Party to delay and wear down each innovation so that it could be assimilated with the least possible change into the body politic. Between this philosophical Conservatism and Chamberlain's constructive radicalism there could be compromise but not synthesis.

If Salisbury was the Peel of his day, Chamberlain was the Disraeli.

Chamberlain's background as an outsider in politics, a businessman amongst landowners and lawyers, a provincial amongst Londoners, meant that he was able to see the implications of political doctrines at the grass roots rather than relying upon inherited knowledge, or the textbooks of political economy. What was required, he argued in the debate over the tariff, was 'not the deductive reasoning of the professors, but the inductive reasoning of hard facts'. Chamberlain moved with the times; he abandoned doctrines when they became irrelevant to the facts of industrial experience. His central contribution to Conservative thought was his instinctive realization at the beginning of the twentieth century that Britain's industrial dominance was gone for good; that the 'informal empire' based upon Britain's control of the seas and financial leadership was no longer sufficient to make her a dominant power; that in twentieth-century geopolitics those states with access to large markets would inevitably exert the greatest influence.

In January 1885, while still a Liberal, Chamberlain said, 'how to promote the greatest happiness of the masses of the people, how to increase their enjoyment of life, that is the problem of the future'. He was the first statesman to concentrate his whole energies upon social and economic reform, the first leading politician to favour the creative use of political power to improve the standard of living of the masses.

But Chamberlain realized that it would be impossible to secure any lasting improvement in the standard of living of the British working classes without guaranteeing Britain's trade position. That is why he came to support tariff reform, a scheme to ensure Britain's access to imperial markets. Similarly, in our own day Conservatives have supported the idea of a wider European patriotism to replace the nineteenth-century imperial dream.

With an assured market for Britain's industry, production and employment could be maintained. Chamberlain proposed to finance old age pensions out of the proceeds of protective duties. But the keystone of his policies was the security that tariff reform offered as an alternative to the constant dislocations and instabilities of the world economy.

There was then a direct link between the programme of social reform and the programme of strengthening Britain's position abroad; as Chamberlain's supporter, Lord Milner, argued, 'amongst civilisations placed of more or less equal size, that one will be, as it will deserve to be, the strongest, which is most successful in removing the causes of class antagonism in its midst'. Chamberlain, like Disraeli, sought to oppose Marxist materialism through imaginative and constructive new policies. If these changes were not carried out, Chamberlain foresaw the growth of a socialist movement. Such a movement did not frighten him, however, for he saw it as basically defensive, a movement to secure working class rights in the face of trade depression, but without a constructive policy for dealing with the economic difficulties.

The mainstream of British Conservatism has rarely been reactionary, resisting all change, as some continental parties of the right have been. The historian A. J. P. Taylor has said unkindly, 'what has called itself Conservatism in the last hundred years has merely consented not to be a brake on the march of progress. Past conservatism has defended the Liberal achievements of the previous generation.'

Joseph Chamberlain certainly did not hold this conception of Conservatism. He wanted to transform the Conservative Party from a party of sound administration and cautious, ameliorative reform into one with a positive and dynamic creed. This creed would avoid the dangers of class conflict inherent in the Conservatism of the market economy. Chamberlain's policy was one of class harmony, both worker and capitalist alike were held to have a stake in Britain's prosperity. For the capitalist, tariff reform offered secure markets and a balanced climate for expansion. For the worker, it offered high wages and, above all, the security of full employment. Thus Chamberlain attempted to alter the accepted categories of British politics by securing a drastic political realignment of the classes and a new electoral coalition for the Conservative Party.

Although the tariff reform campaign failed in the immediate short run, Chamberlain's legacy to the Conservative Party has not been ignored. For Joseph Chamberlain's policies have formed the mainstream of social policy within the twentieth-century Conservative Party. Until the First World War the cause of tariff reform advanced steadily. By the 1920s it had become the Conservative Party's main remedy for mass unemployment. Before the First World War men could not believe that Britain was suffering from a period of economic decline, but after 1919 the collapse of Britain's basic export industries led to the search for new remedies.

In March 1931 the economist John Maynard Keynes publicly announced his conversion to protection. And the new policies which Keynes favoured could only be undertaken in conjunction with a tariff, if they were not to threaten the exchange rate of the pound and ruin business confidence.

The world depression of 1929–33 shattered hopes of a revival of Britain's export industries. In 1931 Britain deserted the gold standard. In 1932 Joseph Chamberlain's son, Neville, piloted through the House of Commons the Import Duties Bill, providing for a general 10 per cent tariff on foreign goods, with a preference to most imports from the Empire. Neville Chamberlain called these proposals 'the direct and legitimate descendants of his father's conception'. By 1938, Sir Charles Petrie, the biographer of the Chamberlain family, could say, 'today the man in the street wonders why he ever adopted free trade and is not certain whether Cobden was a man or a horse'. In a deeper sense also Chamberlain's view triumphed. We are not moving towards the liberal world of free multilateral trade and freely convertible currencies, but to a world of regional economic groups, to a situation in which trade and investment extend between members of a particular group more than between one group and another. Nor does anyone today accept any absolute conception of the economic order, whether free trade or autarchic, *laissez-faire* or socialist.

Through two centuries the Tory Party has inherited a remarkable tradition, the tradition expressed and evaluated by Edmund Burke, Benjamin Disraeli, Joseph Chamberlain and Harold Macmillan. It is a tradition that desperately strives for the creation of one nation, that rejects dangerous doctrines; it is a tradition that Britain needs to turn to today more urgently than at any time in our history.

CHAPTER
III
Equality of Opportunity

THE key to economic and social revival must be a transformation of human relationships in industry. The statistics of the post-war period show the failure of British industry to reach the levels of productivity of our major European competitors, the United States or Japan. Unless we achieve this transformation our relative decline must continue.

Britain has certain disadvantages as a result of its history. The injustices created by the *laissez-faire* economic system of the nineteenth century have done permanent damage to British industrial relations. The nineteenth century was the period in which the uneasy relationship of landlord and tenant gave way to the equally uneasy relationship of master and man. For many the improved incomes available in the towns provided sufficient inducement for them to accept conditions of employment which a more educated population has found unacceptable today.

My own attitudes to industrial relations have been very much affected by the difficulties and unhappinesses of my own father's life. Born the son of a small but successful builder in Wembley, who though without education had built up a business, he had some advantages over many of his contemporaries. His father decided in a typically Victorian, authoritarian way the trade to which each of his sons should be apprenticed, and my own father went into engineering. From the time he completed his four-year apprenticeship at the age of eighteen, he spent the next thirty-five years working unhappily in factories in the London area. For most of my childhood he worked at the H.M.V. factory at Hayes, leaving home at six o'clock in the morning to cycle to work and spending the day in a dark factory splattered by oil in noisy conditions until he was free to cycle home again. With Saturday morning work being normal, there was too little time for my father to get a great deal of enjoyment out of life, even from his own family. That sort of perpetual boredom spent in unpleasant surroundings was suffered by millions of people of his generation, and continues for many millions more today. He was an intelligent man and was able, when in his fifties, to free himself from the treadmill of factory life and open a small shop in Brentford. This liberation was a cause of immense happiness to him, and although in his new life he was never to earn a large income, being in command of his own business, making decisions, working for his own benefit, meeting customers and endeavouring to serve them, and working in surroundings that were light and pleasant, were matters of great joy to him after the decades of dull and miserable existence.

My father, like the majority of his fellow employees, showed no bitterness or hostility to the system which provided him with his poor quality of life.

Being an active trade unionist he regularly attended the branch meetings which took place in the evening; those were the days when he would not be home in time to see my brother and myself before we went to bed. In common with many of today's active trade unionists he used to complain about the failure of others to turn up to meetings.

Many in influential positions still have little real understanding of the way of life and genuine hardships of industrial workers. By providing rural homes and a public school education, many of the original industrialists, who gave Britain such a lead in the industrial revolution, saw to it that their own children became more and more remote from the realities of British industrial life. Harold Macmillan wrote of himself as he was when he first became a parliamentary candidate for Stockton in 1923:

> I had no practical knowledge of the world in which I was to move. I had never been to Teesside and Tyneside. Apart from Glasgow where my printer cousins lived I had scarcely been to an industrial town. I had never seen the great ironworks, steelworks, engineering works, shipyards which had been built up on the banks of the rivers of the north of England and Scotland, nor, except for the war, had I any actual experience of living among an industrial population.

Macmillan was sufficiently sensitive to recognize the very grave deprivation of those he sought to represent at Stockton-on-Tees, and much of his political philosophy, as outlined in *The Middle Way*, and in the programme he tried to pursue as Prime Minister, was influenced by this recognition of the balance between the quality of the lives of the people of Stockton-on-Tees and other industrial towns and those living elsewhere.

My father, like a very large proportion of industrial workers, suffered from deafness by the time he was in his late forties. We now know the immense nervous strains that deafness puts upon people and the generally depressing effects that it has. For most of my father's working life he also suffered, as did the majority of his colleagues in his factory, from dermatitis, a ghastly irritation of the skin, physically ugly and mentally disturbing. For most of their lives men such as these could never wear clean, attractive clothes, and although developments in machinery have reduced the lavish distribution of oil and waste about the machine shop many of the unpleasant features that are associated with factory life continue to the present day. Yet my father's occupation was by no means the least attractive. He was after all a skilled worker. There are certainly more unpleasant areas of industry, such as the foundries, with their choking fumes, or the mines, with their unbelievably hard working conditions and the dangers they involve.

I deplore both the human boredom and unpleasantness involved in much of industrial life, and also the failure to mobilize the basic abilities of the individual. My father could have commanded a job requiring far higher skills than he ever applied, had he only been given the opportunity to train in new skills. But there is no reason for the employer to wish to encourage the skilled engineer, working on the production line, to become a manager. The route to such a post is frequently very different. Men from the shop floor do rise to such positions by showing entrepreneurial instincts at an early age, but many men of immense administrative ability and high intelligence are left to continue in the rut of factory production.

The ghastly waste of human resources that results from our educational and industrial system is perhaps one of the worst features of British life. I was first made aware of this by my experiences as a national serviceman. As an eighteen-year-old I had no concept of military life. A number of my uncles had served as soldiers during the war, but my father had been too old, and I had no relatives who had ever pursued a military career until my brother joined the navy as an artificer at the age of fifteen. I did not gather from him the difference between being commissioned and non-commissioned, nor did I understand the way in which the army was rigidly divided into officers and men. I did not know that the officers came from one social background and the men from another, and that only a small fraction of the men who joined the ranks ever became officers. There was the rare case of the warrant officer who was commissioned, but the division between officers and men was not based upon ability. It was a division in which there was unfair opportunity.

When I did my two years' national service I had no idea that with my educational background I would have been wise to have applied to become a commissioned officer. When I was interviewed for my national service I was asked what regiment I wished to go into. I was in considerable difficulty as I didn't know the names of any regiments and knew little of the diverse sections of the army. I had heard that there was an Educational Corps, however, and I mentioned this and so became an educational instructor in the army.

At the age of eighteen I was suddenly surrounded by young people of similar ability and intellect but with a totally dissimilar social and educational background. I did my basic training with the King's Royal Rifle Corps at Winchester, where for some administrative reason they had suddenly called up a number of young porters from Covent Garden, who all went into one platoon of their own. One of them was called Walker, and when his name got mixed with mine I spent six weeks in the company of the Covent Garden porters.

I soon appreciated their immense wit, keen intelligence and total lack of education. I wrote letters home for some, and filled in forms for others. There was a low standard of literacy but a high standard of intelligence. When later I was posted to the Cheshire Regiment and then to a small unit of the Armoured Corps in Westmorland and I was responsible for the education of the men in these establishments, I discovered quickly that these were men who could be inspired to study for the first time in their lives.

A number of them have had far fuller lives purely because at the age of nineteen or twenty they were encouraged to apply their talents to acquire a better standard of literacy and thereafter to obtain some appropriate qualification that would put them on a new route through life. I realized then that if the small fraction of people that I came across during those two years were typical of the nation as a whole, we were a nation in which much ability was wasted, not developed or never applied, a nation in which the social background of the individual was of far more importance to his future prospects than his ability and intelligence.

The British educational system has failed to provide for modern industrial society. In the later part of the nineteenth century, when it was seen that relative to some other nations Britain was beginning to lose her industrial superiority, campaigns were waged to 'Wake up Britain', but the problems seen and forecast then have remained unsolved.

Scandinavian industry has benefited immensely from having colleges for shop stewards. Throughout this century the United States has been better than Britain at providing an educational system appropriate to industrial society. In 1884 a Royal Commission looked into technical education and made the comment that the ignorance so common amongst workmen in England was almost unknown in Germany.

In 1902 there were only seven universities in Britain providing any form of technical education. At that time there were already twenty-two in Germany. By 1908 there were 3,000 people in technical schools in Britain compared with ten technical universities with 14,000 students amongst them in Germany. By 1921 only 19 per cent of people in Britain between the ages of fourteen and seventeen were in full-time education and only 12 per cent of people in Britain went on from elementary schools. By 1939, when there were 10,000 students in Britain taking technical courses in universities, in Germany the figure was 24,000.

In 1929, in the final report of the Balfour Commission on trade and industry, a report founded on four years of investigations, it was stated:

> The available information makes it clear that the present response of leaders of industrial and commercial enterprises to the educational efforts made to train candidates for entry into higher grades of these organisations is much less certain and widespread than in certain foreign countries, particularly Germany or the United States. Before British industry taken as a whole could hope to reap from scientific research the full advantage that it appears to yield to some of their most formidable rivals nothing less than a revolution is needed in their

general outlook on science. The change of attitude is bound to be slow and difficult in view of our old and deeply rooted industrial traditions. We are aware of no other country that suffers nearly as much as Great Britain from artificial, hard and fast lines of demarcation in different skilled crafts or between workmen of different grades of skill, and this disability is more acutely felt than ever in a period of rapid economic change, when old lines of distinction are necessarily becoming less and less consistent with the realities of productive economy. The conservative habits of mind prevent many British employers from pursuing so energetic and as it appears to them so revolutionary a policy as scrapping old plant and replacing it by new as their competitors have done in America or Germany. Corresponding qualities of mind lead many workmen to cling tenaciously to obsolete trade customs and lines of demarcation and thus prevent them from co-operating to the full in getting the best value out of machinery at the lowest cost.

The Balfour Committee summed all this up as the human factor, and there is no doubt at all that this human factor, resulting from our historical legacy as an industrial power, constitutes a very important part of our problems.

It is true that since that time there has been a massive extension in higher education, and we have also seen the opening of exciting new facilities such as the Open University, but it is still the case that many of those in commanding positions in the commercial and economic world are not there solely because of their abilities. It is likewise the case that a very large proportion of those who are not near the summit in our society have the talents and ability to be there but have never been given the opportunity and in many cases are not even aware of the prospect.

As Secretary of State for Trade and Industry I visited many famous firms. In some cases, after spending an hour or two with the shop stewards and lunching with the board, I reflected that if the shop stewards and the board could change places you would have a lively, energetic, well-informed board and a rather lethargic and apathetic group of shop stewards, which would perhaps be a better combination than that which exists at present.

I spent most of my own business life building up a firm of Lloyd's Insurance Brokers in the City of London. Starting with a former school friend, with one room, one desk and two chairs, in the end, when I became a minister, the firm employed nearly two hundred people. This gave me some interesting insights into the question of opportunity and application of talent.

In Lloyd's, with its worldwide influence, I discovered that many talented underwriters and many of the leading brokers were not, in fact, men of great academic achievement or wealthy social background. While Lloyd's by its very nature recruits to its membership a mass of the more wealthy people in the country, the practical underwriting and the operation of the great broking firms of Lloyd's of London are quite frequently in the hands of men who came to the Lloyd's Market at the age of thirteen or fourteen with no educational qualifications. Starting life as office boys with very small salaries, they eventually developed and applied their intelligence to acquire the professional skills of that particular business and were then given the opportunity to use them to the full.

The City of London's geographical situation is such that Lloyd's recruits its office boys and junior staff from the East End of London. This has meant, over the decades, that many young East Enders of poor background have become men of considerable wealth as part of the Lloyd's Market.

Here was an area where a university education was not a requirement, where one could pick up in a practical way the knowledge of policy wordings and the methods of placing business, where personality rather than social status counted, where individual human ability really was recognized irrespective of background. That Lloyd's managed to utilize such talent shows how disastrous it is that many more spheres of our commercial and industrial life fail to make use of the capabilities and energies of the people they employ.

How then are we to mobilize the wide range of talent and ability in our country? How are we to see that Britain in recovery is a Britain that genuinely provides equality of opportunity and gives every encouragement for ability to be applied to the full? If we can find the key to this we will have found the key to Britain's recovery.

One thing is certain, and that is that industry and society as a whole would benefit greatly if Britain could achieve a higher standard of literacy. One of the great inequalities in our society is the inequality that nearly always exists between the child born into a home where books abound and reading is one of the major pleasures of life itself and the child in the great majority of homes in which hardly a book is to be found.

Inequality of opportunity starts at the youngest possible age. The child whose parents devote themselves to teaching him to read at the age of four or five discovers that he has an immense advantage at school and thereafter at work over the majority of children who obtain no such tuition at that early age. Governments and educational authorities should consider carefully how a new standard of literacy in Britain as a whole could be attained. We have available to us a number of assets that could be utilized to achieve this highly desirable objective.

First we have a substantial number of young qualified teachers who are unemployed. I see no reason why these, together perhaps with former teachers who would like the opportunity to do part-time work, should not be mobilized both to teach four-year-old children to read and to teach their parents how to encourage their children to read and write. Such a programme could be organized without the need for further educational buildings, and at relatively little cost compared with the cost of paying teachers unemployment and social security benefits, and its rewards in terms of a far more literate society in the future would be considerable.

Our other considerable asset, which I believe could be utilized to a far greater degree than at present, is our inheritance of a remarkable public library system. We have no less than 12,000 public libraries; this means an average of nineteen in every constituency in the country. Some are mobile libraries; some are libraries in hospitals and old people's homes; some are well-established and substantial public libraries in their own purpose-built buildings. Altogether our public libraries employ 26,500 people, more than forty people in every constituency, whose occupation is to release books to the public. They own nearly 120 million books, but for more than nine months of each year these books are on the library shelves and not being read by anyone. Over the past five years the number of books borrowed has declined from 648 million to 531 million.

Few countries have a better library system staffed by a more dedicated and well-informed body of people, few nations have a greater literary inheritance or a more lively school of contemporary writing, yet most people obtain little pleasure from reading. With a population of fifty million a novel is considered a success if it sells 5,000 copies in hardback. An outstanding biography of a nationally acclaimed figure would do remarkably well if 50,000 books found their way from the publisher to the reader. With effort these figures could be transformed. The majority, instead of the minority, could be coaxed into the pleasures of reading. Why could not we organize our libraries so that they positively canvass house to house to persuade the residents to become active members? Why should not new lists of books and information be regularly distributed from the library to the locality it serves? Why should not our libraries become the sponsors and inspirers of many more literary and musical groups than exist at the present time. There is no limit to the civilizing effect that turning Britain into a well-read nation would have, and a new dynamism from our libraries could make an immense contribution towards reaching this goal.

The extension of literacy and the creation of a well-read nation would go a long way towards achieving equality of opportunity. At the present time the children of middle-class families, the families who possess books, take five times as many university places as their number would indicate. The children of unskilled and semi-skilled workers, the children in homes without books, obtain but a small fraction of university places.

It has been estimated that children between five and fourteen spend twenty-five hours each week in front of a television set, as long as they spend in the classroom. These same children have many weeks' holiday from school. They have no weeks away from the television set. Television has certainly provided them with wider horizons, but it has also provided them with much that is far inferior and in fact far less enjoyable than what they would have obtained had they spent some of those twenty-five hours reading.

The Bullock Committee recommended that every child should spend part of each day reading with the teacher, who should listen to him several times a week. There is plenty of evidence that this is not done, nor is it done by parents, who have never been persuaded of the importance of doing so. Why could not we use television time to publicize the importance of taking their children to libraries and to teach parents how to teach their children to read?

For far too long the debate on education has been concentrated upon the merits and demerits of comprehensive education as opposed to a selective system. It is an important argument

Harold Macmillan with Peter Walker, then National Chairman of the Young Conservatives, 1959 (*The Times*)

As Shadow Minister of Transport, 1968

As Shadow Minister of Housing and Local Government, 1969 (*G. A. Publicity Limited*)

and one that will doubtless continue, but it has so dominated the scene that we have failed to give proper attention to some of the more fundamental questions about how to provide an educational system that does genuinely create equality of opportunity. The first and fundamental task is to create a far higher standard of literacy and numeracy and to end the disparities that now exist in the attainment of these fundamentals to learning. The second educational question facing us is the degree to which, in a world where knowledge is progressing so fast, we should continue to concentrate our educational effort on the 5–23-year-old rather than the 5–65-year-old. I believe that those now aged forty who completed their formal education perhaps twenty-five years ago should have available to them the means of acquiring new knowledge, whether to enable them to enter new and fresh occupations or to obtain a fuller and more interesting life. Only $2\frac{1}{2}$ per cent of the population over the age of twenty-five are in full-time education. The Open University is a new and important breakthrough, but the numbers involved are small. It has on average less than eighty students in each constituency in the country, and two-thirds of these are under the age of forty.

At the moment there are over two million part-time adult students, a greater number than all of those at schools, universities and colleges beyond school-leaving age put together, yet part-time courses take very low priority in most education departments. They are frequently axed in economy drives. They are closed whenever attendance falls below a certain level, even for one night, under procedures laid down by the Department of Education. Improving these part-time courses and making more generous provision for the maintenance of adult students may well be the direction in which the future expansion of our educational programmes should be concentrated. This is essential if we are to bring greater equality of opportunity to those who did not take full advantage of the educational facilities available to them as children, either because they themselves did not appreciate the importance of education or because their home environments were not conducive to their doing so.

CHAPTER IV

The Tories and the Trade Unions

As well as trying to provide equality of opportunity for the individual we must turn our attention to the institutions that represent individuals. It is vital for governments and unions to have a full understanding of each other's objectives.

When I first became a Cabinet minister I was determined to create a close, and I hoped cordial, relationship with trade union leaders connected with the government department for which I had responsibility. Shortly after becoming the Minister for Housing and Local Government in June 1970 I asked when I would have the opportunity of meeting some of the trade union leaders connected with the department. There was a silence and an uncertainty followed by the remark that the minister did occasionally meet trade union leaders if there was a serious industrial dispute affecting the activities of the department, but, apart from that, meetings did not frequently take place.

I asked for a list of unions directly connected with the department, amongst which were some of the most important unions in the country; the Union of Construction Workers and Allied Trades, the Municipal and General Workers' Union, and the Transport and General Workers' Union, and when later I took over the whole of the Department of the Environment the list included the railway unions, NALGO (National Association of Local Government Officers) and many others.

I sent a personal invitation to the general secretary and the chairman or president of each of these unions, asking them to come in separately to join me for a drink in the early part of the evening so that I could meet them and discuss with them some of the problems of the department. This was systematically carried out in the latter months of 1970.

The response was both interesting and amusing. The two

people invited for a drink would come in somewhat suspiciously and sit uneasily upon the edge of their chairs, immediately asking the reason for their being invited. When I gave as the reason that I simply wished to have a talk with them they seemed surprised.

I discussed with them the many appointments I had to make to the boards of nationalized industries, to advisory committees and to the boards of new towns, and asked them for the names of some of the brighter and abler members of their unions whom they considered had the abilities and talents appropriate to these positions. The list presented to me by the Civil Service had contained few trade unionists and those that were included were past the peak of their careers.

I told the trade union leaders that if there was any point in the policy of the department or in the practical application of policies by the department with which they, as union leaders, were concerned they had only to ask to see me and I would readily be available. I came to know some of these union leaders extremely well, and obtained from a number of them the confession that no Labour minister had ever invited them for a drink or created the type of relationship with them that I had done. They did, of course, say that they knew the Labour leaders better as they frequently met them at various trade union and Labour Party conferences, but they very seldom met them within their own departments and at the invitation of the minister in his ministerial capacity.

I used their suggestions and my own knowledge of a number of these union leaders in appointments I made. Sometimes an unreasonable suspicion would exist on the part of the trade unions. I was responsible for setting up an important committee to enquire into the whole future use of our national parks. I felt that only a small minority was gaining benefits from them, although they were an important part of the nation's heritage, and wanted the whole question of their future use and the development of their facilities looked into. Who better to sit on such a committee than a prominent active trade unionist? Large numbers of trade union members would be spending part of their leisure time in the national parks. I invited John Cousins to take on this important position (I had known his father, Frank Cousins, when he came into Parliament, and I respected his kindness and ability. It was sad that he found Parliament itself so difficult and that he did not obtain the parliamentary success that his basic abilities and talents deserved), but he encountered great opposition from his own union, who were reluctant to agree that he should take an appointment from a Conservative government. To my satisfaction they eventually agreed, and according to the other members he made a very considerable contribution to the work of the committee.

It is a tragedy that when there is so much talent in the trade union movement and such a great need for public appointments in industry, the new towns, and advisory committees, that those trade unionists who are appointed generally obtain their posts as a retiring gift from a Labour government. They are not the new generation of trade unionists, those in their thirties and forties who could contribute so much to future thinking. The close relationship that we at the Department of the Environment established with the union leaders was very frequently of important practical help at times of considerable anxiety. During the strike at the London docks the personal relationship established between John Peyton and Jack Jones was instrumental in getting a sensible settlement. I sought frequently to confer with Vic Feather, a man of genuine patriotism, moderation and common sense, and with an immense pride in the trade union movement. He acknowledged fully the importance in a parliamentary democracy of unions working with the government of the day.

I believe that I am the only Conservative minister in the postwar period who has been invited to open a trade union conference at Congress House. The trade union movement decided to hold a major conference on the problems of the environment and asked me as Secretary of State for the Environment to make the opening speech. The audience was interested and also accepted that my policies on the environment would benefit the majority of its members.

In the same way, my transport policy attempted to give the railways a much more positive and practical future than had previously been envisaged. My relationship with the railway union leaders were extremely good. Sid Greene, who was then the leader of the National Union of Railwaymen and, during the period that I was a minister, was also chairman of the T.U.C., was a person of moderate opinions, kindness and good humour, and with a passionate desire to see the railways succeed. It was perhaps a tragedy for the railways themselves that A.S.L.E.F. (Associated Society of Locomotive Engineers and Firemen) was more militantly led and that there was constant friction between these two unions. I discussed policy on many occasions with Sid

Greene, and if ever he said he would be able to persuade his union on something he was always able to do so.

I envisaged a programme for the railways in which we should link up with the railway systems of Europe through the Channel Tunnel. I also wanted to see the railway termini resited on those ring roads of motorway standard that were to surround our major conurbations. Similarly I wished to encourage inter-city traffic and the long-distance movement of freight by containers. It seems a pity that the protective attitude of railwaymen meant that they were unwilling to accept some of the necessary manpower changes. Perhaps this was understandable in view of the fact that security of employment had always been one of the prime advantages of work on the railways. It was depressing that a freightliner train with no guard's van and no fire, since it was pulled by a diesel locomotive, had under union agreements to have both a guard and a fireman, neither of whom had any particular role to perform. I visited a freightliner depot in London and asked why a second person was joining the driver, as there was no need for a fireman, only to be told that it was a great advantage to have two men rather than one in the event of a crash. A little later a further man joined them, making three in all. I asked the vice-chairman of British Rail why there were now three men there and he said with a smile that in the event of a crash it was probably better to have three men there than two!

There was no atmosphere of hostility or acrimony between myself and the trade union leaders connected with my department, but rather one of shared objectives and friendly relations. The Conservative government had no wish for confrontation with the unions. The controversial Industrial Relations Act created feeling within the unions, but it was certainly not an Act intended to harm them or their members. The whole wording of the legislation was based upon the desire of Robert Carr, a kind and gentle person very much in sympathy with the aspirations of working people in this country, to improve and strengthen responsible trade unionism. It was, on reflection, a mistake to introduce such a major piece of legislation so early in the Conservative government, and for the party, including all of us in the Cabinet, to overrate its importance. It is ironic that those people in industry who had been so passionately in favour of the legislation being introduced were also the first to criticize it. The emotions created by it proved to have an adverse effect on industrial relations in general.

Iain Macleod had committed the Conservatives to abandoning any type of prices and incomes policy. I believe it was a mistake on his part, a mistake that came from his genuine belief as a politician that it was important, whatever else you did in politics, for your policies to be distinctive, clear and easily comprehensible.

I do not think Iain was ever really happy in his role as Shadow Chancellor, or that he would have been happy as Chancellor, apart from the general happiness he got from making decisions. He was somebody I admired immensely and felt privileged to work closely with. After the election of Alec Douglas-Home, when Iain was in the wilderness, Ian Gilmour and I became his closest political friends. We worked with him with the view that Sir Alec would probably retire from the leadership of the Conservative Party long before the end of Iain's political career, our long-term objective being to make Iain the obvious choice of successor. Both Ian Gilmour and I admired, as all did, his eloquence, and his passions. He was a man of very considerable principle, a man who, in our view, fitted into the best traditions of the Conservative Party. When he became Shadow Chancellor I spent several weekends with him at his home providing him with background briefing. I had been one of the junior front bench spokesmen to Ted Heath as Shadow Chancellor and was therefore tolerably well informed on the major Treasury issues of the day and able to provide Iain with a detailed briefing. Each weekend we took a different subject. Public expenditure one weekend, direct taxation another, indirect taxation a third, international monetary policy yet another. While his brilliant intelligence meant that the briefing material he read and the discussions we had were perfectly within his grasp, he never, in my opinion, felt any great enthusiasm for the Chancellor's job itself.

He did enjoy being Minister of Health, with the opportunity it gave for social reform, and he also took great pleasure in being Colonial Secretary, with its wider visions. The opportunity to correct the imbalance between black and white nations was of great importance to him. I never felt he showed the same enthusiasm or passion for economics.

At the famous Selsdon Park meeting he persuaded his colleagues in the Shadow Cabinet that one of the things we needed to do was to rid ourselves of institutions such as the Pay Board, the Prices Commission and the I.R.C. (Industrial Reorganisation Corporation). The only voices opposed to him were those of

Reggie Maudling, who had always seen the necessity of some form of sensible prices and incomes policy so long as union power was exercised in the way it was, Edward Boyle and myself. The majority view was very strongly for pursuing the line Iain advocated.

This meant that in our early years we allowed the unions total freedom of unrestricted collective bargaining. For a period the trend of pay settlements decreased from what was then an alarmingly high figure to a more reasonable one, but eventually a number of unions made large demands and wages again started to rise swiftly. It became clear to us that unions no longer negotiated on the basis of what a particular firm or industry could afford but upon what another union had won. It was a leap-frogging process between unions and no longer a matter of negotiation between union and employer.

Nor was it true that if firms could not afford an increase, they did not pay it. The firm that could not afford it tended to grant the increase more speedily than the one that could, because it found itself in such a position that bankruptcy could have occurred had it been faced with a strike. The more limited the cash resources, the more quick the submission to extravagant union demands. It was in this context that Edward Heath, Tony Barber, Robert Carr, and the Conservative Cabinet as a whole unanimously came to the conclusion that some form of incomes policy was required. None of those who in more recent years has been seen to advocate a return to free collective bargaining opposed this change in policy. We had tried free collective bargaining and it had not succeeded.

Industry as a whole recognized that it could not stand up to the power of the unions under free collective bargaining and that some form of incomes policy should be applied.

We therefore entered into long negotiations with the unions to obtain a voluntary agreement. Those who attended, as I did, many of the talks at Number 10, Chequers, and elsewhere, will always object to the depiction of Edward Heath as a man who sought confrontation with the unions. Every union leader who took part in those talks knows, of course, that this view of him is completely false. He desired passionately to reach agreement with the union leaders, he believed he could, and he very nearly did. It is a tragedy for the British economy that he failed, for if he had succeeded we would have continued with the lowest, rather than the highest, inflation rate in Western Europe. We would have started a new era in industrial relations, of advantage to all political parties, and gained the influence of a new and responsible trade union movement.

The patience that he showed was impressive. He first described in immense detail the problems facing the government and the reasons why agreed restraint on incomes was necessary. He then listened to the unions' views and answered every point put by the union leaders. He asked for creative and constructive suggestions as to what would be needed if a voluntary agreement was to be reached. I was particularly involved over the question of council rents. The government had passed a Bill in which council house rents could be increased by 50 pence per year until they reached what was described as a 'fair rent'. We had introduced for the first time in British history rent rebates for all who could not afford the statutory rent. Naturally the trade union movement was anxious that in a time of wage restraint there should be no council house rent increases. To have accepted this in principle would have done immense damage to the whole future of sensible financing of our housing stock and would have been bad for those on waiting lists by making less money available for new housing. We met the point by giving very substantially improved rent rebates. The lower paid, those who would be most affected by wage restraint, received generous help to meet any rent increases.

On many other issues the government listened to the demands of the unions and either accepted them or gave clear reasons why they could not be accepted, and sought to put forward alternatives. I am convinced that the majority of trade union leaders would have made that voluntary agreement. Two men, I believe, prevented it from happening. One was Mr Briginshaw of the printers' union, a man of fierce left-wing views who was absolutely determined to see that the trade union movement would never reach a voluntary agreement with a Tory government. The other person was Hugh Scanlon, an able, dedicated man who genuinely wishes to eradicate capitalism and create a totally socialist society in Britain, and who won his life-long position of president of a very powerful union on the votes of the extreme left wing. For the rest, I believe agreement was very near, and there is no doubt that with the possible exception of Mr Briginshaw there was not one trade union leader who took part in those talks who did not privately admit his admiration for the sincerity and thoroughness of Edward Heath's approach to these problems.

This, of course, is the reason why, when the government then had to introduce a statutory incomes policy, every trade union in the country with one exception complied without taking industrial action. That exception was the miners' union, which in the unique circumstances of a Middle East oil embargo decided by majority vote to use the economic power of that moment to take political action against the government of the day. It is interesting that in 1973, a year in which the Tory incomes policy was fully applied, the number of days lost through industrial unrest was the lowest figure for four years.

Despite those who say that the Tory government pursued a policy of confrontation with the unions, the government in fact showed a greater depth of understanding of the unions than any of their Labour predecessors.

The Parliamentary Labour Party acted particularly irresponsibly during the period of the miners' strike in the way they supported the miners' case. During the previous six years of Labour government 200,000 miners had become redundant and miners' wages had only gone up by 39 per cent while the cost of living had gone up by 31 per cent. In the first three years of the Conservative government the miners' pay had risen by 50 per cent as compared with a 28 per cent rise in the cost of living. It is totally wrong that Ted Heath should be depicted as a person without understanding of the position of the miner or the trade unionist in general. He understood their aspirations, and he admired many of their leaders perhaps more sincerely and enthusiastically than most post-war Prime Ministers. He was anxious to improve the lot of trade unionists and to see that they obtained at least their fair share of what was available in the national economy.

I first enjoyed a close association with Edward Heath when, in 1965, I was asked by Sir Alec Douglas-Home to join the opposition front bench as number two to Ted Heath. I immediately began to recognize his remarkable range of talents. Our first task was to oppose the 1965 Finance Act introducing Capital Gains and Corporation Tax. It was the first time that a line-by-line, clause-by-clause opposition had been organized against a Finance Act, and I came to recognize then the remarkable stamina, energy and thoroughness of the person who led that attack. We frequently breakfasted at his flat in Albany in order to discuss the tactics for the coming day. I remember one occasion when I had been moving amendments throughout the day and night, and we finally left the House of Commons at 6.15 a.m.; as we walked across Palace Yard together he turned to me and said, 'I will see you at 8.30 a.m. and you might prepare me a brief on Clauses 23 and 24.' He was somewhat shocked at my response!

Perhaps the characteristic that made most impression on me was his honesty. One night one of our backbenchers – a well-known one – made an attack on a particular clause which, while effective in delivery and immediate impact, was totally dishonest in its use of statistics and figures. An angry Ted Heath turned to me and said, 'If we cannot oppose bad legislation without being dishonest we should not oppose it at all.' In the lobbies Ted Heath expressed his disapproval to the backbencher concerned.

One of the reasons for his strict honesty is that he is a very devout Christian. He prays, and prays intensely. He had a mother who taught him that truth was essential and at times his unwillingness to accept something he knows to be bogus has proved to be to his disadvantage.

At the time of the coal crisis the T.U.C. made what was a blatantly dishonest offer to allow the miners to have their increase. From a tactical point of view he could have accepted this, avoided the three-day week, and let events show how dishonest their offer was. Instead, because he knew it to be bogus, he immediately exposed the meaninglessness of the T.U.C. offer, and continued with the problems of the miners' strike.

As Prime Minister, there was never an item on the Cabinet agenda upon which he personally was not exceptionally well briefed, and he always had a barrage of combative questions to put to the minister propounding the particular case.

This technique of combative questioning, interpreted by some as being hostile, was a method that gained him some admirers but rather more opponents. Much of his reputation for obstinacy was due to his way of questioning his colleagues. If, however, your argument was a good one and you managed to sustain it in face of his hostile questions, he would accept your case and press it with enthusiasm himself.

I was with him when the result of the election for the leadership of the Conservative Party following Sir Alec Douglas-Home's resignation was announced. He had not got the necessary majority and there could have been a second ballot, but his lead was such that it was inconceivable that Reggie Maudling would decide to go through with one. We therefore went to my flat at

Gayfere Street, informed the Chief Whip where he could contact Ted Heath, and awaited the decision by Reggie as to whether he would concede.

I then spent a fascinating one and a half hours alone with Ted Heath waiting for the call. There he was, the new leader of the Conservative Party, obviously happy but already recognizing the magnitude of his task.

He had an immense desire to restore the fortunes of his country. Much of his political motivation is in fact simple patriotism, patriotism strengthened by the coincidence of his age with events. His formative days at university were days of pre-war tension; his attendance at the Nuremberg Rally, his visits to Poland and Danzig and his on-the-spot observation of the Spanish Civil War had made him essentially an internationalist before he became president of the Oxford Union. His hostility to Munich was expressed in his campaign against the Conservative candidate in the Oxford by-election, and he immediately joined the forces when war broke out. This all combined to make the survival of his country the initial determining factor in his political thinking.

He now wanted to set about the task of restoring Britain's international influence and domestic strength. One felt, sitting with him, listening to his hopes and aspirations, that the Conservative Party had a new leader with clear objectives. Perhaps more than most politicians, he had thought carefully and in depth about the problems of Britain, and he was now being given the opportunity to apply his solutions.

In the years I have known him there have been only four or five occasions when I have penetrated his deepest thoughts. He is a very self-contained person, and also a fairly shy one, though he is very close to his family and a few long-standing personal friends. There is a simplicity in his motives and affections which gives him a considerable stability. The comment of Anthony Eden that 'the rougher the weather the steadier his advice' is an observation with which many would agree who have worked closely with him during difficult times.

When, at the height of the fuel crisis, virtually every newspaper, both sides of Parliament, and I believe, quite a few ministers were clamouring for the introduction of petrol rationing, I was almost alone in opposing it, and was able to avoid it because of the calm and solid support of Edward Heath. Many Prime Ministers in such an atmosphere would have bowed to the immediate clamour. I never doubted for one moment that, acquainted with the logical arguments for avoiding petrol rationing, he at least would be persuaded.

He has almost certainly tackled the problems of British politics with greater application than any man living. As far as his relationship with the electorate was concerned, his solitude as a politician had many disadvantages, but it also had benefits in terms of his standing and skill as Prime Minister because of the additional time he was able to devote to his work.

He did not, however, pursue his job to the exclusion of all else. Sailing and music received the same total application of his abilities whenever the opportunity arose. To go to a concert or music festival with him was not just to hear a very professional musician admiring or criticizing whatever was being performed, but also to be with one totally happy – if the music was to his satisfaction. When it was not, his criticisms were fierce – as at the Three Choirs Festival when he listened in some discomfort to a new work being played for the first time. When asked for his view by an eager music critic, he said, 'I was interested in being present for its first, and I trust only, performance.'

The impression that Edward Heath is a cold man without family interests is a myth. He was, after all, the Prime Minister who turned Chequers into a real home instead of the country office of the Prime Minister. For the first time since Chequers was made available, it became the scene of an essentially family Christmas when Ted Heath, surrounded by his father, stepmother, brother and sister-in-law, together with Madron and Nancy-Joan Seligman, celebrated a typical English Christmas with all the trimmings and excitement. Likewise, he was probably the only Prime Minister in post-war Britain to fill 10 Downing Street with things that gave him and his friends immense pleasure.

Edward Heath is a totally classless person, and resents class prejudice from whichever quarter it may come. His simple patriotic approach meant that as Prime Minister he was always endeavouring to obtain a sense of national unity. The night when he was defeated as leader, a film was shown cataloguing his immediate past. In his moving tribute Vic Feather expressed his appreciation of Ted's genuine desire for national unity, and it was an appreciation shared by many of his trade union colleagues, for Ted Heath had established a close and friendly relationship with many union leaders.

With them it was easy, for they were discussing mutual problems with experience and knowledge. Where he is bad is in small talk with people who do not share his personal interests. There is a remarkable contrast between his failures to please in the company of people with whom he has little in common and his witty and enthusiastic role when lunching or dining with friends, or with people with common interests.

Where he has made enemies is at dinner parties, frequently with businessmen and men from the City, where he has argued fiercely. Such men do not expect Prime Ministers and leaders of parties to question the manner in which they conduct their activities. They expect them to receive gratefully the advice offered them and not to offer advice themselves, whereas Ted Heath considered that the object of such dinners was to debate current problems. Debating was neither the businessmen's objective nor their skill, and the next day they retailed their resentment of the Prime Minister's failure to listen. An outside observer would realize that he had listened and they had not.

I discovered as Secretary of State for the Environment that he had a deep desire to eradicate the problems of the more depressed areas of the country. As the minister responsible for regional policy he had put into practice the important ideas prepared by Quintin Hogg to bring jobs and improve the quality of life in those parts that had been far too long underprivileged. His many visits to such areas gave him a very genuine and deep admiration for the people who lived there. The story of the appointment of Dennis Stevenson at the age of twenty-six as chairman of Peterlee and Aycliffe New Town provides an illustration of this. Peterlee and Aycliffe had its problems. It was a town that consisted primarily of former Durham miners and with which T. Dan Smith had been closely associated. I was anxious to make an imaginative appointment of somebody who would work enthusiastically to bring real prospects to the town.

I chose Dennis Stevenson, not for any party reasons (all I knew about his political allegiance was that he had been a member of the Labour Club at Cambridge), but because I had immensely admired a piece of research he had done on the problems of young West Indians in London. After reading this I asked to meet him, and was much impressed by his vigour, vitality, and passion to be of public service and to help particularly those who were deprived. When I was confronted with the need to make an imaginative choice for the new town I decided to select Dennis

Stevenson. I wrote to Number 10, a necessary formality, to obtain the approval of the Prime Minister for the appointment, naturally putting in the age of my choice as chairman. Such were the attitudes towards the young at Number 10 that when my letter was received there an official reply came back asking me to confirm that this was a typing error and that I meant sixty-two.

Ted Heath doubted whether I should appoint somebody so young to the chairmanship of the new town and suggested that perhaps I should put him on the board. I pointed out to him that at a somewhat younger age a man called Pitt had carried out duties rather more arduous than those of being the chairman of Peterlee New Town. Alexander the Great had not done too badly by that time either.

Ted Heath then asked to see this young man whom I was supporting so enthusiastically. A rather nervous Dennis Stevenson went with me to visit him at Number 10. Ted asked some pretty tough questions, and for once in his life Dennis Stevenson was very nervous and hesitant, and I could see Ted coming to the conclusion that this had been a lunatic choice on my part. Then the atmosphere improved and Dennis Stevenson's ability began to show, and Ted was obviously much impressed by him.

He then asked, 'Do you really know the north-east?' Dennis Stevenson admitted his limited knowledge of the area but stressed his greater knowledge of the industrial parts of Scotland. Ted Heath then said, 'I'll show you the north-east', and to our astonishment rose from his chair in his study and led us to the flat upstairs where in the hall there was a picture by John Cornish, a former Durham miner who painted mining scenes. It was a picture of a typical Durham miner with his cloth cap, his back to the viewer slumped at a typical public bar of a Durham pub. The surroundings were fairly grim, the background bleak. The Prime Minister turned to Dennis Stevenson and said, 'That's the north-east. If I appoint you as chairman of Peterlee New Town do you think you can see that that man and his children have a rather better quality of life in the future than he and his family had in the past?' The surprised Dennis Stevenson stuttered that it would be marvellous if he could. 'Well,' said the Prime Minister, 'you had better get on with it.'

History will recall the remarkable impact of Ted Heath on the international scene. Remarkable because it was out of all proportion to either the economic or the military strength of the country he led. From his Oxford days he had always essentially been an internationalist. He established close links with Churchill and admired the international views of Churchill in the post-war period. Anyone who has read Ted Heath's Godkin Lectures, delivered in 1967, would recognize his immense vision, foresight and depth of feeling in the sphere of European policy.

His voice will certainly continue to make a considerable impact at home and abroad, for he is a man whose main love for most of his life has been his country and he is in despair that she is doing so badly. He always has been and, I believe, always will be a man determined to achieve things and not just pontificate upon them. He once commented upon his enthusiasm for sailing by saying he always raced and never cruised. I don't believe he is the cruising type.

Ted Heath was genuine in wishing to improve the lot of trade unionists. Nevertheless his government was defeated by the miners.

History may well show that recently the Labour Party has suffered more in its relationship with the unions than the Conservatives have. The total failure of the Social Contract has resulted in an incomes policy which, unlike any previous incomes policy, has had to be toughened rather than relaxed, and which will, in its second phase, if complied with, reduce the living standards of trade unionists more dramatically than at any time since 1930.

The political attitude of the miners was an example of the price the Conservatives still pay for the prejudices created by an era of socially irresponsible capitalism. On the performance of recent governments, and particularly the last Conservative government, the miners should, if motivated by self-interest, have voted Conservative and have been eager to retain a Conservative government in power. It was their traditional prejudice against the Conservative Party and in favour of the Labour Party that led the National Union of Mine Workers (N.U.M.) to use the enhanced industrial power given them by the oil embargo to try to bring down the Conservative government.

The Phase III pay policy was devised after careful consideration of the problems of individual trade unions, and was intended particularly to suit the miners. For not only were the miners to enjoy the full benefits of Phase III, but they also had the chance of referring their case to the Relativities Board, a board set up to see if there was a need for major adjustments in wages of certain industries that had fallen behind over the previous years. There was no clearer case than the miners', and it was very much with the miners in mind that I urged upon my colleagues the necessity for the form of Relativities Board that the Tory government created. The leaders of the miners' union, whom I came to know well, had discussed this with me and were fully conversant with the implications.

Their belief in the justice of such a system was shown by the way they speedily referred their case to the Relativities Board, and the fact that the Relativities Board report, issued close to polling day, suggested an increase virtually identical with the final settlement agreed with the incoming Labour government, showed how fair the system really was, despite its rejection by the miners. There was no need for the miners to take the industrial action that they did. It did immense economic damage and immense damage to the whole principle of democracy in our country, and was aimed at a government that had arranged an incomes policy especially to suit the needs of the miners and had reversed the policy of pit closures.

The miners' reactions to my policies for the coal industry were expressed best by the miners themselves in the official magazine of the N.U.M., *Miner*. Following the publication of my Coal Industry Bill, it carried the headline 'The Coal Bill is a massive victory for commonsense says NUM President' and then the banner headline 'a merry Christmas for Old King Coal'. The front page of the magazine was devoted to the welcome the N.U.M. gave to my Bill. The front page article stated that:

> to many people publication of a Coal Industry Bill giving any assistance to the coal mining industry was a surprise, particularly in view of the Government's defeat by the miners earlier in 1972. When Peter Walker introduced the Coal Industry Bill on 11th December 1972 many people were shocked at the extent of the aid being provided for the industry but apart from seeing the union's philosophy at last accepted few miners will be shocked at his statement to the House of Commons. On 11th December, Peter Walker said, 'There is real uncertainty at future prices of fuels and an increasing awareness throughout the world of the dangerous shortage of energy; we in the United Kingdom must ensure that our national energy assets are widely used. Last year the National Coal Board lost £157 million, it is now losing around £100 million a year.

Visiting West Indian families in Brixton as Minister of Housing and Local Government, 1970 (*London Express News & Features Services*)

Below: At Knottingley Colliery in Yorkshire, while Secretary of State for Trade and Industry, 1973 (*National Coal Board*)

Anglo-Soviet trade talks, Moscow 197 Peter Walker with Mr Kosygin, Prime Minister of the Soviet Union (*Novo Press Agency*)

Peter Walker with Mr Chou en Lai, Prime Minister of China, in Peking in 1973 during negotiations concerning a trade agreement (*London Express News & Features Services*)

Without government aid this would increase and would be eliminated only by a massive contraction. We are not prepared to see such a rapid rundown with all the social and human consequences that it would entail. For these reasons the coal industry must be given the opportunity to establish itself as a supplier of a competitive fuel instead of being a permanent burden on the taxpayer. The industry's joint proposals express a determination to put its own house in order and the government have therefore decided to seek powers to support the industry in this task.'

On the same page was a message from Joe Gormley, N.U.M. president, in which he said:

This is a massive victory for commonsense. Inevitably the Government's declaration of faith in the industry will increase the morale of our lads who have had fears for their future. I am convinced productivity will get better and better and we shall get more use out of the machinery already available in the pits. Our lads will be more willing to accept more mechanization as a result of what the Government have done.

The editorial of the paper said:

The recent joint approach by the mining unions and the Coal Board suggested ten points to the Government which were necessary to give the industry a long-term future. The published Bill covers nine of these points. The only one on which the Government have stood firm is the import of coal. President Gormley said the measures in the Bill could lead to more secure employment in the mines and provide greater security of scarce energy supplies.

This was all in sharp contrast to the 1964–70 Labour government, which had made 200,000 miners redundant.

It was my intention as Secretary of State for the Environment to remove within ten years the slag heaps that have created such ghastly environments in most of the areas where miners live. It was my endeavour as Secretary of State for Trade and Industry not only to improve their industrial conditions but also to give them an industrial future they had not previously enjoyed. It was I who made the decisions to stop the increasing redundancies and to forge ahead with a major investment programme in the Selby coalfield. I think I can claim to have done more for the miners of Britan than any other post-war minister, in both the industrial and the environmental spheres.

I can only regret that they were the cause of the downfall of the government and that their strike was called as a political measure with precisely this object. The incoming government swiftly settled with the miners' union and then returned to the much proclaimed free collective bargaining.

CHAPTER
V

A Programme for Industrial Democracy

THE return of the Labour government to free collective bargaining in 1974 coincided with a change of leadership in the Conservative Party. For a time the new Conservative leaders opposed any form of incomes policy, but in a matter of a year the leadership of the Conservative Party and the Labour Party have both come to recognize that such is the strength of union power at the present time that a policy of free collective bargaining cannot successfully be pursued.

There are four basic choices open to governments in respect of future industrial relations in Britain. The first is to allow free collective bargaining while making no attempt to alter the attitudes or the power of the unions. Both parties have tried to pursue the policy, but in their first eighteen months of office it achieved disastrous results for the present Labour government: earnings increased by 49 per cent while industrial production dropped by 10 per cent. We suffered the worst inflation in Western Europe, and the public sector wages bill soared by £6½ billion, creating a massive increase in public expenditure and thus in the government's borrowing requirement.

The second choice, favoured by some members of the Conservative Party and some employers, is to allow free collective bargaining but to reduce the power of the unions. Its supporters argue for the abolition of social security payments to strikers' families, changing the law of picketing, and training specialists who can replace strikers in the maintenance of essential services. I believe that such a policy would also be disastrous. It would divide the nation and create a bitterness in society not experienced since the Jarrow Hunger Marches. Taking away social security payments to strikers' families would penalize the wives and children of strikers, irrespective of whether the strike was justified or even of whether a particular man had voted against the strike. It would also be a policy quite impossible to administer, for the strikers could live with relatives or neighbours during the strike so that their wives could claim that their husbands had left home and that they and their children were therefore dependent upon social security payments. There would be no way in which one could possibly establish that the men had not temporarily left their wives and children. There would be loopholes in the system which would make it totally ineffective. One can imagine the emotional reaction to the death of the first child that was said to have suffered from malnutrition. It would certainly not be a policy that could be followed by any Tory government that was serious in its desire to establish a good relationship with the unions.

The third option is a national incomes policy, the option taken by the last Conservative government and now by the present Labour government after the calamitous effects of a period of free collective bargaining. All incomes policies have a multitude of defects and injustices, but recent experience has shown that in total incomes policies have been far less unjust and far better at combating domestically created inflation than a 'free for all' in wage claims.

Those who argue that incomes policies require political concessions that increase public expenditure fail to realize the immense contribution that wage increases make towards increasing public expenditure.

In 1976 the total public sector wages bill amounted to £24 billion. Every 1 per cent increase adds £240 million to public expenditure. The wage inflation created in the free collective bargaining allowed by the Labour government in their first two years of office put up public sector wages by £6½ billion; coincidentally the public sector borrowing requirement increased by an almost identical amount during the same period.

A perpetual incomes policy, however, would create an undesirable lack of flexibility within the economy. It would do much to create a corporate state. It would destroy the right to bargain responsibly over the division of rewards between the firm and the employee and, in the longer term, it would create an undesirable tendency towards collectivism. Normally an incomes policy fails to share rewards fairly between the skilled and the unskilled, and fails to give sufficient incentive and encouragement to the hardworking. While essential in the economic circumstances of 1976 following the two years of totally irresponsible wage and salary increases, an incomes policy does not in itself lead to the type of industrial society that a Conservative government should wish to seek.

This leaves the fourth choice – the choice that a Conservative government should adopt – the creation of a new industrial society that can be relied upon to see that the distribution of rewards is more objectively and responsibly decided.

Such a programme gives us the only chance of avoiding the two extremes of impossible inflationary wage demands on the one hand, and a permanent bureaucratically controlled incomes policy on the other. It would mobilize the fullest sense of responsibility in all who work in industry. It should consist of five points:

1 Secret postal or factory ballots.
2 A reform of company law to ensure that information is provided to all involved in industry.
3 Action to obtain widespread employee participation.
4 An industrial assembly which would institutionalize the conflict of powers within industry.
5 Widespread profit-sharing.

1 *Secret Postal or Factory Ballots*

This is a simple and practical measure that would genuinely increase democracy within the trade unions. Postal ballots or secret ballots within the factories concerned should become a statutory requirement in the election of key union officers. It would also be necessary that there should be elections for union officers at tolerable intervals. There would then be a maximum period for which a general secretary of a trade union could be elected. The period could well be five years, the same as for members of Parliament, or if unions wished to have more opportunities for change it could be less than that.

It is not enough for the Conservative government to say that it will pay for postal ballots if requested: the union leaders who have been elected as a result of minority voting under the present electoral systems are not going to ask to be provided with money to finance a system of voting that will result in their defeat. Mr Hugh Scanlon, who was originally elected to his office, the all-powerful office of president of the engineering union, on the votes of 5 per cent of the total membership of that union, is unlikely to go rushing round to a Conservative minister saying, 'Please will you finance a new system of voting whereby people like me will not be elected.' The postal ballot has in recent times been shown to increase industrial democracy and to decrease the unjustified power of extreme minorities. It is in the national interest that it should become a reality for all unions.

I reject the argument that it is up to the unions to decide what form their election shall take and whether or not to change the ballot system. This can be tolerated only with institutions of less national importance than the trade unions. Company law in this country imposes very considerable restrictions on the rights of shareholders to vote. There are no similar restrictions as far as the unions are concerned.

Will any Conservative government introducing postal voting and secret ballots create all the emotional hostility that the Industrial Relations Act tragically brought about? I do not believe so, because it would be very difficult to stir up such hostility. No union leader could claim that such a measure was against the interests of the members of that union. Nor could he claim that it would do other than make the leadership more truly representative of the union membership.

2 *Reform of Company Law*

There is also a need to change our company law. This is something I would have done had a Conservative government continued in power after 1974, for I had already published a White Paper outlining the preliminary views of the government. The object of my reforms was to see that both the interests of the employee and the interests of the community were recognized.

The present principle of British company law is that directors have responsibility only to the shareholders. But modern society must accept that the directors of companies have considerable responsibility both to their employees and to the community in which they operate.

One of the major purposes of company law reform must be to insist on the disclosure of relevant information to both employees and shareholders. This should be done at frequent intervals. There is no information that is disclosed to shareholders that should not be readily available to employees. There is, on the other hand, a whole range of information that employees should be given but which need not be made available to shareholders.

Under our present system of company law it is only the shareholders that receive information as a right. I welcome the experiments carried out in recent years by a number of firms who have held annual general meetings of employees. It must be sensible for the directors of a firm to have an open meeting with those they employ at least once a year, to inform them of the prospects for the coming year, to hear criticisms, and to accept questions from those whose whole lives are given to the firm. In the future, information concerning training, the working environment, health and safety factors should become an essential part of an annual report to the employees.

3 *Employee Participation*
This, however, is only part of the process of creating fuller industrial democracy. In the debate on industrial democracy both sides of industry have tended to take a defensive attitude towards policies which, if successful, would replace confrontation with collaboration and would make one side in industry instead of two.

The unions for their part have been suspicious and reluctant that much progress should be made in employee participation. They realize that if participation succeeds the traditional role of the trade unions will be transformed. Some of them also see that the overwhelming power given to trade unions under a system of free collective bargaining in the short term provides very substantial wage increases for their members and in the longer term will bring about a change in the very nature of the economic system itself.

The power to demand of firms more than they can pay and the knowledge that if they refuse to pay strike action will quickly bring them to insolvency is considered by some to be the means of bringing about public ownership. During the worst cash flow problems of British Leyland the unions did nothing to modify their pay demands. The cash flow problems of British Leyland aggravated by wage demands and industrial action resulted in a major industry going into the public sector.

There are some politically motivated leaders of major unions who see genuine employee participation as endangering their political objectives. For the rest there is a reluctance to change from a system of negotiation in which they are experienced and successful to a system in which they would have to share some of the responsibilities of decision-taking with those who provide the capital.

It is not surprising that the Trades Union Congress has looked upon employee participation not as a means of transforming the existing power of the unions into a power with a wider responsibility but as a method of extending their present power and giving them yet further advantages in their comprehended role of collective bargaining. Their main objective has been to persuade a Labour government and the Bullock Committee to pursue policies that would increase union power rather than create genuine participation. They do not wish the twelve million people who are members of unions to have any participation other than through their existing trade union representatives. Nor do they envisage any participation for the fourteen million employees who are not in unions. Participation would then mean the participation of a small handful of people elected by something like 10 per cent of British employees. There will not be much change in industrial attitudes or relationships if this particular route is followed.

Employers in their turn have looked upon employee participation as a pretext and excuse for the unions to extend still further their power over management decision-taking. It is true that a number of our major firms have improved their communication with the shop floor and by delegation within their firms achieved a considerable degree of participation in the taking of decisions. Such firms are in the minority; in the majority of firms there is a very distinct pride in the management's power to make decisions and a jealous belief that this power should not be shared with those who are managed. It is very difficult to persuade the managing director who has spent perhaps thirty-five years of his life reaching a position of power and authority within his firm to study ways in which he can share that power and authority with others. There is therefore an in-built reluctance to make much progress, and yet while the appalling 'two sides of industry' concept dominates British industrial thinking, the damage done by it will remain, and that damage will certainly prevent our economic revival.

When I was Secretary of State for Trade and Industry the subject of employee participation came to the forefront of discussion in industrial and political circles because of our joining the European Community. On a visit to our embassy in Bonn I asked whether it would be possible for me to discuss privately the experiences of industrialists in Germany, where employee participation has been a statutory requirement since the war. A dinner took place in Cologne and was attended by twelve top German industrialists.

I had suspected, when I read the reports of British industrialists as to how ineffective and troublesome the Germany system had been, that these men, the tycoonery of Western Germany, would tell me they had accepted the system reluctantly. And the two industrialists from the steel industry, where 50 per cent of the supervisory board was elected by the employees and 50 per cent by the management, were indeed hostile to the system. They said that it had resulted in considerable stalemate in their industry, and in long periods of indecision, creating friction between the two sides rather than improving the relationship.

What was impressive, however, was that the remaining ten industrialists, whose experiences of participation had been with a supervisory board on which a third of the members had been chosen by the employees and two-thirds by the management, were unanimous in their praise for the system. They had not publicly acclaimed their enthusiasm and praise for the system, they told me, because, had they done so, it might have aroused suspicion amongst their employees that this was some system particularly advantageous to the employers. They genuinely considered that it had been to the mutual advantage of employee and employer. It had also prevented the irresponsible militant making much progress in German industry. Since employees' representatives had access to confidential information and were able to discuss the firm's investment programmes and the need for profit if those investment programmes were to be completed, the employees realized the full implications of the firm's policy. It had created an atmosphere in German industry far more conducive to the putting forward of constructive suggestions by employees. It was this unanimous view of ten German industrialists from a wide range of industries that convinced me that there was much in the German system which could sensibly be incorporated in Britain.

The very fact that Germany has operated such a system during the post-war period and has achieved a G.N.P. double our own, with a somewhat similar population, does at least indicate that employee participation is not disadvantageous to industry.

There are other factors in the German industrial scene which have played their part. A closed shop is illegal in Western Germany; the unions have no direct political tie with the major parties; collective agreements are legally binding on both sides;

strikes are illegal if they are against what has already been agreed in a collective agreement, if they are purely sympathetic strikes not affecting the pay or conditions of the striker himself, or if they are strikes made before the agreed conciliation machinery has been fully exhausted. Strikes then have to obtain the approval of more than 75 per cent of the workforce in the factory concerned and must not be for a purely political purpose.

All German firms have to have a works council representing all the employees. The tasks of the works council are first to study the effects of statutory requirements on employees of the firm, to receive suggestions, to recommend policies considered good for both employees and the company, to help the disabled and those in need, to promote the employment of the elderly and to encourage the sensible integration of foreign workers.

There are also a number of very important spheres where the works council enjoys co-determination with the management. These are : job evaluation; working times and holidays, and times for breaks; recruitment, promotion and redeployment policies; training and accident prevention; redundancy plans, should they prove to be necessary, in which case a social plan must be agreed between the employers and the works council. Set into all these procedures there is compulsory arbitration in the event of a dispute.

The works council must be consulted on hirings and dismissals and has the right to object on the grounds of social hardship, in which case the matter is referred to the Labour Court. Where there are more than 100 people employed in a firm an economic committee is formed of four to eight members of the works council, and they are provided with financial information concerning the company, some of which may be of a confidential nature.

Where more than 500 people are employed a supervisory board is created which meets four or five times a year, appoints a management board, discusses and comments upon annual accounts and is involved in the decision-taking on any merger or takeover. The management board, which is full-time, is responsible for the day-to-day operation of the firm, and its members are not allowed to be members of the supervisory board. The proprietors' interests have in the past controlled two-thirds of the membership of the supervisory board. Now new proposals have been made whereby firms with more than 2,000 employees must have a supervisory board consisting of ten members representing the shareholders' interests and ten the employees' interests. Of the ten representing the employees' interests one must be from senior management. The ten employees chosen are from an electoral college elected by all the workers. The deputy chairman of the board will be an employee, the chairman being from the proprietory side and in the event of a dispute having the casting vote. One member of the management board in all such companies must be solely responsible for personnel and social matters.

Works assemblies are held quarterly to hear the reports of the works councils. Elections for such bodies take place throughout Germany at the same time. There is a very high percentage poll in these elections, for all employees, whether members of unions or not, have a right to vote. In practice, however, although not quite a third of the working population of Germany are members of trade unions, the majority of places on works councils have gone to trade unionists. In any British application of the system of employee participation it would be vital to keep the principle of each employee having to vote but to give the trade unions the right to put up trade union candidates, many of whom would have a very good chance of being elected.

When the European Community prepared a discussion paper on employee participation their proposals differed considerably from those of the British T.U.C. It was considered essential that all employees should have a vote in the creation of any form of supervisory board, and that the ultimate authority, perhaps provided by the casting vote, should be with the owners. It was also decided that a free and secret ballot should take place in all cases and that the workers would have to accept full corporate responsibility when they received the powers concerned. Seemingly the T.U.C. in Britain are opposed to all employees being represented and wish to disenfranchise more than 50 per cent of employees who are not members of unions. They have made no suggestions that appointment to supervisory boards should be other than by the existing trade union leadership and therefore reject the proposal for a free and secret ballot. Nor do they accept that any trade union official taking part on a supervisory board should accept the full responsibilities of a member of that board. Their proposals are not for an extension of democracy to industry so as to create a social and industrial partnership between employer and employee but for the increase of the existing power, knowledge and influence of the trade unions themselves.

Such proposals would present considerable dangers and

hazards; for example, the same union might appoint people to competing companies and work within the union to try to come to work-sharing arrangements which would cut across the interests both of the consumer and of the employee of the better run company.

Britain has been very much behind Europe in industrial democracy. Although Germany has been way ahead of any other country, in Belgium and Luxembourg works councils are required by law, they operate on a wide scale in Denmark and Italy, and in France not only is there widespread profit-sharing but supervisory boards have also become an accepted possibility. If industrial democracy is to succeed here time is needed for preparation and training. The present trade union movement would not be able to play its full part, for its experience is frequently limited to the area of pay negotiation and its staff are not sufficiently trained.

We need to do far more in Britain about the training of employees' representatives, whether they are elected representatives on works councils, representatives on supervisory boards, or shop stewards. The trade union movement does not have the financial resources or the means of providing this training, and it is therefore a matter of urgency that the government should enter into an agreement with the trade union movement as to the manner in which more time and money should be made available for this vital task.

If a new atmosphere in industry is to be generated employees need to have a far greater comprehension of how firms operate. This means that each firm will have to take the trouble to provide tuition in the procedures and concepts of marketing and in the technological developments affecting the company. Industrial democracy can only succeed if all employees are interested in the firm. What must be avoided is a top-heavy consultative structure in which large numbers of people are involved but without making very much impact upon the individuals who are supposed to be consulted.

A number of firms have carried out experiments in which middle management is removed and groups of employees are left to organize themselves in the most efficient way possible. One of the breweries has been particularly successful in this sphere. The employees eliminated all supervisory management in many areas of their work, and created groups of employees to decide jointly upon investment programmes and methods of increasing production, and were naturally allowed to benefit from the additional rewards resulting from their decisions. The result was a very considerable increase in productivity and in the incomes of the employees.

Delegation is in itself a very important form of participation. Each manager should operate with a small area of control but a wide area of autonomy. The delegation of responsibility all along the line is a very important part of proper and just consultation procedures. There is an increasing tendency in British industry to make liberal use of the employee attitude survey. If we are to delegate responsibility adequately, and if industrial democracy is to become meaningful, there are only three ways in which management can convey its views. One is to tell the employee what is going to take place. The second is to tell the employees' representatives and discuss it with them. The third is to tell all concerned and discuss it with them. In many cases the formation of a works management through which employees are told and have the opportunity of discussing what is going on has proved by far the best method of management. It is vital to move away from the present position in which the unions are suspicious of anything that means collaboration and not negotiation.

Many employers agree with the C.B.I. that employee participation should be allowed to evolve and develop naturally. If their view is accepted large numbers of firms who wish to continue upon the master and man principle and not to make their contribution to improving industrial relations will continue to take no action. Legislation should be produced to the effect that within three years every firm employing more than 300 people should agree to adopt one or other of a listed range of schemes for increasing industrial democracy. If none of the listed schemes was applicable the firm could introduce an alternative scheme for which it had obtained the agreement of both employees and management. By such an approach we would make considerable progress and a great deal of important experimentation would begin.

Among the choices that should be listed is the introduction of a supervisory board similar to those operating in Germany. Such is their success there that they have been given the genuine support of all the major political parties in Western Germany.

The German experience of employee participation is important. It has been examined by a commission of experts which was set up in 1970 to see how well co-determination had worked. They found that there was no case where employees' representatives had refused to consent to investment projects that were for the future good of the company. They also considered that it had been important from the point of view of the dignity of the human being and his free development. The idea of the dignity of the individual is founded both in Christian doctrine and in the basic ethic of democracy itself. It is true that the owner runs a substantial risk when he makes entrepreneurial decisions, but there is also very substantial risk on the part of the employees involved. The loss of invested capital is frequently less painful than the loss of a job, and this must be recognized in our ideas about industry. Capital ownership certainly gives control over goods and machinery, but it should not in itself give the same control over persons. Human abilities and human skills are even more important than fixed capital.

Managers themselves do not risk their capital; if we are not careful we shall be reaching a position where the major decisions of corporations are taken by people who have neither invested their capital or savings in the industry nor are directly adversely affected by measures that may affect the majority of employees whom they themselves manage. The importance of employee participation is that it is the only way to dismantle the authoritarian structures that characterize relationships in industry.

A second possibility is to make provision for employee directors to go on to the existing board and play their role upon a single board of directors. If such a system were adopted it would again be essential that they should be there not upon the appointment of the board but as the choice of all the employees in the firm and that they should be re-elected perhaps every three years, in the same way as the majority of directors are elected by shareholders.

The third choice is the election of a democratically constituted works council with rights of consultation and powers of co-determination.

The fourth possibility is the creation of a trustee council, in which a number of trustees appointed by the employees and a number appointed by the shareholders would jointly be provided with certain information and would have powers of decision or co-determination in certain spheres.

A further option is co-operative ownership. There are, of course, a number of highly successful famous co-operatives, apart from the Co-operative Societies themselves, in Great Britain – the John Lewis Partnership is an example – though it was a blow for the concept of employee co-operatives that those selected by Mr Benn were those that had the least chance of success. Co-operative ownership has considerable advantages over nationalization because it is those engaged in the economic activity of a company rather than politicians and civil servants who control its destiny. The co-operative principle may well be the best chance that we have of ridding ourselves of the disadvantages of nationalization.

A sixth method of obtaining a new degree of employee participation would be for employees to be given membership of the company on the same terms as the shareholders, except that they would not enjoy the right to dispose of or diminish the shareholders' capital.

A seventh method, which has proved successful in certain types of firm, is for employers and employees to agree to compulsory departmental meetings at which both management and employees are represented. They would also agree what sort of thing should be dealt with at the meetings, and in which matters there should be consultation and in which co-determination. This is a variation on the works council scheme, but instead of a works council consisting totally of employees there would be a series of mixed committees dealing with each facet of the firm's business.

A further possibility is to create a scheme whereby over a period of years a proportion of the equity of the company is transferred to employees and employee interests, resulting in a steady diminution of the shareholders' interest and a steady increase in the power, in every sense of the word, of those employed in the firm. There have been family businesses in which the line of inheritance has ended when this has proved a viable method of steadily handling over control to those who have joined in building up the business. If such schemes were fully operative it would mean the transfer of power over a number of years and it would necessarily involve considerable consultation over that period.

The extension of employee participation is equally possible in both public and private companies. A substantial part of British industry lies in the unquoted company. Such companies account for something like 51 per cent of the employment and 53 per cent of the output in Britain. Productivity in smaller firms is high, one would imagine, because of the better communications within those firms. Firms with assets of over £15 million show a return on capital of 14.6 per cent, whereas firms employing assets of between £½ million and £5 million show a return of 17.8 per cent. It has been estimated that 70 per cent of inventions and new ideas in British industry originate in the smaller firms.

An O.R.C. survey carried out for the Organisation of Unquoted Companies showed some interesting views upon the manner in which employee participation should develop. When it came to the possibility of supervisory boards with employee directors only one out of ten employees considered that these directors should be appointed by the unions. This is in stark contrast to the demands of the unions themselves that they should make all such appointments. Strangely, 35 per cent of employees considered that the directors should be elected by the employees. A further illustration of the widespread feeling against union-appointed employees was provided by the Swiss referendum in 1975, when the trade unions sought to give themselves power to appoint directors to supervisory boards and lost the referendum by a two to one vote.

The market economy in a democracy depends on the support of the majority of the population. It cannot be argued that in recent years capitalism in Britain has been very popular with the majority of British people, although most have considered it preferable to the even less favoured system of nationalization. People are more likely to be committed to objects and goals that they themselves have played a part in setting than they are to those imposed upon them. Work is perhaps the most important single feature in life. Half an adult's waking life is spent carrying out his or her occupation, and the nature of the employment determines to a great extent the style and quality of the life of the individual. Unless industry can make its products and values consistent with social values outside industry it will be less effective, and ultimately management will lose control altogether.

4 *An Industrial Assembly*
The Heath government was perhaps the first government to recognize the importance of bringing the trade unions fully into consultation on economic and industrial matters. The succeeding Wilson government to some extent stole the clothes of its predecessors and developed still further this consultation with the

trade union movement. Their disadvantage was that their relationship with the unions was not on the basis of partnership; in consulting the unions they were dealing with those responsible for their party funds and a great deal of their party organization. The nature of modern industrial society demands genuine dialogue between management, trade unions and government.

We may need to find some institutional means of establishing better understanding in industry. I wonder whether we cannot find inspiration in Winston Churchill's Romanes Lectures of 1930. With wonderful prescience Churchill analysed the challenge to parliamentary government, a challenge in many ways similar to that of today. The British Parliament, Churchill argued, would not be overthrown by political agitation; 'It will pass only when it has shown itself incapable of dealing with some fundamental and imperative economic need; and such a challenge is now open.' Churchill suggested the creation of a Parliament of Industry to deal with the pressing economic problems of the day. Today we have Neddy. But Neddy is an organization that makes little impact upon the majority of the people of Britain. It is a small 'in' group meeting in private. Occasionally its deliberations result in some passing mention in a few newspapers. What we need is machinery which is watched by the public at large, which has an impact upon the personal views of each individual citizen, which debates the great issues of industrial relationships knowing that the quality of its debate will be judged by the people.

What we face is, in some respects, a parallel with the anti-parliamentary agitation of the nineteenth century. Parliamentarians made sure that this agitation was contained by giving the vote to those outside the political system. Similarly today we face the need to enfranchise the various economic power groups if we are to deal with our economic problems. It is not possible to abolish conflict in industrial life – but we must institutionalize it so that its effects are not disruptive. We have succeeded in doing this with political conflict; we have not yet succeeded in doing the same with conflict in industry.

The creation of an assembly of industry, with the membership drawn from all sections of our industrial life, to discuss matters relevant to the immediate economic and industrial conditions of our nation, could make a substantial contribution to the creation of a new climate in industry.

5 Profit Sharing

If we are to move towards responsible industrial society we must also consider the sharing of profits by all involved in the profit-making industries. Some think this would be unfair to those who work in the non-profit-making sector, people such as nurses, doctors and teachers, but if we are to have the wealth to expand our basic services our profit-making industries must be successful. If the result of giving specific tax inducements to profit-sharing arrangements was to bring about a movement of people from the non-profit-making sector of British society to the profit-making sector, this would be to the advantage of Great Britain, particularly if this came from the vast administration that now manages many of our public services.

When he was Minister of Finance, Giscard d'Estaing, now the President of France, recognized the importance of profit-sharing. My first meeting with Giscard d'Estaing was not in the happiest of situations. He was leading the French delegation to the Gatt (General Agreement on Trade and Tariffs) talks in Tokyo in 1973 and I was the leader of the British delegation. Prior to the Gatt talks, after protracted haggling, primarily between the French and the Germans, we had agreed a Community approach to the conference. I arrived in Tokyo after the long flight from London at ten o'clock in the evening, with the conference due to start next morning, to be greeted by our ambassador at the airport with the message that there was a meeting of European ministers at midnight because the French had decided to go back upon the agreement we had reached in Brussels. I was tired, annoyed, and angry. Giscard opened the meeting by explaining the French reservations in his usual articulate way. There followed several hours of acrimonious argument, in which I led the opposition to the French suggestions for change. It must have been three o'clock in the morning when Giscard said that there was no possibility of us obtaining agreement that night and we should meet again in the morning. With the conference starting at eleven o'clock there would have been no possibility of us deciding anything then, so I said that I considered it monstrous that the European position should be weakened by our failure to come to any agreement. I was supported by all the other European ministers, and then in the early hours of the morning a reluctant Giscard came to an understanding with us.

After this unfortunate start to our relationship I came to admire his vision and his awareness of the changing social trends of European society. I rejoiced at his decision to stand for the presidency, and in spite of the current problems of France, I believe that he is the Frenchman most likely to unify France and perhaps Europe.

It is his view that of the many changes he brought about in the long period when he was responsible for French financial policy his introduction of the profit-sharing incentive was one of the most important. We should learn from his example and from the experiences of the French in the few years during which their profit-sharing schemes have been in operation.

The basis of any profit-sharing scheme should be a range of tax incentives given to all firms making profits to enable them to distribute a portion of those profits to their workforce. There would obviously have to be limitations set out by government on the tax exemptions given, as it would mean loss of direct revenue to the Exchequer, but in my opinion this would be more than balanced out by the greater volume of profits upon which tax would be levied. Any firm to agree a profit-sharing scheme with its employees would have the payment of those profits, within fixed limits, deducted from its Corporation Tax. Instead of the government taking 52 per cent of all profits, it would agree that if 12 per cent of profits were given to employees then the rate of corporation tax would be reduced to 40 per cent.

Another method is to distribute equity to employees. The dividends on equity so distributed would be added to the stock and remain there for the benefit of the employee. The voting in such schemes could either be tied to the holding of the stock or, as is sometimes done in America, be vested in the hands of a trustee.

Such a system could be used as an alternative means of providing a pension, and as a satisfactory way for ownership of a family business to be transferred to its employees. If there is no one to inherit the business and the owners want to transfer it over a period of time to those who work in the company profit-sharing represents an obvious way to achieve this end. The very famous card firm, Hallmark, for instance, have planned to distribute the majority of the equity in their company to the employees using this scheme.

There is a need to provide increasing profits in order to encourage greater investment, but hostility to increasing profits arises from the lack of any experience of profit-sharing amongst employees. If we are to restore the earnings of capital it must be because there is general agreement that capital, being widely spread, should obtain its due reward. We will obtain a reduction in corporate taxation only because the benefit is acceptable and generally shared. Dividends under these schemes should be a pre-tax expense. This would give a further encouragement to accelerate substantially the spread of equity ownership in British industry.

An incoming Conservative government could achieve a transformation in industrial relations, and without any possible accusations of trade union-bashing or of acting other than in the interests of all working people. It could do this by adopting a programme that would result in the growth of genuine employee participation, the creation of a more democratic trade union movement, and the achievement of a wider distribution of profits to all concerned in industry.

If we succeed in this we will have created a Britain that can at last escape from the vicious spiral of industrial decline and defeatism.

CHAPTER VI

Government & Industry working together

IN the post-war period Labour governments have been noted for their extensive nationalization programmes, for increases in taxation on industry itself and upon those willing to invest in industry, and for a desire to restrict and interfere with industry so as to make it subservient to the concepts of the politician. The combination of these attitudes has meant that periods of Labour government have been marked by considerable friction and hostility between government and industry.

During the periods of Conservative administration there has been a tendency for governments to react against their Labour predecessors by endeavouring to have the most limited of relationships with industry and only to interfere on matters of necessity, though even that they have considered most unfortunate.

Our major competitors have been in a very different position. In France the close relationship between the Civil Service and industry has enabled the French government to work with French industry to the advantage of both. The way senior French civil servants frequently become the leaders of French industries and vice versa has resulted in a partnership which is personal and remarkably effective.

In Germany, collaboration tends to take place through the remarkable power of the Central Bank. During the first years after the war, Herr Abs, the head of the Deutsche Bank, played a very large part both in arranging the original investment programme and in seeking the help of the Americans with the reconstruction of Germany's new post-war industries. Today government, industry and the banking system continue to work together for Germany's economic success.

In Japan, the great merchant houses have been closely tied to all post-war governments, in order to develop the internal industries of Japan and then to conquer world markets.

The British government and British industry must work together in close collaboration in order to overcome foreign competition. When I was Secretary of State for Trade and Industry I endeavoured to create new relationships between the department and industry. There was a considerable reluctance to achieve this better relationship on the part of both the Civil Service and industry itself. When I made speeches on this theme financial journalists and business leaders began to write nervous articles suggesting that I was trying to impose upon the City or that I was encouraging a trend towards much greater interference in industry.

On one occasion when I made a speech at the annual dinner of the Finance Houses Association a remark that I had made was taken out of context by *The Times* and written up as if it were an indication of a major clash between my own thinking and that of the then governor of the Bank of England, Sir Leslie O'Brien. In reality the relationship between Sir Leslie and myself was always cordial and friendly and he welcomed the idea of the City and government working closely together. Amusingly, the article was based upon the quotation, prefaced with the magic words, 'Significantly departing from his press handout Mr Peter Walker said . . .' As I hardly ever speak from notes most of my speeches are departures from my press handouts. On one occasion my chief information officer came up to me after speaking at a lunch and said, 'Thank you very much Secretary of State.' 'What for?' I asked. 'For saying something that was in the press handout,' he responded.

Relationships with the City of London were the responsibility of that part of the Department of Trade and Industry that had previously been the Board of Trade. Unfortunately there was a belief within the department that its duties were simply those of a policeman. People had the impression that they were there to observe that the City complied wth company law, that insurance companies complied with the appropriate solvency agreements, and that the banking institutions followed what were considered to be acceptable practices. They felt they would be in some way compromised if they came to know the City too well and hence less effective in their policing activities.

At a time when our invisible earnings from the City were of such importance and when we were discussing a European system of company law and European insurance regulations, it was vital that leading officials of the department came to know the ablest and liveliest minds in the City. I urged merchant bankers, stockbrokers, insurance companies, Lloyd's brokers, commodity firms and others to see that they came to know senior civil servants. My purpose was to create such a relationship that at any time the civil servants could telephone and obtain their views and advice, and indeed vice versa.

The major clearing banks and merchant banks, with a few exceptions, had failed ever to get to know any senior civil servants. I sent them a list of the key officials in the hope that they would try to establish close acquaintances. This did begin to happen and the civil servants soon came to realize the advantage, not least that of having rather better lunches! I am told that since the last election these relationships have continued to improve. The decision taken by the Departments of Trade and Industry, Energy and Consumer Affairs and by the Treasury itself have immense repercussions upon the success or failure of British industry. There is a wide area in which a close relationship should exist.

Sir Jack Callard, chairman of I.C.I., once complained to me about a particular decision of my department. He expressed the view that there was a lack of communication between I.C.I. and the government and we agreed to put into operation a very simple system. At the beginning of each month he would write a personal letter to me in which he would convey any information available to him which he considered that I, as the Cabinet minister responsible for Trade and Industry, should have, and mention any problems or complaints in the remedying of which the government could possibly play their part. I undertook to reply immediately and in depth to the letter and to deal with any specific problems that had come up in the previous month. This arrangement proved to be of immense value both to I.C.I. and to my own department. The moment the letter came in the various problems were relayed to the relevant sections of government and within a short time a full and detailed reply was prepared. As a government we were able to take action on points which would not otherwise have been brought to our attention.

I tried to see that a much better relationship was created with our major motor corporations. Each month three of my top officials met with three of the directors of British Leyland to discuss areas of joint interest and points where the government could be of some assistance to British Leyland in its export drive. We were also informed of progress in their major investment programme. There were times when the results of all this were rather a disappointment to us in the Department of Trade and Industry.

Donald Stokes complained to me about the immense difficulties of exporting British Leyland cars to Japan. He described how, while there was no open tariff discrimination or import control, in practice the Japanese prevented any successful penetration of their domestic market. He described to me how sometimes cars would be delivered and British Leyland would be informed that the regulations had been changed; for example, engine numbers might need to be in a different position and the cars would then have to be returned so that this could be done. It was undoubtedly true that the great Japanese merchant houses that handled British Leyland's affairs were not successful in selling very many cars and that British Leyland cars would frequently be found in the worst showrooms in the worst areas at the worst times. A whole list of other minor problems were listed by British Leyland which seemed to amount to a very considerable discrimination against British Leyland exports to Japan.

I called in the Japanese ambassador and spoke to him and other officials about these problems, telling him that unless things changed quickly I would take discriminatory action against Japanese export to Britain. He pointed out to me that this was against the General Agreement on Trade and Tariffs, but I argued that a discussion of our grievances in an international forum such as Gatt would have a healthy effect upon removing these irritating restrictive practices. The Japanese came to quick agreement. It was agreed that British Leyland would be able to sell a much larger number of cars to the Japanese market.

Donald Stokes was elated at this success, and it was arranged that a new range of British Leyland cars should be launched on the Japanese market, and that Sir Geoffrey Howe, one of the ministers in my department, should go to Tokyo to open the sales drive. I was amazed and shocked when I received a phone call from Sir Geoffrey, who was about to open the exhibition, to say that whereas Japan is about the only country apart from Britain where right-hand drive cars are used, British Leyland had sent twelve left-hand drive cars for the launching of their new sales campaign! This was a prime example of managerial inefficiency and of the frustrating experiences that can face government departments when dealing with industry.

The next Conservative government will have to debate what its attitude is going to be towards planning agreements. I do not believe that the planning agreements envisaged by the present Labour government will succeed. They will fail because of suspicion on the part of industry and a reluctance to provide information to a socialist government, and because there are no civil servants (at the moment) able to deal with the information that would be made available. This is not to criticize the civil servants that I encountered at the Department of Trade and Industry, who were of high calibre, but they were already under considerable pressure in carrying out their existing functions. The talent for scrutinizing the long-term investment plans of industry has yet to be developed.

It would be wrong in any case to want too many men of such talent in Whitehall, for their proper place is in industry itself. We do not have sufficient commercial talent in this country to be able to spread it over both industry and the Civil Service. A system which required the submission of plans for scrutiny by civil servants would also lead to much duplication of effort and to damaging delays during the inevitable protracted correspondence.

On the other hand, one should be able to establish a position in which all parties concerned can react sensibly to major investment decisions, whether made by government or by industry. When I announced the go-ahead for the £3,000 million modernization of British Steel, I spoke to the leading steel plant manufacturers and told them of this programme, which would provide them with plenty of work in the coming years. I was anxious to see that they used this investment programme not just to give them a few fat years but to enable them to be competitive and successful abroad. I agreed with them that we should use all the resources of government to make a survey of the worldwide steel plant manufacturing requirements over the coming decade, and that we should then decide from which countries we would seek orders, using the influence of both government and industry to defeat foreign competition. We agreed that they would examine their capacity to provide the British steel industry with its requirements and to provide for the world markets. The steel plant manufacturers found this an exciting and totally acceptable approach to their future strategy and joined in enthusiastically both in surveying the potentialities of world markets and in examining their own capacity.

The incoming Labour government decided to defer decision-taking upon the modernization of British Steel, and the uncertainty has continued since then. With a clear programme for future steel investment and a knowledge of worldwide demand for the construction of steel-making capacity, there is no doubt that the British government and British manufacturers together would achieve much better results than when the plant manufacturers are just left alone to get on with satisfying orders from this country, while neglecting the potential of world markets.

Collaboration between government and industry would also mean that industry could obtain government help in extending its capacity. If, as a result of the survey of future demand, it had been clearly illustrated to government that there was a considerable potential for obtaining a wide range of international orders and boosting our exports, it might have been sensible to use the Industry Act to help the steel plant manufacturers to increase their basic capacity so that they could satisfy both the home and the international market. Certainly that is the type of injection of capital that would have taken place in France, Germany or Japan.

Nationalization has not provided governments with the economic power that socialists contemplated, but has produced a series of seemingly insoluble industrial problems.

Nationalized industries are responsible for 17 per cent of U.K. output, employ 8 per cent of our workforce, and carry out 15 per cent of our total capital investment. It is therefore vital that we find ways of improving their performance and overcoming some of their major handicaps. When recently a list of the chairmen of the nationalized industries was published, twenty in all, I discovered that no less than ten of them had been appointed by me during the period when I was Secretary of State for the Environment or Secretary of State for Trade and Industry. I remembered the difficulty I had had in making these particular appointments. It may be that some criticisms of the chairmen of some of these industries reflected upon the poorness of my own choice. What critics would never know was whether the person chosen was my first choice, my second choice, or, as was the case with one nationalized industry chairman, my fourteenth choice.

What do you say to a person you are approaching to be a nationalized industry chairman? If you are truthful you say to him: I want you to take a job where your salary will be somewhat lower than you are receiving at the present time; where the provisions for your pension will be somewhat less; where the general benefits you will enjoy from being in an important industrial position will certainly be far less than in the private sector; where you will be assured that all the major decisions you will want to make will be scrutinized first of all by civil servants, then by myself, then by the Treasury civil servants and then, if it is a sufficiently important decision, by the Prime Minister, the Chancellor and the Cabinet as a whole. You can be assured that whenever you do anything which is unpopular with the public, such as increasing your prices or failing to deliver or produce goods on time, you will be abused far more than if you committed similar sins in the private sector. You can also be assured that anything which is successful will go unnoticed. You will find that any decisions of government to reduce investment, fix prices or influence wages, will be far more total in their effects on your industry than on those in the private sector. Added to this, your appointment is but for a short period of three or five years; almost certainly by then a different minister will be responsible for this industry, and in all probability he will decide not to reappoint you for another period of office. This would be the truthful approach to the man you wish to head one of the largest industries in Great Britain.

The socialist formula of nationalization is a formula for failure, where decision-taking in what is essentially a commercial activity is totally perverted by the close proximity of an industry to a politician. As long as so much of our industry continues to be dominated by the politician and the civil servant, we will see these basic industries fail to attain the effectiveness that is necessary for a country seeking economic revival.

What can be done? A number of ideas have been propounded at various times. One very simple approach is to seek to denationalize these industries, but denationalization is almost as impossible in the majority of industries as the unscrambling of eggs. Most of them would in any case have no willing buyers.

An immense amount of permanent damage can be done to Britain's economic scene by the nationalization and denationalization battle. Perhaps the classic example of this is once again the British steel industry. From 1960 to 1972, while every other steel industry in the world was forging ahead with massive investment programmes yielding modern steel production methods, the

British steel industry undertook little investment. First of all the threat of nationalization deterred the private sector from investment. Then a Labour government came to power in 1964, and though it did not have a sufficient majority to nationalize steel it made clear its intention of doing so. In 1966 it was returned with the appropriate majority, and in 1967 it nationalized the industry. Vesting date took place in 1968 and the new nationalized steel industry was born, a massive conglomeration of companies that first had to spend years trying to sort itself out. It was only then that it could start to prepare its future investment programmes. Those future investment plans came up for consideration in the 1970s, and it was not until February 1973 that I was able to signal government approval. For twelve years one of our major and most fundamental industries had remained void of investment due to the battle over nationalization. Even now the programme that I agreed has been totally frustrated by the continued political interference of Mr Benn and now Mr Varley.

I spent two intensive months cross-examining the late Lord Melchett, who was then chairman of the British Steel Corporation, and Sir Monty Finniston, on their modernization programme. I persuaded the Cabinet it was essential for Britain's future industrial strength that we should proceed swiftly with a £3,000 million modernization programme that would by the early 1980s increase steel production by 50 per cent while reducing the manpower employed in the steel industry by 50 per cent. Britain would no longer be alone among the major industrial countries in being without the most modern steel-making techniques.

The drop in manpower requirements would, of course, create important social problems. It was for this reason that I pledged that the government would act to see that a diversity of new job opportunities were introduced in the places most affected.

I was naturally unpopular in those towns which would see a drop in the number of jobs in steel. I immediately visited Cardiff, where I was booed and shouted at by a demonstration of local steel workers. I went to Ebbw Vale and had a long and detailed meeting with the shop stewards, and I met representatives from Shotton, who also had the opportunity of a meeting with the Prime Minister.

It is a tragedy that constituency interests, and much worse, short-term constituency interests, motivated the Labour Party to promise prior to the 1974 election that if they were elected they would stop the modernization programme and have it reviewed. Mr Callaghan and Mr Michael Foot both had constituency interests. Shotton was in a marginal Labour seat, and none of the politicians concerned was courageous enough to explain that if Britain was to continue with a presence in steel at all, modernization had to take place.

As a result of technical changes after a more detailed examination of the schemes concerned the steel modernization programme would now cost £3,600 million at 1973 prices. Due to the massive inflation of Labour's years of office and the delays in starting, this same programme will now cost at least £6,500 million, and on current estimates of future inflation and continuing delays, even if the government did now proceed with the programme, it is likely to cost £9,000 million. Labour's pathetic procrastination and high inflation rate will probably have cost Britain £5,400 million.

Had the steel board been allowed to proceed upon the lines I agreed with them, the major development of Port Talbot would now have been completed and would have doubled steel-making capacity there, making a total of 6 million tons. The major coastal project at Redcar would be completed in the first half of 1977, and this would result in an increase in steel-making capacity of $3\frac{1}{2}$ million tons.

This means that because of the government's delays, originally instigated by Mr Benn, by the autumn of 1977 we will have $6\frac{1}{2}$ million tons less annual steel production than we would have had, had my modernization programme proceeded. If current projections of the up-turn of world trade and the British economy prove to be correct, that $6\frac{1}{2}$ million tons of steel would have been used in a combination of domestic consumption and increased exports, and by the end of 1977 we will be losing £520 million annually in import savings on exports – a terrifying blow to our balance of payments.

A further disadvantage of existing steel-producing methods, as opposed to the modernized methods, is that they are probably something like £12 per ton more expensive. From this month onwards, therefore, the failure to have new facilities at Port Talbot will be costing £36 million per year in increased steel prices, and by the middle of 1977 the failure to bring to fruition the Redcar project will add a further £42 million to steel prices. In addition to this the quality as well as the quantity of steel produced will be worse.

Under my original proposals by 1979 we would have had a steel capacity of between 33 million and 35 million tons, and by the middle of the 1980s of up to 38 million tons. Because of the three and a half wasted years of Labour's indecision, by the year 1980-1 our maximum capacity will be 31 million tons, and the original target for the late 1970s cannot possibly be reached before 1984-5. During the period of Labour's delays the French and Japanese have substantially increased their steel-making capacity.

In addition to all this the original plan also envisaged a major increase in iron-making capacity by the creation of three major blast furnaces, one at Port Talbot and two at Redcar. The delays in the government programme will mean that in the near future they will only complete one of these furnaces, that at Redcar, and that one will be in replacement of three existing blast furnaces and will in no way increase capacity. If an increased demand is created, therefore, there will be immense competition for all available scrap which will create considerable problems for the private sector of the steel industry and, of course, for the price of steel itself.

It is an incredible reflection upon the Luddite attitude of socialism that the socialist government is incapable of proceeding with such a programme.

I did succeed in one measure of denationalization: the sale of Thomas Cook. But this is a business that no one could consider fundamental to the economy; it is not one of the commanding heights of the economy which the socialist party lusts for. This was the exception, however. Any denationalization will be frustrated so long as one major British party states that anybody who invests in such a firm will be penalized if and when they return to government and renationalize. The power of a socialist party to deter rational free enterprise policies is very great. It is great even where there is a very strong case for denationalizing a range of existing nationalized industries. It has also been disastrous in housing, where the elimination of the private sector of rented housing by socialist measures of rent control has done immense damage and made thousands of innocent families homeless.

What other courses are open? What should be considered in a range of nationalized industries is the possibility of conveying the ownership of these industries from the politician and the bureaucrat to the employees in some way. It is vital to recognize that public ownership has done little to give the public any real sense of participation. The people employed in nationalized industries do not feel that they enjoy a different quality of life as a result of nationalization. In the years 1970–4 I frequently reminded the House of Commons that in the previous six years of Labour government no less than 404,000 employees of nationalized industries had been made redundant. And such employees find that when redundancies are decided upon they are fighting a much stronger employer than in the private sector. The same, of course, is true of pay negotiations. Far from giving a lead in pay negotiations the nationalized industries have often been way behind the private sector. Except in those areas that are vital to the whole running of the economy, employees have little strike power because of the unlimited cash resources of the public sector.

Nor can it be said that the consumer has enjoyed a period of ecstasy in the post-nationalization era. Every M.P. will vouch that he receives many complaints about nationalized industries. Saturday morning surgeries are filled with people complaining about them. A far higher proportion of the consumer complaints one receives as an M.P. are about nationalized industries than about private firms.

Nationalization is a socialist experiment that has resulted only in increased power for politicians and civil servants, and substantial taxes to meet the very large deficits of many of our nationalized industries. In the British experience of 1945–75 I can find very little to support the argument for nationalization. It is true of most of the industries concerned that had they remained in the private or semi-private sector the consumer, the employee and the nation as a whole would have benefited.

In looking for a solution one is seeking a formula which will remove the threat of renationalization. It is primarily for this reason that I suggest that we examine the possibility of making the employees the future owners of some of our nationalized industries. Equity in these industries could then be passed partly to the present employees, partly to a trust fund representing the interests of future employees, and partly to employee pension funds, both funds connected directly with the industry and pension funds elsewhere.

Instead of these industries being directly owned by the state, represented by the politician and the civil servant, they would then be in the hands of a combination of employee interests which would benefit from any improvements in efficiency that the employees attained. Clearly the consumer would have to be protected in such a situation, particularly in the case of a nationalized industry with a near monopoly position. We have in this country very powerful consumer monopoly legislation, and through this it would be possible to protect the consumer interest.

There are a number of areas where this formula would not be applicable. It would not be applicable in the coal industry because the miners would want the industry to remain as a single entity, owned directly by the state. They would not want to be involved in the social problems of the uneconomic mine that should on all reasonable assumptions be closed. Furthermore, my own experience of working with the N.U.M. leads me to believe that at this phase in their history they would be unwilling to change the system of ownership. This does not mean that the opportunity should not be provided and the possibility discussed with them. Nor do I believe it would be possible to transfer ownership of the other energy industries. They are basic services that it is sensible to operate nationally, and the relationship between investment and manpower is such that it would be wrong to transfer them.

I think, however, that it would be possible to handle the steel industry in the way I have suggested. We should see that the different parts of the steel industry are operated separately in future and in direct competition with the private sector steel producers. I think it would be necessary to complete the investment strategy agreed in 1973 first, for it would be unfair to convey to an employees' combination a steel industry that had been starved of capital investment for such a long time. It would take five to seven years for the investment programme to be completed, and after this there is no reason why the industry should not be broken up into smaller organizations controlled by employee interests. The dual advantages of competition and freedom from outside control could be achieved simply and quickly. I believe that the National Bus Company, British Leyland and Rolls Royce could be denationalized in a similar way.

British Rail presents a greater problem because of the massive burden of the cost of its track. I believe in this instance careful examination should be made of the possibility of forming a national track company which would take on full responsibilty for running the railway network and maintaining the track and signal equipment, in the same way as the Department of the Environment maintains and operates our major trunk roads. We would then have, within the railway system, a number of activities which could again be free from the disadvantages of nationalization: the Inter-City rail services, the freightliner trains and those major operations serving the large conurbations. All these separate entities, released from the heavy burden of track costs, could be profitable enterprises run far more efficiently than they are at the present time, if the people working on them had a direct incentive to do so. The ports and airlines could also benefit from a change in ownership. It might also be possible to sell part of the Post Office, although here there is a national service at stake and it might well be that this would have to remain part of the nationalized sector.

If we did transfer the ownership of industries I have suggested it would mean that only 4.1 per cent of our production, 2.5 per cent of our manpower, and 7 per cent of our investment continued to be under the existing form of nationalization. This would be a very substantial shift and one that would, I think, be of immense benefit to the economy.

In those industries that did remain nationalized, apart from trying to improve the calibre of board members and putting into practice the fullest employee participation schemes, I think it would be important to appoint a number of people to act as spokesmen for the shareholders, i.e. the state. The present system of making an annual report to Parliament which receives only minor notice in the press and very little interest in Westminster is not an effective way of controlling and influencing a board of directors. It would surely be better to select half a dozen people with a wide range of abilities and talents who would publicly question the board upon its annual report. This would provide something like the annual general meeting of shareholders, although probably more lively and with a wider range of interest. The shareholder committee would be well aware of general public criticisms of a nationalized industry and would make sure that they were raised at the public hearing on the annual report. Unless far more lively and active attention is given to the annual activities of these great nationalized industries, complacency and indecision are likely to continue. Success stories (of which there have been many) will continue to go unacclaimed and those responsible for these successes will be given no encouragement to continue in their efficient ways.

It would also be important when handing over the other nationalized industries to employee ownership both that agreement should be reached as to the best methods of employee participation in that industry, and that provision should be made for proper reporting to the public at large about the effectiveness of the industry under its new management.

Government and industry must also work together in bringing about a successful regional policy. The Industry Act, which was created by my predecessor John Davies, is a flexible instrument for achieving this purpose. There are those in the Conservative Party who would argue that regional policies should be scrapped and that market forces should be left to determine the location of industry. They also argue that regional policies take jobs away from one area and give them to another, increasing the prosperity of one group of people at the expense of another.

I do not accept this argument. There are a number of parts of Britain which, because they have retained the industries which developed there during the Industrial Revolution, need to diversify their economies. If we do not provide new jobs for the regions, then there will be either unemployment and the consequent heavy burden on the remainder who are at work, or alternatively a very substantial drift of young people from the areas of high unemployment to the areas of prosperity.

In Britain this implies a drift of people from the north-east, the north-west, Wales and Scotland to the south-east and the Midlands. Such a movement would be massively expensive. It would mean new housing, new schools, new roads, a new infrastructure, to be paid for from public expenditure, in order to enable people to take up jobs in areas with less unemployment. None of these costs is met by industry other than through direct taxation and higher rates. It would be wasted expenditure when we have already invested massive social capital in hospitals, roads, houses, schools and factories in the regions of high unemployment. It would be disastrous to neglect that investment through an unwillingness to give incentives and inducements to industry and to have some sensible form of planning control to encourage industries to locate their new plants in areas where the social capital has already been provided.

The success of this policy is illustrated by the fact that Scotland and the north-east, previously so adversely affected by any downturn of world trade, have been less affected than other regions by the recent recession. Three hundred thousand jobs have been created directly by regional policies over the past ten years, and a multitude of other jobs stem from the prosperity and purchasing power these new jobs have brought to certain regions. It is essential for industry to understand the benefits of playing its part in regional policies. They must know what grants are available to enable them to go to a certain region and the advantages and nature of the local workforce. The Industry Act is an ideal instrument for this task. It means that minor decisions can be made quickly at regional level and that the major decisions are only made after some of the best commercial talent in the country have considered whether it is in the basic long-term interests of the country to provide a grant or loan.

The Industry Act created the Industrial Development Advisory Board. When I first became the minister responsible the chairman was Gordon Richardson (now governor of the Bank of England). The rest of the board consisted of men of immense commercial ability and talent. It is these men who examine applications for substantial investment programmes and advise the Secretary of State as to whether, in their judgement, the investment will prove to be commercially viable or not. The quality of their advice is exceedingly high, and certainly the investments they have recommended have proved excellent. Occasionally their belief that a firm would become commercially viable has proved to be unjustified. This, of course, is true of the decisions made by every clearing bank and every merchant bank in the country. The failure rate on their advice is much lower than that generally obtained in the private sector and their proportion of successes is very high. It is a tragedy that when Mr Benn was the minister responsible he rejected their advice on five occasions with results that have proved to be disastrous.

The flexible powers of the Industry Act are an essential instrument of government, both in the pursuance of a positive regional policy and in the pursuance of an export and import saving strategy. A safeguard that we do need, however, is a far more vigorous monitoring of investments than has taken place and the requirement that the minister must go to Parliament for permission if he wishes to invest against the advice of the Industrial Development Advisory Board.

An active regional policy minimizes differences in levels of economic activity between regions. Unemployment rates differ between regions because the wage differentials that exist are incapable of attracting sufficient extra employment and because migration out of depressed areas is too slow to eradicate economic imbalance. Regional aid does not distort the operation of market forces but assists them. Faced with frictional problems in the process of economic adjustment, government must act not only to ease large-scale unemployment but also to preserve regional communities.

The case for regional policy is not purely economic. It has important effects on the attitudes and ideas of the areas which it affects, but above all recent studies have shown that not only has regional policy no resource cost but under certain circumstances it saves the Exchequer money. 1973 figures suggest that each job created in the development regions costs about £6,000. From 1963, when active regional policy can be said to have begun, to 1970, about 220,000 new jobs were created, an encouragingly large number. Most of these were in directly productive manufacturing industry. Manufacturing employment in the development areas rose 12 per cent above the figure that was expected for 1970.

The body of evidence that is available suggests convincingly that regional policy continues to have a substantial effect on the amelioration of unemployment and low levels of investment. Much remains to be done, however, and any sensible government would continue with the programme, even at a time of great financial stringency.

One of the weaknesses of the British economy is that in times of prosperity the south 'overheats' while the regions are still barely warm. Government action to increase the rate of growth runs up against the bottlenecks of labour and raw material supply in some areas while unemployment rates in other areas are still intolerably high. The logical way out of this difficulty is to spread the country's industry more uniformly. Governments have therefore successfully diverted the building of new factories to the less prosperous areas of Britain. This will enable future administrations to pursue policies which include higher levels of overall employment.

No present output is sacrificed by the diversion of new factories. Regional policy is one of the few areas of government expenditure which raises both the short-run and the long-run productive potential of the economy and, in fact, generates an extra supply of resources. The Exchequer flow generated by the British regional policy during the period 1963-70 is as follows:

Exchequer outlays, gross	£1,240,000,000
Directly recoverable costs such as rents and interest payments	£240,000,000
Fall in social security payments and rise in taxes after job creation	£1,248,000,000
Reduction in expenditure (net) on infrastructure in rich areas	£54,000,000
Total gain to Exchequer	£296,000,000

It seems that the Treasury gains money by the operation of regional policies and loses none of its control over the economy. Income is lower than it would have been from the prosperous areas but much higher from the regions. Job creation means less unemployment benefit paid out, more money from income taxation and more tax from the companies concerned. Similarly it means less expenditure on social capital in the prosperous areas. It makes financial sense to operate a regional policy.

There is a political case for regional policy as well. There is little doubt that inequalities of income are at the root of demands for devolution. It is felt that Westminster has allowed the poorer cities of the peripheries of Britain to drift downwards compared with London and the south. Urban deterioration and a lack of prosperity are traced to the selfish accumulation of resources by the rich corner of Britain. It is important to show that the government is prepared to take action to correct this. Abandonment of the regional programme would deservedly mean the end of the United Kingdom in its present form.

Both government and industry would also benefit from an improvement in the ability to forecast economic trends and to comprehend each other better when it comes to the allocation of the nation's resources.

We have not yet found the right mechanism for achieving these ends, nor is government well served by its heavy reliance on the Treasury in these matters.

Authorities agree that French economic development since the war has been substantially aided by the institution of their planning mechanism. Before 1939, output levels had been stagnating and France had immense problems of economic co-ordination and integration. Furthermore, certain facts suggested strongly that there was a lack of interest in industrial development and insufficient private entrepreneurship. Many of these problems have been alleviated by the Plan system, though its nature has changed considerably since 1946. The first Plan ran from 1946 to 1950, the seventh Plan is now in operation. In the first years of its existence the Commissariat General au Plan (C.G.P.) could count on the prevailing socialistic mood of the country. Then, as now, the staff of the Commissariat was small in number but of unquestionable ability. The first decade of reconstruction was the period of the Plans' greatest importance, when specific targets were set and planning agreements, or contracts as they are called, were instituted.

In the first twenty years the Plans were essentially indicative, for except in the case of investment the French government has no power to coerce. Gradually the Commissariat's strongest weapon came to be seen as its ability to forecast. As employers followed forecasts, each Plan became a self-fulfilling prophecy. At no stage were Plans comprehensive. They were always intended for the medium term and were not concerned, for example, with the alleviation of cyclical unemployment.

About ten years ago, the French were in the process of replacing the demand expectational model with a greater emphasis on the promotion of competitiveness and the removal of factors that impede it. The growing importance of prices and exports focused attention on the necessity for increasing productivity and lowering costs. In such spheres an indicative approach is no longer of any great use.

The sixth Plan specifically focused on growth industries with an emphasis on manpower training, improving competitiveness and increasing productivity. The sixth Plan's industrial policy had three objectives:

1 The removal of legal and other barriers to competition.
2 The improvement of the environment of industry, a doubling in the capacity of schools to retrain labour, more flexible arrangements for obtaining loans, and guaranteed expenditure by the government on social capital.
3 The setting of criteria for government action, implying 'help to the strong, not the weak'.

Up to the sixth Plan the emphasis had been on industrialization, but the recent trend has been to stress the necessity for social capital. The era of the 'industrial imperative' is over, and political considerations are becoming far more important. The most recent Plan is concerned only with public policy; it tries, for example, to upgrade the attention paid to the whole question of social environment. Overall, therefore, there is evidence of a much less technocratic approach. The Plan continues, however, to be the outcome of an extremely thorough consultation process.

No method of economic management is directly transferable from one country to another. It would obviously be wrong to exaggerate the success of the French planning system and its suitability to Britain. Nevertheless, planning would remove the emphasis from the huge short-term problems of Britain and give the economy a chance of sustained recovery. It is not a panacea, under any circumstances, and it should be more permissive than directly aggressive in intent. Our present problems do not dictate a panic descent on to *'dirigiste'* policies for their own sake. The French success with such measures just after the war took place in very special circumstances. What is needed today is an appraisal of the measures required to relax medium-term constraints on the British economy. We also need a much better grasp of the workings of the economic system than we have at present. A proper theoretical framework of econometric complexity is vital. At present only the French and the Americans possess this framework, and the Americans do not make full use of it. Gallic independence in the development of economic theory has resulted in British economists being about fifteen years behind in the use of optimal control techniques.

The Plan system would have to be introduced into Britain slowly and with care. The full process of consultation that occurs in France would have to be gone through. It is not enough to produce a National Plan, as in 1965, and then expect everybody to take notice. The French experience suggests that we should go through the stages of gradually tightening demand targets and then, as confidence in the Plan system increases, it should be possible to concentrate on the supply side of the economy. The present need in Britain is for a considerable degree of restructuring. This should come through government co-ordinated action, perhaps indicative, as the present administration is beginning to attempt, so that confidence and the will to grow are restored.

One of the reasons why planning in the French style appears unlikely to succeed here at the moment is that the Treasury is far too closely tied to the government of the day. It therefore has low credibility as a forecasting agent and as a formulater of policies. Forecasts are biased, for electoral reasons, and policy decisions are too influenced by political considerations. While it is not necessary to copy the French system in its entirety, several changes in the British style of economic management might be effective in preparing the ground for a successful introduction of sensible economic planning. We should aim to create the equivalent of the C.G.P. office here. Its main features would be that it would work directly under the Prime Minister's office, that it would have a small staff of very highly skilled people, and that it would be independent and so able to gain the confidence of all sides. Properly constituted, it would change the shape of economic management in this country. For too long the Treasury has been burdened by its over-reliance on the use of demand as the prime tool of government control. This stems from government's political need to engineer short-term stability; because the Treasury is directly influenced by overtly political considerations, medium-term planning has to go by the board.

Separation of a number of influential civil servants with the addition of talented outsiders, would act as a powerful countervailing force. Independence of thought and action would give the institution much greater standing than any equivalent at present existing. In time, it would be able to attract first-rank academics, who are put off government work at present by its political overtones, and its understanding of the economy would come to be as great as that of the French C.G.P.

Under present circumstances this could not be a rapid process, and attempts to speed up the pace of change would fail because the scope of the institution's action could only increase in step with the confidence that it had generated. The relatively minor scheme that I have outlined would represent a first step on the way to the gaining of sufficient confidence to initiate a proper planning system. If nothing else, the French have shown that planning is not incompatible with a free society, and if we are to avoid the full impact of a corporate state we should look to a similar system in this country to solve some of our medium-term problems.

The government must also play a leading role in our export strategy. Many of the commercial decisions that are taken throughout the world are taken by governments and not by individual enterprises. Most of South America, nearly all of Africa, much of Asia, communist China, the whole of the Soviet bloc and the majority of the OPEC countries have a commercial decision-taking process based upon governments. It is important that a relationship should be established between the British government and those governments to enable private British firms to participate in their development plans and major purchasing policies. I took a leading part in endeavouring to create such a trade relationship with Iran. The background and circumstances of this relationship proved important for Britain in economic terms, and also showed how governments can promote their industry successfully if they make the effort.

My first connection with Iran was when I had to preside over the biennial Anglo-Iranian trade talks in 1973. These had taken place regularly in the past and it was the turn of the Iranian Minister of Economics, Mr Hushang Ansary, to lead a delegation from Iran for three or four days' talks with me in London.

These biennial reviews are a common feature of trade relationships between Britain and other countries. They are desperately boring and a total waste of ministerial time. Officials of both governments normally agree beforehand what is to be discussed and what each minister will say. They are the sort of occasion where the minutes could be circulated before the meeting takes place. Appropriate lunches and dinners are arranged, toasts are given to the Queen and the foreign head of state, and at the end a communiqué, usually prepared long before, is issued. The communiqué says that successful talks have taken place, and that both countries express their satisfaction at the manner in which their trade has increased and look forward to further increases in the future.

On this occasion Hushang Ansary, a highly intelligent man, asked if he could see me before the first meeting took place so that we could have a personal chat together. For some reason, after a few minutes with him I took the risk of saying that I felt that our meetings were a total waste of his time and mine and that no great business would result. We would all drift on in our own merry way, the tragedy being that if he and I really put our heads together we could transform the trade between our two countries.

Hushang Ansary, who had obviously had to suffer as many of these talks as I had, rejoiced at this approach. We agreed that instead of spending the next few days going through the tedious process of formal discussions he would let me know some of the things that Iran wished to purchase in the near future and I would get the managing directors of the appropriate companies to London. He was delighted. In a few hours he had obtained a list of commodities that he would be interested in purchasing to fulfil the Iranian development programme. Some of them were items that were in short supply and difficult to obtain, others were products that we were delighted to sell. I and top officials phoned up managing directors of leading firms that could supply these goods and asked them to come themselves or send someone to London immediately to negotiate with the Iranians. Within three days we succeeded in doing £250 million-worth of business. Instead of the usual communiqués, we were able to put out a statement of the business that had actually been transacted. We were both delighted with the impact we had made on Anglo-Iranian trade and said that this was only the beginning.

I agreed that in the following autumn I would lead a British delegation to discuss joint investment projects in Iran and take with me many leading businessmen. This meeting took place at Persepolis in November, and once again we brought to the conference a practical approach. The result was that at the end of the conference we were able to announce £237 million worth of joint ventures between British and Iranian firms.

It was as a result of the success of this conference, which received considerable publicity in both countries, that I had my first opportunity of meeting the Shah of Iran. The meeting had been scheduled for the Friday morning at the end of the conference and I was expected to have half an hour's audience with the Shah. He had been told by Hushang Ansary that we had made exciting practical progress of the type which the Shah was eager should take place. The Shah is an impressive man to meet. His English is of course perfect, and he certainly has the charisma one would expect of someone who enjoys the title of His Imperial Majesty. Above all he is exceedingly well informed upon the economic and military realities of the modern world.

Within minutes of the beginning of our conversation we found that our assessment of the dangers presented by the Soviet Union and of the potential long-term benefits of the readjustment of oil prices made us share a common viewpoint on major issues. It often happens that when you first meet somebody either you find the relationship difficult and tense from the start or you find immediately that it is one of mutual enjoyment and enthusiasm. Instead of a thirty-minute audience our meeting extended to two hours, and within those two hours we agreed on the exciting possibility of creating a new kind of industrial and commercial partnership between our two countries.

The Shah was very enthusiastic about obtaining a new

relationship with Britain for a number of reasons. First, I think he admires the history of Britain and its monarchy. He greatly enjoyed the Queen's visit to Iran on her way back from Australia. Secondly, he is an admirer of Edward Heath, who was at that time Prime Minister. The Shah considered him to be immensely able and realistic, and the one man capable of transforming the atmosphere in Britain and bringing us back into the mainstream of European development. He also appreciated his attitude towards defence, and felt that he could regard a Britain led by Edward Heath as a staunch ally in the defence of Iran against possible Soviet attack. He regretted the way the British defence effort had diminished over the years; he was now willing to play his full role in the defence of the Indian Ocean but wished to do so in close collaboration with ourselves.

The Shah agreed with Hushang Ansary and myself that the initiatives of our trade talks, followed by the investment conference, were matters that should be pursued energetically. He agreed to deposit substantial amounts of his oil revenues in London and to invest a good proportion of them in the procurement of goods for the Iranian five-year plan and for their defence effort. Similarly he was interested in entering into collaboration with major British firms in joint ventures. He also discussed how the OPEC countries should come together to deal with the international monetary problems created by the enormous increase in oil revenues.

The international monetary system is largely in the hands of the central bankers of the major manufacturing countries, and the Shah felt, correctly in my view, that the influence of the OPEC countries on decisions about changes in the world monetary system was not commensurate with the position they now enjoyed. In an ideal world, of course, one would be able to assess the real wealth of each nation and the issue of world currencies would be related to these assessments of real wealth. This would mean a monitoring of raw material prices and raw material reserves. It would also mean some form of agreement as to the value of the productive power of the manufacturing countries.

For 200 years manufacturing countries improved their standard of living by processing primary products and then selling them throughout the world. The primary producer was given very little margin to improve his standard of living. This is a fact of economic history. The first step towards adjustment came when the OPEC countries recognized their power. That adjustment will continue in the next decade. It is a process which creates massive monetary problems for the Western world in the short term and demands of them a reduction in their standard of living. In the longer term it must be of immense benefit to the world as a whole that large populations will enjoy enormously increased consumer purchasing power which will bring to the world a much greater total prosperity.

Primary producers will now wish to be protected from the ravages of inflation, just as the manufacturers have been protected in the past. They must be able to improve substantially the quality of life in their countries, just as we have done over previous economic cycles.

The oil embargoes in the latter part of 1973 presented tremendous problems for Britain, but our new relationship with Iran was of considerable assistance. I negotiated with Iran to obtain a substantial amount of oil, additional to what would otherwise have been available to us, in exchange for a range of British exports to Iran. These negotiations took place in London between Hushang Ansary and myself. Top officials were sent out to Iran, led by Sir Peter Carey, now permanent secretary to the Department of Industry, who did a marvellous job in negotiating with the Iranians, and a deal was agreed, to be ratified by the Shah himself. This brought about my next meeting with the Shah, which took place in his villa at St Moritz in January 1974.

I was anxious to take with me on that visit the Chancellor of the Exchequer, Tony Barber. He was our spokesman on international monetary policy, and I very much wanted the Shah to have a talk with him, both so that the Shah could influence British policy in this sphere and so that Tony Barber could gain a better understanding of the OPEC aspirations.

The Treasury was extremely reluctant that the Chancellor should go to St Moritz to meet the Shah. It was a monstrous attitude, since we were suffering from a considerable adverse balance of payments as a result of the massive increase in the price of raw materials, and although the projections of British exports into 1974 were very encouraging we undoubtedly needed to have substantial oil revenues deposited in London. The British economy depended upon getting further supplies of oil, and this was one way of getting them. In terms of our future relationship with OPEC it would be immensely important to have the Shah on good personal terms with our Chancellor. Treasury officials felt that the fact that the initiative for this visit had come from the Secretary of State for Trade and Industry was in itself a justification for not taking advantage of the invitation. Added to this there was a feeling that the Chancellor should not be seen dashing off to St Moritz at the behest of the Shah. All of these were absurd and ridiculous reasons; it was in my judgement a unique opportunity of establishing an economic relationship between the two countries. I argued this case strenuously with both the Prime Minister and the Chancellor, and I am glad to say that Tony Barber agreed to come and felt that the meeting was of great value for the future.

At that meeting we agreed upon the deal whereby we would obtain £120 million-worth of oil in exchange for £120 million-worth of exports. We then discussed the possibilities of a very close and detailed collaboration on industrial and economic matters between our two countries. There was a whole range of industrial machinery that Iran required as part of its industrialization programme which Britain could supply. There was also a wide range of British industries that could do with an injection of capital. I therefore suggested that we should identify a number of industries, such as the motor industry, the machine tool industry and the electronics industry, in which the Shah was anxious to build up a presence, and that Iran should make an equity investment in these industries. By injecting fresh capital into firms Iran would take a minority stake in them, and that stake would be an important investment which would enjoy substantial growth within the European Community. The British firm could then build a plant in Iran which the Iranians themselves would own, and thereafter the production plant in Iran would supply the markets of the Middle East and many parts of the Far East, while the newly re-equipped British industry could be the supplier for Europe and North America.

I believe an arrangement such as this could have been made for British Leyland, for Herberts the machine tool manufacturer, and for a number of aircraft industry and electronic industry manufacturers. It would have given these industries a much needed injection of capital and stopped them becoming part of the nationalized sector. Helping in the industrialization of Iran would have provided an immense amount of work for Britain in the years that lie ahead. There would have been a commercial relationship between Britain and Iran of lasting significance. With a whole range of products we would have been able to conquer markets to a far greater extent than we had ever achieved before.

The Shah agreed with this basic idea, and it was then up to Hushang Ansary and myself to see that it progressed. We were to meet for several days each month alternately in Britain and Iran, so that we could build up a solid partnership over the next two years. A general election took place, however, and this spirit of partnership did not develop with the incoming government. The Shah considered that Britain under a Labour government would not be as interested in defence, and that for some of his procurement programmes he would be better going to nations such as France and America who would continue with their defence effort. Furthermore, investing in a range of British industries during the period of a Labour government probably did not appeal to the Shah for he suspected that a Labour government would not be as enthusiastic on making British industry profitable. Nor would they take the same interest in defence that the Conservative government had certainly taken under Mr Heath's leadership. Whatever the reasons, while it is true that the Department of Trade continued to put every pressure it could on improving our exports to Iran, the spirit of partnership between governments that could have been created, which would have been of immense benefit to the private sector, did not, in fact, evolve.

The major development schemes for Iran are now primarily in partnership with France, Germany and the United States and even to some extent Japan. Of the major capital investment programmes we have not had anything like the proportion we could have had if a true spirit of co-operation had come into being. We would have done far better than France, Germany or America in the coming years if that new relationship could have been created. Iran, of course, will continue to be a prosperous nation. The next Conservative government will still be able to make new relationships and new initiatives, but they will need to be made at the highest level.

There is a general need for government and industry to work together more to boost our export drive. The government has a unique service to British exporters whereby information upon future contracts and tenders is readily available to any firm that is interested. The method is a very simple one: our commercial attachés abroad send daily to London the information they have concerning possible orders. This information is fed into a computer, and cards are run off and posted each day to any interested firm. So, for £25 a year, a manufacturer of umbrellas is able to receive information from throughout the world on people interested in buying umbrellas. It is a very effective system. When, shortly after becoming Secretary of State for Trade and Industry, I asked how many firms participated in this system, the figure was small. I then asked for a list of those who were operating the system in my constituency. A number of names were given to me. I phoned up the managing directors of those firms, all people known to me, and asked them how they had found the system and whether it had been advantageous. All four of the managing directors whom I phoned professed complete ignorance of it. I told them that they had certainly paid £25 a year to receive the cards. I discovered from all four that the only use to which the system was being put was to provide employment for a girl who filed the card each day under the appropriate national heading – except that when the sales manager went abroad he was given the file and would look up the cards that had arrived during the previous six or twelve months. Not only were many firms unaware of the existence of this service, but those that had discovered it had relegated it to such an unimportant place that it had had very little effect.

I also discovered at this time that in Germany many of our goods were selling well below the price that could have been obtained because British exporters had not adjusted the prices of their goods in line with changes in the currency exchange rate. Our ambassador told me that he knew of a whole range of products that was selling 20 or 30 per cent below the true market price. I obtained from him a list of six such products and phoned the managing directors of the firms concerned. After persuading them that I really was the Secretary of State and that my name was Peter Walker, I told them that I felt they were selling products to Germany below the realistic price. Their immediate reaction was that this was very unlikely, but they all agreed that they would look into it. They all came back with the confession that what I had told them was correct and that they would be adjusting their prices. This failure to obtain the best possible prices came as a shock to me. The export managers of firms are primarily interested not in the profits made from exports but in the volume of exports they sell. If selling in Germany becomes very much easier and the volume they sell increases substantially they are delighted with their progress. The last thing they would do is go back to their management and ask for prices to be raised. This experience in Germany indicated how unsatisfactory the relationship between sales and profit often was, and on the strength of this and other instances I decided to make a real effort to communicate to industry the range of services that government could offer the exporter, both in providing information about markets with immense potential for growth and in pointing out the markets in which British goods were grossly underpriced.

I enquired how many firms exported or could export and found that there are about 15,000 such firms in Britain. This brings you down to very small firms employing as few as ten or fifteen people.

The problem was how to make an impact on 15,000 firms. If I sent a circular letter it would have little effect. I decided to ask all the managing directors or chief executives of these companies to meet with one of my ministers for an hour; he could then go through a list of facts and information which would be of interest to them. I discussed this with the department and said that as I had eight ministers working under me we would have a total of nine meetings in different parts of the country and that I would send out a personal letter inviting all 15,000. The Civil Service were very sceptical of the possibility of success in such an offensive. First they thought that it was impossible to send 15,000 personal letters; then they wondered if people would turn up in large numbers for such a meeting. We discussed the timing of the meeting and I came to the conclusion that the ideal time was 8.30 in the morning: it could hardly then be said that other appointments had stopped them coming, and would mean that after the meeting instead of going home they would go to their offices and immediately start making enquiries and taking action.

The meetings did take place at 8.30 in the morning, and I addressed the one at Birmingham, which was attended by nearly 2,000 West Midlands businessmen. Other meetings were held at the major commercial centres throughout the country. More than 11,000 businessmen turned up that morning for those meetings. It resulted in a very substantial increase in the number of firms using the various exporting services offered by the department. Much more important to Britain at the time, over the coming weeks there was a very considerable rise in our export prices throughout the world.

This is an illustration of a practical way in which government and industry can work together to their mutual benefit. Even the most independent businessman, hostile to government interference, could not object to the services or the information that were detailed to the business community that morning. I had never expected that at the end of a series of slides and illustrations and a talk about commercial information, I would be enthusiastically applauded by 2,000 Midlands businessmen at 9.30 in the morning, but that is what happened. There is no reason why the information given at those meetings should not be updated every three months and circulated directly to the managing directors of all the companies concerned. Having found a way of contacting the majority of chief executives at once, similar operations could take place on other topics. In this way a direct relationship between government and industry could be established on issues of importance to the business community.

There is no reason why the computer service providing information to firms in Britain should not be substantially improved. The foundation of improvement would be the strengthening of our commercial offices abroad. This has been done to a certain extent, and during the period I was Secretary of State for Trade and Industry the quality of our commercial attachés certainly compared favourably with those of our major competitors. Nevertheless, the total amount expended on this effort compared with the results that could be obtained is relatively small. If those responsible for decision-taking in the Foreign Office would look seriously at recruiting far more powerful teams of people to fill commercial posts overseas they would find their efforts repaid. There is no reason why a career diplomat should not be the commercial ataché, but he should have under him, perhaps seconded for periods of two or three years, men of immense ability and talent who could at the same time acquire important training themselves and put a new zest into our commercial offices abroad.

Since the war we have never pursued a satisfactory trading strategy. Immediately after the war Britain was uncertain whether to concentrate on her former imperial trade, but this prospect was undermined by the terms negotiated for the American loan to the Labour government. After taking action that put that government in considerable economic jeopardy, the Americans agreed to provide a loan only on condition that the imperial preference system, which had been so beneficial to Britain in the 1930s, was ended. No longer would Britain be able to have a system of imperial preference which discriminated against countries that were not part of the British Empire.

There followed the years in which we decided not to enter Europe and had to look elsewhere for trading partners. Successful negotiations with our Scandinavian friends resulted in the creation of EFTA. At one point in 1960 we were in a very strong position to negotiate trading arrangements beneficial to the British exporter. We were then the biggest single customer of the European Community and by far the biggest economic power in EFTA, and the trade between us and our former empire remained substantial. It was at this time that I argued against my own government negotiating for Britain to join the Community. Instead of joining what certainly appeared to me to have all the weaknesses of an inward-looking organization, we could force the Community to be outward-looking, to the benefit of Europe and, specifically, of Britain. I wanted to create an economic agreement between EFTA and certain Commonwealth countries. At that time Canada, Australia, New Zealand, India and Nigeria were amongst the more important Commonwealth countries that would have been interested in entering negotiations for such an agreement.

Had we succeeded the new grouping would have been in a very strong bargaining position when attempting to make an economic treaty with the Community itself. The Community would have been very dependent upon these countries for raw materials, and they would also have provided a vast new market for the Community. This course was not pursued, and might not have succeeded even if it had been. The opportunity did not last for long, and by the end of the 1960s the pattern of imperial trade had been transformed. Australia and New Zealand had begun to look far more towards Japan, while Canada had continued to become more and more entwined with the economy of the United States. Many of the EFTA countries themselves wished to join the Community, and when Britain and Denmark became members of the European Community EFTA ceased to function.

Since joining the E.E.C. great emphasis has been placed upon improving our trading relationship with the Community itself, but the British businessman has yet to be persuaded to look upon the Community as a domestic market. This is perhaps due to the barrier of the sea, perhaps to language differences, but whatever the reason we are failing to obtain the full benefit of being members of the European Community. We still look upon Europe as being very much 'abroad'. We must train a new generation of British management to think in terms of Europe and to make their investment decisions with the E.E.C. as their domestic market.

Although Europe is a major consumer market, I believe there are opportunities in other parts of the world which provide an invaluable chance for Britain. I have discussed the arrangements that I made with the Shah of Iran and the missed opportunity of 1974 when we failed to create a true economic partnership with that country.

Iran and Brazil are both suffering from serious problems of a current balance of payments deficit, for they are both attracting inward investment on a scale far greater than their current exports. As their current deficits are calculated and temporary, both countries have ambitious programmes of first, import substitution and then, export penetration. Brazil will by 1980, as a result of her current investment programmes, be saving no less than twenty-two billion dollars of foreign exchange by means of import substitution; more than half of this by the massive expansion of their production of steel products, and more than half a billion dollars as a result of the most incredible expansion of their pulp and paper industry. Within the same period, Iran's current investment programme will provide her with a massive increase in exports and saving in imports that will transform Iran's balance of payments.

The rapid expansion of any economy brings problems of administration and inefficiency; problems also of congestion at the docks and problems linked with the shortages of skilled manpower. These problems, though currently proving both frustrating and expensive to the overseas investor or exporter, are also, however, essentially short-term problems. My fear is that Germany, Japan, and France will stay close to these countries during their difficult stages of transition into major industrial powers whilst Britain will withdraw. If we do, the result will be calamitous and would add another reason for Britain's further decline.

Britain should concentrate on four countries: Brazil, Iran, Nigeria, and Venezuela. They all have rapidly growing economies and are investing at a phenomenal rate.

In 1976 I visited Brazil, Venezuela and Iran in order to meet the political and commercial leaders of these countries and to ascertain for myself the potential for Britain in contributing to the economic development of these fast-emerging nations. I could not have been more impressed by the men I met and the progress I saw.

Brasilia, Brazil's capital of one and a half million people, had less than twenty years before been a bare scrubland, 500 miles from the nearest road. The new ministries created in Brasilia concentrate on the rapid development of a nation geographically bigger than the United States, populated by over 100 million people from a mixture of races still free from racial tension – a nation containing almost every known type of raw material resource and with unlimited supplies of hydro-electric power.

The ministers I met there were certainly impressive. Mr Simonsen, the Minister of Finance, has perhaps one of the finest intellects engaged in international monetary questions at the present time. He is fully aware of the financial strains of Brazil's rapid expansion, but also appreciates the immense basic assets of the country for which he bears financial responsibility. The Governor of São Paulo, Engo Paulo Egydio Martins, has been invested with considerable powers over the most industrialized state in Brazil. He is advised and supported by industrialists, bankers, and trade union leaders who are all determined to obtain rising living standards by a combination of industrial activity and social investment. The city of São Paulo alone now has a population of nine million. The nationalized Brazilian Oil Company, headed by General Araken de Oliveira, is engaged not only upon substantial off-shore oil exploration but also in bringing to Brazil the full benefit of their vast natural gas resources and the potential of major petro-chemical industries.

Mr Paulinelli, the young and dynamic Minister of Agriculture, has in Brazil the biggest potential farm the world has ever known. The country is fast becoming self-sufficient in wheat, it is already a major exporter of soya beans; there are going to be a lot of other agricultural products apart from coffee in the Brazil of the future.

Venezuela is a genuine democracy that has twice in recent years peacefully changed governments under its universal electoral system. It is currently led by President Perez, again a man of energy and talent, backed up by an able Cabinet. He is carrying through a programme that will require within four years the importation of £20 billion worth of goods, resulting in an increase of nearly 50 per cent in Venezuelan agricultural production and the same increase in manufacturing production. Within the same period a massive construction programme for roads, railways, housing, and sewerage will be undertaken. £3,000 million will be invested in manufacturing industries, £2,500 million in hydro-electric power industries and their oil industry, and more than £2,000 million in transport and communications. Venezuela has a small population, desperate to obtain technical advice and the application of skills and it is, furthermore, a country by nature friendly towards Britain, governed by ministers who would welcome a major British initiative.

There is a tendency for Britain to fail to recognize the new centres of power in world affairs. First, we should remember that it was Perez Alfonso who provided the initial rationale for OPEC, and that it is another Venezuelan, Perez Guerrero, who is now the most formidable spokesman for the third world. Second, we must realize that Brazil will be having a major influence on the events of Southern Africa, and third, that it is Iran that has an active political and military influence upon both the Persian Gulf and the Indian Ocean.

Brazil, Iran, Nigeria and Venezuela have a total investment programme over the next five years amounting to more than 400 billion dollars. Exports to these four countries from the countries of the O.E.C.D. (Organization for Economic Co-operation and Development) have risen from 5.6 billion dollars in 1970 to 27.6 billion dollars in 1975, which represents an annual growth rate of nearly 40 per cent. Britain contributes only 10 per cent of these exports, but if that figure was 20 per cent, a figure certainly feasible when one looks at both the Americans and the German performance, in 1975 Britain's exports would have been £1,400 million greater than they were. It is not enough for Britain to regard its main objective as holding its share of the market in these countries; we must, on a commercial, political and economic level, pursue policies that will give us a sharply increasing share. Even if we only hold our share of these markets, by 1980 exports to these four countries could well be worth £7,000–£8,000 million per year.

Three of the countries, Iran, Nigeria, and Venezuela, have the benefit of substantial oil resources. It is the massive increase in oil incomes that has transformed their economies. All three have now embarked upon development plans to turn into industrial nations. Brazil is different in that it is not an oil-exporting country and has to rely heavily upon petroleum imports. It is now developing its own oil industry, both off-shore and on-shore, and it is currently going through a period of deficit financing in order to import a vast quantity of capital goods. In 1975 its debt servicing amounted to 44 per cent of its export earnings. The rise in oil prices increased its import bill by 2 billion dollars a year, but even if this had not happened it would still have been in deficit. The growth of the Brazilian economy is such that it can afford to have current deficits of substantial proportions. In the years 1970-2 the Brazilian economy was growing at a staggering rate of 33 per cent per annum, though with the restraints on their financing now current it is down to the much lower rate of 6-10 per cent. Brazil has a growth plan which concentrates on the development of the infrastructure necessary for an industrial nation. It wishes to develop a whole range of industries and to obtain greater self-sufficiency in energy by developing off-shore and on-shore oil, hydro-electric power and nuclear energy programmes. The latter has been arranged by Western Germany, but there is no reason why, with her unique knowledge and expertise both in off-shore oil development and in the hydro-electric industry, Britain should not play a very major part in these developments.

We should look at the combined development plans of these four countries. Brazil anticipates that in the year 1975-9 her investment expenditure will amount, at current prices, to 250 billion dollars. Iran anticipates that her programme will cost 65.6 billion dollars, Nigeria 53.5 billion dollars, and Venezuela 37 billion dollars. The Iranian programme is for the years 1973-8. The Nigerian and Venezuelan programmes are for 1975-80. Taking the four countries together, the total development expenditure in the remainder of this decade will exceed 400 billion dollars. During this period Brazil anticipates an industrial growth rate of 12 per cent and an agricultural growth rate of something like 7 per cent. Iran expects a growth rate of 26 per cent, Nigeria 10 per cent and Venezuela 15-20 per cent. These are the dynamic economies of the world, and yet so far the British government and the British commercial community have failed to exploit the unique opportunities they offer.

Britain provides Nigeria with 24.6 per cent of her imports. This has dropped from a figure of 36.3 per cent in 1965. Currently Nigerian imports amount to 4.4 billion dollars, and they are likely to rise to 12 billion dollars by 1980. If therefore we even retain our share of this market by 1980 our exports to Nigeria could amount to 3 billion dollars.

In 1975 Britain provided Iran with 10.4 per cent of her imports from O.E.C.D. countries. This compares with 11.7 per cent in 1970 and 16.1 per cent in 1965. In the same period American exports to Iran have increased from 24.4 per cent in

1965 to 28.7 per cent in 1975. And Japan's exports in the same period have virtually doubled from 8.8 per cent to 16.8 per cent. If as a result of positive measures and efforts we could restore our position to that of 1965, with the current rate of growth of Iranian imports by 1980 our exports to Iran could be worth 7 billion dollars.

Britain provides 4.1 per cent of the O.E.C.D. exports to Venezuela, as compared with 5.3 per cent in 1970 and 6.2 per cent in 1965. During the same period Japanese exports have risen from 5 per cent in 1965 to 8.3 per cent in 1975. The French proportion of the market has also risen during this period. America still provides more than half of the O.E.C.D. exports to Venezuela. If Britain restored its position to that of 1965, as Venezuelan imports are expected to grow to 8 billion dollars by 1980 our exports to Venezuela would then be 500 million dollars.

In 1975 Britain had only 4.7 per cent of the O.E.C.D. exports to Brazil. This had remained fairly static during the previous ten years, whereas in the same ten years Germany had increased her exports from 13.9 per cent to 15.7 per cent and Japan had more than trebled hers from 4.1 per cent to 12.1 per cent. If we could increase our share of exports even to $7\frac{1}{2}$ per cent, half that achieved by Germany, and once achieved by ourselves, then with the projected Brazilian imports of 27 billion dollars by 1980 Britain would enjoy a 2 billion dollar export to Brazil. With these not too ambitious targets, by 1980 Britain could have an increase in exports to these four countries of no less than £7 billion per year, a massive contribution to solving our inherent balance of payments weakness.

What needs to be done if we are to be really dynamic in these four markets? The first thing is to establish proper relationships between the British government and the governments of these countries. This means top level talks and negotiations and a constant interest by our Cabinet ministers in these countries' affairs. The French government has done this with Iran. After the Labour government came to power in February 1974 it was many months before any British minister went to Iran. I would envisage a series of meetings at prime ministerial level. I would then ensure that co-ordinating machinery was constructed between the respective ministers responsible for industry and trade. This would not mean that they had the formal biennial talks, but rather that they corresponded frequently and spoke to each other weekly on the telephone and that frequent visits took place between the two countries. I believe that in all four of these countries, where government plays a leading role in all commercial decisions, the personal relationships between their ministers and British ministers should be something quite special. This would demand a very positive political action on the part of the British government. The permanent secretaries and top leading officials of the appropriate government departments should also liaise with their opposite numbers in each of the countries.

A detailed study should be made of the development plans of each of the countries, and Britain should decide in which parts of these plans she wishes to participate, choosing those areas where we know our industries are competitive with our main rivals. The leading commercial personalities in the relevant industries should then be called to Whitehall, and visits should be organized to the countries concerned to discuss in detail the potential participation of Britain in these development plans.

More positive suggestions should be made to these countries as to how we could help with their industrialization programmes. We should not simply ask for payment for building factories but should suggest genuine partnership arrangements between British firms and the firms of these four nations. It is natural and sensible that countries should wish to own the new industries they are going to create, and one should accept this at the beginning of all negotiations.

We should agree with the partner countries on the provision of training programmes, a division of world markets and future collaboration on research and development. The creation of new commercial partnerships abroad is essential if Britain is to obtain a new commercial greatness.

British governments should also be far more positive in attracting inward investment into Britain. The combination of the mechanism of the City of London, the availability of a skilled labour force and our membership of the European Community should be attractive to nations outside the Community interested in making a penetration into Europe. There is an absurd reluctance on the part of Britain to encourage positively a flow of new investment. A suspicion on the part of the trade unions that multinational companies are dangerous and the reluctance of existing British companies to increase competition combine with a lack of imagination on the part of government departments to prevent an important injection of capital and creation of jobs within the British economy.

If a Japanese television manufacturer wishes to invest in Europe because of the shortage of space and rising costs in Japan and because of the heavy costs of shipping from Japan to Europe, it must be in the interests of Britain that he sites that factory in the U.K. and not in another Community country.

Let us look at the differences to Britain if that company invests in the U.K. as opposed to another Community country. If it invests in another E.E.C. country:

(a) The British television manufacturing industry will lose still more jobs because its products will meet stronger competition within the E.E.C.
(b) There will certainly be a net unfavourable effect on the balance of payments.
(c) The benefit of the creation of jobs, and more importantly of the indirect job creation through sub-contracts, i.e. through the building of factories, will be lost to the U.K.

If the investment is made in the U.K.:

(a) Jobs will be created to replace those which are being lost in our own industry.
(b) A net favourable effect on the balance of payments will almost certainly be achieved.
(c) Considerable spin-off benefits, such as sub-contracts, rates and taxes will follow.

The arithmetic is unexceptionable, and when one considers that there appear to be a lot of international companies who for the sake of repatriating a small percentage of their turnover are prepared to invest in re-equipping British firms, it is in many ways remarkable that the U.K. has not made a more direct and crude attack on the international capital market to attract her fair share.

At the moment such effort as is being made is made by the commercial wings of our embassies, and a motley crew of local authority 'jollies' going to foreign parts, and these provide very little in the way of a long-term, serious and sustained attempt to attract foreign investment. This is the worst of all possible worlds. The commercial wings of the embassies are selling something they neither know nor care about. The miscellaneous 'local authorities' going round the world are too fragmented and unprofessional for what is a major task.

After all, the attraction of foreign capital is probably one of the supreme export selling jobs. In attracting international capital you are not persuading somebody just to buy £2 million-worth of raw materials but to make a long-term commitment probably involving greater sums.

If we are to increase inward industrial investment we must reduce the number of selling points from the U.K. and make them far more professional and commercial.

In the next five years we should create a series of regional development agencies and they should be given this job of selling (and no one else should do it). One national institution would be unnecessarily centralized and bureaucratic and would lose in enthusiasm through not having local knowledge of a region. The markets we were selling to would not resent reviewing five or six competing agencies in the U.K., whereas at the moment they do get fed up when town after town comes through their front doors.

We should look at the major sources of international capital in an attempt to 'estimate' the market and to judge how we should approach it.

We should then set out our priorities: Japan first, because the Japanese have become a major net exporter of capital. The United States, with its common language and its diverse industries, should also be high on our list of priorities. We should obtain a list of the major American corporations that have already invested in Britain, and take as our target the hundreds of American companies within a fifteen-mile radius of major American corporations already working in Britain. In this way we would be able to refer these American firms to neighbours who had some experience of the advantages of operating in the British economy.

We would need to make permanent contacts with overseas banks and institutional investors so that we could obtain from them leads to companies who were thinking of investing in Europe. We should also see that the major potential sources of inward investment are constantly monitored and that consulting firms are constantly operating amongst new contacts. We must, in fact, set up a very professional selling machinery.

British trade union representatives would be an integral part of this machinery, so that they could provide information about the basis of industrial relations in Britain and they themselves could feel they were participating in what is essentially a job creation programme. When working with me as a minister, Christopher Chataway went on a number of missions to both Japan and Germany for the purpose of encouraging inward investment, and was very much helped by being accompanied by a prominent trade unionist.

New partnerships abroad and new inward investment at home must both contribute to our future commercial strategy. In achieving a new commercial success at home and abroad the government does have a positive role to play. It is not a socialist role of minimizing reward for both the individual and the corporation, nor a role based on an arrogant belief that government knows best, but a role based on a genuine desire to encourage British industry to defeat foreign competition both at home and abroad.

Government action is needed to take advantage of the productive capacity of all our people in every region of the country. It is needed to help open up new markets and forge new international trade links. Government must act to enable our nationalized industries to take commercial decisions without the unnecessary interference of the politician and the civil servant. It must endeavour to provide industry with more accurate forecasting and greater economic stability. It has the ultimate responsibility in deciding how best to utilize the rich assets of the North Sea.

If government can succeed in these spheres, it will cease to be an aggravation to industry and at last become an ally.

CHAPTER VII

Our Inner Cities

HISTORY will judge that the most significant trend of the twentieth century has been the trend towards a world in which the majority of people live in urban areas. At the beginning of the twentieth century only one person in seven lived in a town. By the end the majority of people will be leading an urban life, and its transformation will have come about during a century in which the population of the world will have trebled.

At the start of this century the world possessed only eleven cities with a population of more than a million people; within the next few years we will have 300 such cities, and we will have seventeen cities with populations of 10 million or more.

The massive urban conurbations have a new dominance. One-third of the population of Japan live in Tokyo, and one in five of the people of France and Britain live in their capital cities. Within some of these great conurbations there is a new tendency for the inner city to recede. Glasgow and London are two classic examples of cities originally built around industries that are now either disappearing or moving out. It is the middle class who tend to move out and the poor and the coloured who move in. Nearly 2 million middle class people have moved out of the centre of New York and nearly 2 million poor, black Puerto Ricans have moved in. Such a transformation creates impossible conditions for any city, even one that can call upon the resources available to New York; the available resources are no longer sufficient for the growing liabilities.

The city is the most important of our products. It was Winston Churchill who once said, 'We shape our cities and then they shape our way of life.' Britain's urban problems are aggravated because of the way the majority of our cities developed in the early stages of the Industrial Revolution. These cities contain old housing, old factories and old civic buildings. They have allowed their rivers to become polluted and suffer from a lack of any total concept or vision. The Western world faces problems that arise because a society with a disorganized mixture of competing objectives is unable to provide a high quality of life. The several self-interests do not add up to common benefit. It is the way we tackle the problem of improving the quality of city life that will determine whether our cities will prove to be the death or the revival of our civilization.

There are a number of major mistakes that we are continuing to make. One of the worst is to allow our cities to spread. It is terrifying that cities in Japan will be 600 miles of unbroken urban sprawl from end to end. Such sprawl has colossal disadvantages: it means that for many of those who live within it travel time to work, play and worship is very much extended and takes up a considerable proportion of that part of life that is available for leisure; it tends to be both ugly and dull; it is inhuman in that it is out of scale with people, and being inhuman it creates an environment in which neuroses, divorce and other social problems tend to increase.

It is a tragedy that Britain has so far failed to learn from the disastrous trends that have become apparent in American urban life. The inner city areas of America have deteriorated steadily over the last fifteen years, and there has been a continuous reduction in the number of people living in these city centres. The number decreased by a sixth between 1960 and 1974, and at the same time the comparative incomes of those remaining in the city centres declined sharply. In 1960 the incomes of those living in these areas were well above the national average, by 1974 they were well below. Whereas in 1960 only 26.9 per cent of the people living in the inner city areas were living below the poverty line, by 1974 that figure had leapt to 34.7 per cent. The number of families with a woman as head of the family had increased by 50 per cent, and the percentage of the population that was black had risen from 16.4 to 22.3. The American city centre had become an area of poverty, one-parent families, racial tension, unemployment, truancy, and crime. This same pattern is developing year by year in Britain's cities.

It has been estimated that Chicago will have its population reduced by one-third by the end of the century, and if that happens it means that the population of the inner city area of

Chicago will have halved during the second half of the twentieth century. There are trends developing in London which show that a similar movement of people could take place there.

It was the late President Kennedy who first awakened America and the world to the horror of the inner city problem. It is now fashionable to deride the Kennedys, to look upon Jack Kennedy's presidency as a failure and upon Bobby's contribution to American politics as of little importance. I do not share this view. They were both men who saw the big issues of the day, and who could communicate their views well and, when necessary, courageously. They brought a new vision and excitement to world politics, and in particular restored the confidence of the young that the politician is motivated by a deep desire to eradicate the injustices and the sufferings of the world and to create a better and fuller society.

When Jack Kennedy started campaigning for the presidency I was seventeen, and spent some pleasurable and inspiring weeks following the young presidential candidate around different parts of the United States. One certainly sensed his determination to confront the American people with the crisis of their cities. It was a crisis that had been ignored too long, and those in Britain who cite the American failure to solve the inner city problem by increased public expenditure should be reminded that it was the decades of ignoring the needs of the city areas that created conditions that were beyond redemption. Jack Kennedy's presidency was too short for him to have the impact I know he wished to make – besides which, presidential powers to intervene in city problems are very limited. His leadership, however, did bring to the fore a generation of young Americans who have made some impact on America's urban problem.

Bobby Kennedy's death prevented him also from making the contribution to this problem that he desperately wanted to make. Of the two brothers he was the more passionate, the more intelligent and the more energetic. The last time I talked to him was some weeks before his death during his period of actively campaigning in the primary elections, and one sensed then that he had a premonition that he was neither going to win nor lose the fight for the nomination. Had he lived he would have been the Democrat candidate after his successes in California. He would have defeated Nixon for the presidency and the fortunes of the Western democracies would have been transformed. This was not to be, but Bobby Kennedy's passionate desire to eradicate the deprivation of America's inner cities continues to be an inspiration for those of us who still see this as one of the most fundamental issues facing the modern world.

While the deterioration of our inner cities takes place those suffering from it remain relatively silent. One of the worst features of a democracy is that the poor and underprivileged are far less articulate than the wealthy and prosperous. I discovered when I was Secretary of State for the Environment that if there was a project, perhaps the building of a road or a new airport, which adversely affected a middle-class area, then petitions were organized, protest meetings took place, there were demands to see the minister, there was publicity in the local and national newspapers, even on the radio and television networks. All this occurred when articulate and informed people felt that their interests were being threatened. When some of our more depressed areas were affected by major schemes of reconstruction, or a road programme, few voices were heard. These people had become accustomed to bad, noisy living conditions and one further blow was not going to make very much difference to the quality of their lives.

It is also a poor reflection upon the Labour Party that although throughout this century the most deprived areas of the country have tended to return Labour Members of Parliament with large majorities, those M.P.s have made few vigorous demands for the deprived areas. It is seldom that Labour M.P.s from the safe seats of Liverpool, Birmingham or London bring to the attention of Parliament the awful conditions in many of their constituencies. The Labour Party has tended to take these conditions for granted, and the lack of political pressure and competition from the Tory Party for these seats has resulted in parliamentary complacency. This in turn has encouraged governments to believe that there is no urgent necessity to channel resources to improve the quality of our urban life.

Labour Party thinking has been dominated by a paternalism that requires the urban dweller to live in a local authority house and become the permanent tenant of a public authority with a colourless standardization imposed upon him. The same paternalism demands there should be no alternatives in education. It is conformity rather than equality of opportunity that is the main aspiration of the socialist. The dreariness of this aspiration presents the Conservatives with a unique challenge to provide the urban dweller with a far better alternative.

The people who live in the most deprived areas of our major cities have a bad record of voting, perhaps because over the years they have felt that voting for one party or another did not make very much difference. In these areas communications are bad: many of the people do not read widely, they do not listen to news programmes, and they concentrate upon lighter entertainment if they have television. They do not feel they have much power to influence authority, for what complaints they have made in past years have sometimes been listened to but seldom acted upon. The officers of local authorities and government departments appear to them rather remote, both physically and culturally. They have reached a stage of permanent despair in which there is little hope, and as hope disappears tacit acceptance takes its place.

I was not only the first Secretary of State for the Environment in Britain but the first person to hold such a position in any democracy, and I was excited by the possibility of using the resources of a large department to improve radically the condition of our inner city areas. I quickly discovered that the realities of inner city life in Britain were relatively unknown to both local and central government. They knew how many people were on social security in certain localities. They were aware of areas of high unemployment and areas where the crime rate was high. But there were no plans to transform these areas. Primarily, there had been no assessment of what was necessary to improve housing conditions. Certain areas were scheduled for demolition, a process that tended to add to a locality's misery for a considerable period of time. The bulldozer was used not just on houses that needed to be replaced but on countless thousands of houses that could well have been improved and would have provided far pleasanter houses than the multi-storey blocks to which their occupants were transferred. There was no accurate information about those people who needed social security and other benefits, and were not obtaining them. There was no basic measure of the horrific conditions that currently existed or of the quality of life that it was so desperately important to obtain. I was determined to discover the scope of the problems and then to pursue policies that would transform the reality of today, ghastly and awful as it is for many communities, into a decent and tolerable life in the future.

I decided to examine the underlying problems in six urban areas. Three of these areas were to be complete towns, Sunderland, Rotherham, and Oldham, and three of them districts of major cities which were known to suffer from multiple deprivations, Liverpool, Birmingham, and London. I decided that this was not an enquiry that should be in the hands of officials, because I felt that it was important that from the very beginning politicians, and politicians with power, should be immersed in the study. I asked that each of these enquiries be under a steering committee of three people: a minister from my department, the leader of the local council (being the person with most political power in the locality concerned) and a senior partner of a major firm of consultants on urban problems. I took the chair at the enquiry looking into a district of Birmingham. Others of my ministers took the chair at each of the other enquiries. The six leaders of the councils agreed to take their place, and six different firms of consultants were chosen so that we would get a genuine diversity of ideas, observations and solutions from the reports. The store of knowledge thus obtained would enable us to tackle vigorously and competently the problems of our cities.

It is a matter of deep personal regret that within a few months of starting these studies I was moved to another department to become the Secretary of State for Trade and Industry. I regret even more that thereafter these studies took a lower priority in the work of the Department of the Environment. Ministerial interest gradually lessened, and when the reports finally appeared, with little publicity or comment, they remained almost totally unknown, not only in the country as a whole but even in the towns and localities upon which the reports were based. Nevertheless they have provided a fund of knowledge for future ministers to draw upon, for they do show the way to future progress, and even more devastatingly they point out the terrible mistakes of the past and the present, demonstrating clearly our continuing failure to provide the resources that are needed.

The Liverpool study covers a district that has all the problems associated with the worst of our inner city areas: the district known as Liverpool 8. Liverpool 8 contains 9.6 per cent of the population of the city but it has a much higher incidence of the worst urban problems. At a time when the city was suffering from an unemployment rate of 8 per cent, Liverpool 8 had a rate of 11 per cent and the worst ward 18 per cent. Whereas 4 per cent of the population of Liverpool as a whole are immigrants, Liverpool 8 had 8 per cent and the worst ward 13 per cent. Liverpool had a far greater concentration of families with large numbers of children. In Liverpool as a whole 6 per cent of the families have more that four children. In Liverpool 8 the figure is 9 per cent. The number of educationally subnormal children in the worst district of Liverpool 8 is almost twice the figure for Liverpool as a whole. The proportion of adults who are mentally ill in the city as a whole is 0.5 per cent; in Liverpool 8 it is 2.8 per cent, in the worst ward 4.5 per cent.

The housing conditions in Liverpool 8 are very much worse than in the rest of the city. There are over 1.5 persons to a room in only 3 per cent of the households in Liverpool, but in the worst ward of Liverpool 8 the figure is 9 per cent. In the city as a whole 71 per cent of the population have a bath, an inside toilet and hot water, but only 43 per cent of the people in Liverpool 8 have such fundamental facilities. As to the housing stock in the area, 8 per cent is either due for clearance or has been scheduled as having a short life of only fifteen years or less. Future plans for redevelopment will result in the closure of over 100 of the 180 businesses in the district.

With 9.6 per cent of the total population of Liverpool living in an area of such multi-deprivation, one would anticipate that much more than 9.6 per cent of Liverpool's expenditure would be put into the area. The inner city study discloses the horrifying fact that in this part of Liverpool they do not even obtain the 9.6 per cent of the expenditure which they would get if they were just getting the average allocation for the city as a whole, for they obtain only 6.1 per cent of the money available. The basic principle of the greater the problems the less the effort is, I am afraid, typical of many of Britain's cities.

The first task in tackling our inner city problem is to ascertain the facts. Let us have a look at some of the basic facts concerning four of our major urban areas, the Inner London area, Birmingham, Liverpool and Glasgow.

	Inner London	Birmingham	Liverpool	Glasgow
No. of households	1,120,000	360,000	190,000	320,000
No. of households that are council tenants	2 in 7	1 in 3	2 in 5	more than half
No. of households with someone on social security	1 in 6	1 in 4	2 in 5	1 in 4

	Inner London	Birmingham	Liverpool	Glasgow
No. of households with no bathroom	1 in 7	1 in 12	1 in 6	1 in 5
No. of households with no inside toilet	1 in 12	1 in 7	1 in 4	1 in 11
No. of households where there is a one-parent family	1 in 12	1 in 11	1 in 10	1 in 10
No. of households where there is someone suffering from a substantial permanent physical handicap	1 in 18	1 in 19	1 in 12	not available

There are other terrifying facts about these cities. In the Inner London area there are 12,000 children who have been taken from their parents into the care of the local authorities. There are 4,000 such children in Birmingham, 2,000 in Liverpool and 6,000 in Glasgow. The incidence of mental illness in these areas is very high. In the Inner London area, in 1975 alone, 14,000 people were discharged from hospital after being treated for mental illness. The figure was 6,200 in Birmingham, 3,000 in Liverpool. Three-quarters of those discharged will have to continue with treatment. Some of them were discharged against the wishes of their medical advisers.

The crime figures for our cities are bad, and accelerating. In the Inner London area in 1973 one in every twenty-five children between the ages of ten and sixteen was arrested. This proportion has grown worse since. In 1975 in the Metropolitan Police area young people between the ages of ten and sixteen accounted for half the arrests for burglary and a third of all arrests.

What are the underlying problems that create these conditions? There is the growing problem of unemployment, a problem that increases as our public transport system breaks down. Many lower income families living in inner city areas are unable to provide their own transport, and as public transport ceases to function they become immobile. A second problem is the crime rate itself, for not only is it increasing and self-reinforcing but it creates further problems which encourage delinquency. It is very difficult to attract new businesses to the areas of high crime rate in Birmingham and Liverpool. Businesses that are perpetually burgled and have to have windows barricaded find other locations. More people become unemployed and the crime rate rises. This particularly affects young people.

These inner city areas suffer from a great deal of pollution. The rivers and canals are sure to be polluted, and the air is full of smoke and dust. They also suffer from traffic congestion: most warehousing is in the centre of a city rather than on the ring road, and this means that most of the goods for the city come into the centre. These are the areas with the oldest school buildings and the most difficult children, a combination that makes it much more difficult to attract good teaching staff. And even if they had the best teaching staff available the children would still return to deplorable housing conditions. The truancy rate in these districts is very high. In the Inner London area the truth is constantly concealed by the authorities, these are the areas with the highest levels of illiteracy, which makes communication that much more difficult.

These districts contain a large proportion of elderly people who have nowhere else to move to and are trapped in the locality. They are the reception areas for those who move to our bigger cities, be it from Glasgow, Cork or Bombay. They are areas where there is very little proper professional advice available. The best solicitors do not site their offices in such localities, so the quality of legal advice is inferior. Doctors prefer to live and work in pleasant areas rather than where their professional skills are most needed.

Fundamental to the improvement of life in our inner cities is the task of creating better job opportunities. A combination of high unemployment and low earnings brings about a rapid deterioration in the quality of life in these areas. As jobs become scarce, longer journeys are needed to obtain work, and as public transport breaks down job opportunities are reduced. As the price of public transport increases the expenses of travelling considerable distances become a factor in still further reducing living standards. The necessity for mothers to work longer to supplement the family income means that the children receive less attention and the likelihood that children will play truant and commit petty crimes is correspondingly increased. The prospects of employment and good earnings are worse for the unskilled than the skilled, worse for black than white, worse for the school-leaver than those already established in their jobs. The inner city areas contain predominantly the unskilled and the blacks, and they also have a very substantial volume of school-leavers in proportion to their total populations. The difference between the aspirations and the qualifications of many of the younger people represents a basis for discontent.

We must provide more job opportunities in these districts and reduce the difference between the earnings of the inner city areas and the nation as a whole. There are clear potential employment opportunities precisely because these are areas in need of renewal. There is an urgent need to modernize houses and to provide them with bathrooms and inside toilets. We need to turn the derelict sites into places of relaxation and beauty. We need to clean the dirty buildings. These are all labour-intensive tasks. They are also very substantial tasks and would need to be tackled over an extended period. Such a programme would provide job opportunities for a good number of unemployed construction workers and a basis for training many other people in the skills of the construction industry. The announcement made by Mr Healey of methods by which he hopes to stimulate the construction industry illustrates the very small net costs of providing work in this sphere. There is little difference between the cost of unemployment pay, tax rebates and social security payments and the cost of putting a man to work in the construction industry, for at work he pays tax and his employer pays tax, and he pays his national insurance contribution. The net difference between the cost of employing a man and not employing him is very small, but the improvement in the quality of life that could be brought about by a major renewal programme, well organized and planned over a period of years, is considerable.

Much more should be done about training and retraining facilities in deprived inner city areas. The inner city study on Lambeth showed that the nearest training centre was Croydon. There is little prospect of the untrained person in Lambeth travelling to Croydon daily to obtain training. There is little in our training programmes for the young who have missed out on apprenticeships, and the paid allowance for trainees is too low. In the inner city areas too few school-leavers have the necessary standards of literacy and numeracy to take advantage of the existing type of training programme. The last year of school should be spent in preparing for future employment, and also in engendering a new state of mind in the sixteen-year-old leaving school so that he recognizes that this is not the end of his education process but the beginning, that if he is to lead a fuller and better life he must take advantage of the many opportunities for education and training that will still be made available by the public sector.

A positive programme for improving employment opportunities in the inner city areas should include the following features:

1   The government's industrial development certificate powers should be applied so as to benefit selected areas. At the present time they are applied to benefit whole regions of the country, the north-west, the north-east, Scotland and Wales. There are districts in Birmingham and London in which unemployment is so high that it is imperative to direct more industrial and commercial activity to them. Selected districts of our major cities should, like the regions of high unemployment, be designated regions where industrial development certificates will no longer be required.

2   The government's job creation programme should concentrate on the inner city areas with high unemployment as well as the regions of high unemployment.

3   The effects on job opportunities should become a far more dominant factor in decisions about redevelopment. In far too many parts of our major cities reconstruction programmes have meant the elimination of many small businesses and their replacement with housing, educational and recreational facilities which provide no work for the people concerned.

4   In looking at future land designation for planning purposes and in the allocation of land which central or local government already has in its ownership, the provision of space for commercial and industrial activities should be an important consideration.

5   Small business advisory services should be developed in inner city areas with high unemployment. As Secretary of State for Trade and Industry I instituted such a programme when I realized how many of the small firms which contribute so much to our employment and export prospects did not have available to them the same range of information and knowledge that the larger firms naturally possessed.

They were not as aware as the larger firms of the availability of different forms of government aid and government grants. Nor were they aware of the range of government export services. They were ignorant of some important and up-to-date methods of marketing. The provision of an advisory service to small firms and small industries is highly cost effective : it is relatively cheap to run and the benefits of the expansion of these small businesses more than compensate for any public expenditure involved.

6 The percentage of public investment programmes that create employment in inner city areas should be substantially increased. The government has a considerable purchasing power which should be mobilized to provide better job opportunities in the areas of need.

7 We should take advantage of unemployment in the construction industry to transform the built environment of our inner cities. When in 1971 I was faced with rising unemployment in the construction industry, I persuaded the then Conservative government that it was an absurdity when there was so much to be done that these men should be idle and drawing unemployment or supplementary benefit. I increased to 75 per cent the improvement grants for modernizing older houses and saw to it that the grants for the clearance of derelict land and slag heaps were increased. The unique scheme of 'Operation Eyesore' was started, whereby any local authority that had a dirty building, a derelict site it wished to landscape, or indeed any other eyesore, could obtain a substantial grant to remove it. This was given on condition that the work was completed within two years, the two years in which there would otherwise have been high unemployment in the construction industry.

The impact of these programmes was considerable. This would not have been the case had it not been for the way we, as ministers, made sure that the availability of such help was brought to the attention of those with the power to make decisions.

In the north-east and the north-west there were on average eighty Operation Eyesore schemes in every constituency. When I went to see the remarkable progress that had been made in Stoke in the clearance of derelict land I discovered that the five town halls of Arnold Bennett's *Five Towns* had all been cleaned as a result of Operation Eyesore. The citizens of Stoke were so amazed at the elegance of the buildings they found underneath the grime that they decided to floodlight them in future.

To see the worst environment suddenly enjoy a transformation and to realize that there is hope of changing drab cities into areas of beauty is exciting.

Such transformations also have an immense economic impact.

One of the reasons why firms leave some of our drabber industrial areas is that management is unwilling to live in a bad environment. A programme of urban renovation and renewal is beneficial not only in actually providing employment but also in encouraging further employment to come to the locality.

From the very beginning of my period as Secretary of State for the Environment, I made it clear in speech after speech and action after action that the first priority had to be to enhance those places in Britain where the environment was worst. I spelt out that these were primarily the old industrial areas of Britain, and indeed the surroundings of the factories themselves. It was for this reason that I put a new emphasis upon the damaging effects of noise pollution in factories. We also brought in tougher controls of air pollution and stepped up massively the programme to remove the dereliction left by the early stages of the Industrial Revolution.

I was very moved when I was invited to meet a District Council in Durham, which consisted of twelve members, all Labour, and all miners or ex-miners. They presented me with a specially engraved miner's lamp at the end of my visit and said they had been able to do more as a result of the measures I had introduced to improve the quality of life in their particular district than they had under any previous government. But the best vote of thanks I have ever received was when I spoke to a conference of housing and planning chairmen in the north-east, nearly all of whom were from socialist-controlled councils. At the end of the speech a prominent socialist, leader of one of the Labour groups in the north-east, was asked to give the vote of thanks. It was very simple: 'You may wonder why we have invited you, a Tory, to speak to this conference which is virtually all Labour councillors. It is not because we agree with your government. It is not because we agree with the policies of your party or ever will do. It is because we are agreed that as far as the north-east is concerned you are the best bugger we've ever had.' He then sat down, I'm glad to say, to loud applause. The truth was that I had directed a substantial portion of the budget of my department to improving the areas where the environment was worst. The north-east more than most regions had slag heaps, houses in desperate need of modernization, dirty air and dirty rivers. The progress that was made in the first few years of the 1970–4 Conservative government was far greater than ever before or since.

During that period almost every pre-war council house in the north-east was modernized, using the grants we provided, and Operation Eyesore was bringing about major environmental improvements. I agreed with the Durham County Council and the district councils of the north-east a programme for clearing derelict land and slag heaps at the fastest possible rate they could technically achieve, a programme that would have meant the elimination of every acre of derelict land in the north-east by the end of the 1970s.

8 As the drift from our cities continues we must take great care over the distribution of population. What is happening at the moment is that the skilled workers and the middle classes are leaving our inner city areas (as they have done in America) while the unskilled and the poor remain. This unbalances the workforce, the result of which is that firms do not move into such areas because middle management and the professional skills that the middle classes provide are lacking.

Housing schemes should be designed to see that the middle classes have available to them the quality of housing that they require at lower prices than in more desirable areas.

It is also important that in pursuing our new town strategies – and I believe they should be pursued in the south-east of England – the dispersal of people from London does not involve only the skilled but a balanced population of both skilled and unskilled, both black and white.

9 We should substantially improve training facilities within the areas of high unemployment in our inner cities.

10 We must see that in these areas the schools and other educational facilities place a far greater emphasis on preparing people for the work opportunities that are likely to exist.

11 We must provide better schools. If we are to revive these areas, less crime and better schools are the best way to bring back the future leaders, the future managers and the middle classes in general to these localities. Such people will not live in areas of high crime and bad schools.

Frequently the areas with the worst housing also have the worst schools. A Ministry of Education enquiry showed that whereas over the whole country 40 per cent of school buildings tended to be inadequate the corresponding figure for areas of bad housing was nearly 80 per cent.

The E.P.A. (Educational Priority Area) report on primary schools will show that in the London project area 25 per cent of children change schools during the school year. In Birmingham the figure is 37 per cent. The teaching staff in urban stress areas also show a high turnover rate and only a small proportion of teachers have more than five years' experience. A large majority of teachers in these schools come from middle-class or white collar backgrounds and live outside the areas where they teach. Evidence collected before the recent slump in teacher employment showed that special allowances for working in difficult schools were no longer effectively checking the staff turnover.

Attainment tests suggest that there are many more low-attaining children in the urban stress areas than elsewhere, while a high proportion of children have serious linguistic difficulties. The problems caused by past immigration will be with the schools for a long time. What is essential is to provide a more extensive programme of English teaching for immigrant children. The social problems created by immigrants' inability to communicate with the rest of the community are self-evident. If this prevents them getting jobs it will only intensify the cycle of deprivation.

12 We must organize local government finance in such a way that the declining inner city areas are not the areas where local taxation is at its peak. One of the disasters of the United States has been that high local taxation in the inner cities has pushed out industry and commerce and the more prosperous people. Inner city areas have to meet the high costs that follow from poverty and bad housing, which means that the amount of tax they have to raise per head of the population is very much higher than elsewhere. In these areas the child population is normally much higher, which means that they also have more school children to support. As industrial firms and the more prosperous families move away, they deprive the areas of major sources of revenue and so add a still greater burden to the already impoverished people that remain. It is vital that whatever system of local government finance is adopted it is one that prevents this scenario.

13 Crime prevention must be increased in these areas. The relationship between crime and high unemployment must be recognized. The two are very closely interlinked. In areas of high crime, job opportunities decline swiftly, in areas of high unemployment crime increases swiftly. There could not be a more vicious circle. It is vital therefore not only that crime prevention is increased in such areas but also that jobs are provided so that

the young do not turn to crime as they always have done in areas of high unemployment.

In inner city areas three times as many major crimes are committed as in other parts of the cities. But even this is not a true index of the realities of crime in those areas, for the statistics of crime tend to be the statistics of arrests. For much of the petty crime in these districts there are no arrests. There is a mass of vandalism, to public housing and to commercial premises, which is seldom detected and for which there are few arrests but which does immense damage and harm to the prospects of the locality itself. In New York the crime is so bad that the situation has been reached that there are many localities into which the police hardly go. It is vital, if our inner city areas continue to decline, that we do not create no-go areas. It would be interesting if one could produce statistics about the vandalism and theft in these localities, but they are not available.

14 We should apply to the inner city areas the methods developed by the Local Enterprise Development Unit established in December 1970 in Northern Ireland. This unit was designed to try to reduce the very serious unemployment that was aggravating the problems of Ulster. Its object was to promote new industrial development, and assistance was particularly to be extended to small manufacturing and services businesses, excluding transport and distribution, with the aim of increasing employment. The unit has not supported projects where demand was not expanding or where it was already adequately met. Nor has it encouraged businesses that were not suited to small-scale manufacture. Area panels have been established, some members of which possess detailed local knowledge and work closely with local bank managers, chambers of commerce and technical schools. The incentive to co-operate is the financial assistance, 30–50 per cent of the new capital requirements, and for this reason local bank managers have proved a useful source of contacts. However, the enterprise has also benefited from accountancy, marketing and engineering advice, partly provided by local experts once they had become involved with the unit.

The Local Enterprise Development Unit has built small factories and workshops that are available for immediate occupation by new or expanding firms. The premises remain the property of the Department of Commerce. The marketing and advisory section has aimed to educate the entrepreneurs about the importance of good design and customer orientation. It has in addition organized exhibitions both inside and outside the province which have been particularly important in encouraging craft industries, one of the aims of the unit. Two discoveries that have been made since it was set up have been the suitability of small businesses for sub-contract work and the advantages of manufacturing established products under licence. The unit itself has attempted to inform firms of potential licencing and sub-contracting opportunities.

Since 1970 the unit has provided 4,500 jobs in firms with less than fifty employees at a cost of £1,500 per job. This is a far lower cost than that of most job creation programmes. This programme of course will be of lasting benefit, and the initial investment will almost certainly result in substantially more than the 4,500 jobs resulting directly from it. The establishment of such units in each of the major conurbations, concentrating specifically on the districts of high unemployment, could have a very important impact.

Although all of these fourteen proposals are extremely important, housing is perhaps the most fundamental of both our social and urban problems. I remember listening to Harold Macmillan in his capacity as Minister of Housing. We had set ourselves a target of building 300,000 houses a year. It had become a major political issue. The then Labour government had said that it was a physical impossibility. Harold Macmillan was given the task, and it was vital for the standing of the Tory Party and the Tory government that he achieved that objective. He did, and he came to a Tory Party conference as the hero of the piece. I remember his final peroration, delivered with perfect timing in that splendidly slow and effective voice: 'My hopes are expressed in the words of an English folk song, words that my children used to sing at my feet [I have always found it difficult to visualize Maurice Macmillan singing at his father's feet], words, simple though they may be, that I hope one day will ring true in every heart of every family in the land. The words "ours is a nice house, ours is".' It was an important aspiration, but it is far from being reached. Housing conditions in our inner city areas are in decline. 'Ours is a nasty house, ours is', would better express the feelings of a very considerable proportion of those who live in such areas.

These people are caught in a housing trap. Their incomes are not high enough to enable them to buy a house. There is no private rented accommodation available to them other than the accommodation they have already been able to obtain. Nor can they move to a privately rented house in another part of the country or leave to buy a house elsewhere. The decline in relets in the private sector, a decline substantially hastened by the foolish piece of legislation of Wilson's government, has meant more homelessness, more squatting, and longer council waiting lists. The worst housed tend not to get the best opportunities in the new towns. The need to have a job before you get a house in the new towns has tended to discriminate both against the unskilled and against coloured people.

There are still further deprivations suffered by those who live in some of the poorer areas in the inner cities. All the statistics show that the child density is very much higher and that the number of mothers who have to go out to work is much greater, and this combines to put many more children out on the streets. This increases noise, vandalism and litter, and adds to the friction between the elderly and the young with their large families. There are none of the social ties that previously existed. Married children often cannot rent or buy a home near to their parents. Massive redevelopment programmes have knocked out whole communities, and families are separated.

There are tremendous variations in housing costs in this country. For the first-time buyer the combination of very high repayments, because of high interest rates, and the high cost of new houses, makes an exorbitant demand upon his existing level of salary. The person obtaining a £10,000 mortgage today, if he is without capital, has interest payments alone amounting to £1,100 a year which, together with the capital repayment, means that he has to find something like £30 a week to meet his housing costs. There is a massive disparity between this and the £3 to £6 per week which is required for either public or private sector controlled rents. On the other hand, the existing house purchaser, who bought his house some years ago when it was valued at perhaps only £2,000 to £3,000, finds that relative to his present salary his housing costs are exceedingly small. And the person who has already purchased his house has no housing costs at all other than maintenance. In the rented sector there is a massive disparity between the very low rents of the controlled and regulated sector and the exorbitant rates that are paid by those who are forced to obtain furnished accommodation.

The Lambeth inner city report shows quite clearly that after ten years of London local government reorganization a clear and agreed set of planning and housing policies has yet to appear. But during those ten years the pattern of London's problems has changed, and the fear of an ever-expanding population has been transformed into concern at a decline in population, a decline that leaves the poverty, leaves the homelessness, and leaves the bad housing.

It is just this type of problem that London, and increasingly many of our other urban areas, are going to have to meet, and it demands a total new approach to housing. For one thing we need housing schemes that depend far less on management services. The way such services in, for example, many of the multi-storey flat developments of London have failed to maintain decent standards is indicative of the need to mobilize the family itself to provide its own services rather than to depend upon others to maintain housing standards.

Housing policy in future should concentrate much more on variety. The ghastly conformity of British council housing is but a trailer of what George Orwell's *1984* would be like. Inner city housing should concentrate on small schemes on small sites and avoid the mistakes of the large redevelopment schemes of the fifties and sixties. The decline in the population of our inner city areas will provide space, space previously not available. It must be sensibly used, to encourage the middle-class professional worker to return to the inner city, to provide better cultural and recreational facilities.

So long as public housing continues one must avoid the terrible mistake of concentrating the poorer families in the worst estates. There is plenty of evidence that local authorities have given immigrants and poor workers the worst of the available public housing. The families with rent arrears tend to be concentrated together. Tenants are charged lower rents for houses in certain estates because they are substandard, so existing tenants in such estates find themselves surrounded by the rougher and poorer families, and are desperate to move. It may well be that there is a desire for the concentration of ethnic groups on the part of the groups themselves, but it should be a voluntary choice and not a choice made for them as a result of their current high level of unemployment.

An analysis as to who the deprived are, both in terms of housing and income, will show that primarily they are families with three children or more, families with only one parent, families with teenage parents who had children at a young age before their incomes were sufficient to support them, immigrant families and the old and the handicapped, who share the problems of lack of mobility. In the inner cities there is a concentration of all these categories. There is no way to remove the deprivation suffered by them in a civilized way other than turning to the tax credit scheme.

There is a failure on the part of deprived people to make use of those agencies and services that can help them with some of their problems. They do not know where to go. When they actually attempt to use the services that are available, they often find them complicated or beyond comprehension. The various departments of local authorities offer a range of social services, but people often have to go to one building to discuss one benefit and to another building sometimes many miles away for another benefit. There is a desperate need to establish one community service centre in these inner city areas of multi-deprivation. There should be created, if possible, multi-service teams so that the whole range of benefits and facilities are available to the individual when he enquires at the joint community service centre. There is also a need to establish a much more positive link with the deprived. It should be possible after appropriate surveys have been done to organize localized information channels whereby, through voluntary help, important information as to new benefits and new services can quickly be communicated to those whom one wishes to help.

The Lambeth inner city study has carried out four projects which should have general application. First, the multi-space project, designed to examine all spaces in the locality and to see how they can best be used to enhance the environment. Secondly, the multi-service project, to bring all the services available to individual citizens under one roof. Thirdly, the local information post project, designed to see that communications to individuals are much improved so that they can take advantage of the services available. Such a service also very much adds to the sense of community identity. Fourthly, the day care project, an attempt really to analyse the needs of families for proper day care facilities so that the total incomes of those families can be substantially increased by the mothers being able to work. These four projects together will be a very important armoury in the battle for improving our inner cities.

The inner city studies have come up with new and differing

approaches to the management structure that is needed to tackle effectively the problems of inner cities.

The inner city report on Lambeth emphasized the advantages of concentrating upon administering well numerous short-term projects. They suggested an annual programme of short-term projects for each local authority. Projects should be submitted by all the departments of the local authority and an appropriate programme selected. They argued that in London there were many small districts and some large districts suffering from multi-deprivation, and that if one created an area management for these districts one would in some cases return to the former boundaries of the old London boroughs, so one would merely be continuing with the old system of local government under a new title. They advocated, therefore, the flying squad principle, whereby teams from different local government departments would tackle the problems, sometimes of an area and sometimes of an issue.

In contrast to this the study on Liverpool considered that area management had an important contribution to make, and they are currently carrying out an experiment in area management. District D of Liverpool covers 60,000 people, and they have set up four institutions there. The first is a consultative committee consisting of all the councillors for the district. The second is an area management unit consisting of a top executive, three assistants and a secretary. The third is the area management group, which has representatives of the various departments of the local authority and comes under the leadership of the chief executive. The fourth is a community forum which tries to bring about a relationship between the various community groups in the district and the area management unit.

I fear this experiment is unlikely to have very much success. The area management unit has made relatively little impact in its first year. The main executive was chosen in July. He did not get the first of his assistants until October. Two further assistants were then appointed in December, as was the secretary. The original decision that their offices should be in district D was rejected and they are now in the offices of the city council itself. They have no budget of their own, nor any powers of their own, and the project is very much under the control of the existing political organization and bureaucracy of the city council. The community forum has met monthly but most of the discussion has been on procedural matters and at present they are in dispute as to how they will liaise with the area consultative committee and the local councillors.

We must move to a new concept of district management applicable to those inner city areas designated by the Department of the Environment as areas urgently in need of action as a result of their multi-deprivation. The designation of these districts would be agreed with the local authorities, as would the duration of the programmes necessary to tackle effectively the problems involved. The first task would be to identify the problems, and skilled teams would be recruited quickly to assess accurately the housing, educational, social and job creation problems of the districts. There would then be an agreement as to the programmes required to tackle these problems and an order of priorities would be worked out. From that point onwards the new area management executive would be responsible for implementing the various schemes involved and for producing an annual progress report. In some districts the programme would last five years and in others it would be for a longer period. The Rate Support Grant mechanism could be used to see that resources were largely directed to these districts so that they received the correct priority in expenditure.

There would be no difficulty in recruiting the people to lead the executive side of these management organizations because they would provide one of the most satisfying opportunities for applying administrative skills.

Of course this form of management would only be appropriate to a few designated districts. There would be many other smaller communities with problems that needed to be tackled where the flying squad techniques recommended in the Lambeth report would be applicable.

To succeed we must have more than management; we must have vision, energy and enthusiasm. By harnessing the full energies of the younger generation we can most speedily make progress in tackling the problems of our cities. The youth services frequently fail because they cannot become a self-generating movement without young people at the helm. We have failed to stimulate a movement that harnesses the idealism of the young and draws them into practical long-term involvement in the community. Too often we have fallaciously assumed that they want ping-pong rather than responsibility. Too many bodies concerned with the organization of youth and the planning of youth services have no young people on them. Too many youth officers are middle-aged. Too many youth committees have no contact with the generation they seek to organize. Policies are needed for educating the young and adults alike so that the young have an equal footing with the older generation in the future of this country.

There are many spheres of community activity where the young themselves should take charge. Their enthusiasm must be accepted as a substitute for the leadership given by better trained adults. A British task force should be created, a task force aimed at improving the communities in which we live. This task force should be manned by the young and organized by them. Giving them this kind of responsibility will make them commit themselves to the country and to the local communities in which they are innovators and improvers.

The problem of our inner cities is caused by the concentration of people living on the economic and social margins of society. This concentration is increasing. The economic and social conditions are deteriorating. The problem of the inner city is the most serious social problem facing British government. Urgent action is needed if the problem is not to become as intractable as that of the United States.

The cost of failure to solve the problems of our cities will be paid in lives of misery for many of the inhabitants. The reward of well-thought-out dynamic policies could be cities of beauty and opportunity where men and women can decide for themselves how they will work, live and enjoy their leisure.

This is a reward of such magnitude that it should command the highest priority in any political party.

CHAPTER VIII
Racial Harmony

IN the years prior to the 1970 election I visited some of the worst slum areas in Liverpool, Birmingham and Glasgow. I saw the results of the use of the bulldozer and the building of multi-storey flats and became convinced that wherever possible it would be far better to modernize and improve the older properties and retain the existing communities. I looked upon this as a high priority. I decided to make a number of visits to areas of bad housing. My first was to Brixton.

The first house I visited was a nine-roomed house in which there were no less than thirty-two people living. I spoke to a West Indian couple who had four children. The whole family was living in one room, a room that had no natural daylight of any description. The room was clean. The furniture was colourful and there above one of the two large beds was a dominating picture of Mary with Jesus. Yet here was a failure of the Christian faith in Christian Britain.

It is totally incompatible with Christianity to practise discrimination against other human beings. Yet the small minority population of coloured people in Britain are deprived and discriminated against, have housing and educational standards below those of the nation as a whole, and as a result are handicapped for the rest of their lives.

Some Church leaders have tried to persuade the Church to be more militant and active. Perhaps the most important appointment of a bishop in recent years has been the appointment of David Sheppard as Bishop of Liverpool. David is a person who exudes his Christianity; he is intelligent, passionate and determined to devote his life to overcoming the problems of deprivation that a Christian society should never allow. He was largely responsible for the resolution of the British Council of Churches in April 1976, supporting the document 'The New Black Presence in Britain: A Christian Scrutiny'. This paper set out very clearly the reasons why the present treatment of the coloured population is against any acceptable Christian principle.

In an introduction to that report David Sheppard wrote: 'We shall argue persistently for the principle of positive discrimination and practise it whenever it is within our powers to do so. People, including Church members, sometimes grumble about situations in which they feel that discrimination is made in favour of black people. If it is sometimes the case we should not apologise for it but explain why it is necessary.'

To succeed with race relations in Britain would be an immense prize, for it would set an important example to the world as to how the races can live and work together, and benefit from each other's culture and background, overcoming the prejudices of centuries past. To fail is not just to perpetuate the misery of large numbers of coloured people in Britain, but also to bring misery to the white indigenous population. For failure would mean an increase in crime, increased burdens on the social services, and deteriorating industrial relations. Failure in a task so small relative to our available resources would show that the nation was incapable of tackling a problem the details of which were known and the solutions to which were readily available.

The Council of Churches made a good summary of the disorder within the coloured communities in Britain. They identified the following elements:

1 Large numbers of potentially creative young people defined, labelled and stigmatized by being condemned to spend years in inferior schools and finally emerging to incur the disrespect and rejection of society, unable to earn a wage.
2 Even larger numbers emerging each year as semi-literate school-leavers doomed to exist on the fringe of society.
3 Young people without roots and without hope, often unemployed and homeless, gradually drifting into a life of crime.
4 Conflict between these young people and the police and the other control agencies, with a high proportion being removed from society and placed in custodial institutions.
5 Parents incurring humiliation and blame for not caring for their children, or for dealing with them too harshly, losing all hope and self-confidence and creating further problems for the social services.

6 The co-opting of potential leaders into organizations that are intended to control discontent and to do ambulance welfare work, so that they are not available to engage more radically with the structures of society, based on exploitation, which create the casualties in the first place.
7 The white working-class population clamouring in some sections for repatriation and the denial of citizenship to black people, and in other sections expecting black people to join them in allegiance without taking upon themselves any concern for the black people's own claims; black people working harmoniously alongside white people on the factory floor but being excluded from joining them after work in the working men's clubs.

The report went on to say:

> We are in danger of losing a whole generation of youngsters to institutional care in prisons, borstals, psychiatric units or ESN centres. In their eyes society offers only one place to them and that is the bottom of the heap doing the jobs that their parents are doing and that they reject. So they leave home and live on the streets and take what they want from the society that has refused them a fully human place, and the police, the protectors of the social order, are in open confrontation with them. The battle lines are drawn and in clubs where black youngsters gather to play their music there is a sense of solidarity and comfort and territorial right where police who dare to invade are liable to physical attack. 'They want to stop our sound' the youngsters cry as complaints of noise, of drugs, and of protection of young criminals grow in relation to these clubs. The alarming thing is that the rest of society does not hear what the sound is saying and see it only as something threatening, alien and hostile.

In March 1969 Coretta Scott King, the widow of Dr Martin Luther King, came to deliver a sermon in St Paul's Cathedral. The next day there was a public meeting at Central Hall, Westminster, and an address was delivered by a West Indian clergyman, Wilfred Wood, who had worked hard and successfully in Lewisham and Brixton. In his address at that meeting he said:

> From time to time I am invited to speak on the immigrants'

contribution to this country – remembering the word 'immigrant' is a polite form of reference to black people – and dutifully I repeat that in the Health Service nearly 50 per cent of all junior staff (doctors below the status of consultant) are immigrants; that the mental hospitals, the district hospitals, and the geriatric wards of large hospitals rely heavily on immigrant nursing staff, that the building industry, public transport and other public services could possibly grind to a halt if all immigrant labour was withdrawn. But I would be doing both black and white sections of our community the greatest disservice if I paraded these facts as the grounds on which black people's claims for civilized treatment and the right to live peaceably in the world were based. It would be a disservice because it might suggest that the status of being human is to be earned by being useful, and in this way we make communication even more difficult between those who have never doubted that they are human, and those who require proof that this is so.

It is fashionable to equate colour prejudice with patriotism, and because the presence of black people in this country is represented as a threat to the fine British heritage passed down to the present generation of Englishmen and which must be passed on to future generations, I feel I must refer to some words spoken by Sir Winston Churchill just before the Second World War:

The West Indies, two hundred years ago, baulked large in the minds of all people making Britain and the British Empire. Our possession of the West Indies, like that of India – colonial plantation and development as they were then called – gave us the strength, but especially the capital, the wealth at a time when no European nation possessed such a reserve, which enabled us to acquire not only this world-wide appendage of possessions which we have, but also to lay the foundations of that commercial and financial leadership, which when the world was young, when everything outside Europe was undeveloped, enabled us to make our great position in the world.

The task to which we must apply ourselves is that of ensuring that this country thrives not in spite of its black minority but because of it. As Wilfred Wood went on to say in his address:

No, the immigrants' contribution does not lie in cheerfully providing labour, keeping essential services going, until such time as they can be modernized and improved by automation. It lies in sharing the same ambitions and achievements as a good citizen of a good country. If, in the years to come, he is able to do this regardless of what may be the colour of his skin or the birthplace of his grandfather, then it will be because England has become a country in which there is equal opportunity with cultural diversity and mutual tolerance. He would then have made his contribution to the finest country in the world.

Surely to create an England in which that prospect can become a reality is an objective worthy of any politician.

What is the scale of the problem that we have to tackle? The total coloured population of Great Britain is less than 3.5 per cent of the total. Only a small percentage of these were actually born in the United Kingdom; 92 per cent of them have come to Britain during the last twenty years and half of them in the last twelve years. Nine out of ten of them were over fifteen when they came. Approximately 43 per cent of these immigrants are West Indian and the majority of the rest are Asian. Seventy-four per cent of the Asians and West Indians are located in the West Midlands and in south-east England. In south-east England they are almost totally in the Greater London area. The degree to which the immigrant population is concentrated is illustrated by the fact that in the 1971 census those districts containing 10 per cent immigrants or more accounted for only 4.8 per cent of the general population but for over half the immigrant population. Not only are the immigrants geographically concentrated but they are also literally concentrated in their own houses. The average English household consists of 2.86 persons, the average West Indian household 4.31 persons, the average Asian household of 5.19 persons. The West Indian community suffers greatly from the problem of the one-parent family. The percentage of West Indian families with lone parents is half as much again as for the country as a whole. This partly accounts for the high proportion of West Indian women who work, 74 per cent compared with 43 per cent for the adult female population in general.

With an immigrant population of only 3.5 per cent of the total, in spite of the concentration of immigrants into certain areas, the problems are still within our abilities to solve. We should concentrate on solutions to the existing problems, however, and not aggravate them by further large-scale immigration. Attitudes towards existing immigrants could well improve if some finite limit was agreed on the extent of further immigration. The Conservatives are right to propose that a register of relatives who may in future be allowed to enter the country should be agreed, and that no others should be allowed entry except students and those to whom we are offering training facilities that will further the development of their own lands.

The housing conditions of immigrants are very much worse than for the country as a whole. Only 4 per cent of white families have to share accommodation with another family. Amongst the coloured population one family in four is in shared accommodation. Whereas 18 per cent of white families do not have the exclusive use of a bathroom and toilet, for the coloured population it is more than twice that percentage. Nearly two coloured families out of every five do not have the use of a bathroom. The Asians, by very hard work and by economizing on other consumer expenditure, have succeeded in becoming house owners – and in many areas the proportion of Asians that are owner-occupiers is higher than that of their British equivalent – but the coloured population as a whole has not acquired its share of council house accommodation, and many coloured people are concentrated in the impoverished privately rented sector, paying high rents for bad accommodation. In the G.L.C. area the coloured population forms 7.6 per cent of the total but occupies only 3.5 per cent of local authority houses, and is concentrated in the least attractive of those houses. They have 13.7 per cent of what are classified as the least attractive houses and only 0.6 per cent of what are classified as the most attractive. There are four times as many coloured people living in pre-war flats as in modern houses. Whereas only 8.6 per cent of the population as a whole live in privately rented accommodation, nearly 20 per cent of the coloured population are living in these conditions. A further dramatic contrast becomes apparent if one looks at the number of persons per room, perhaps one of the best ways of measuring genuine overcrowding. In Britain as a whole we have 0.59 persons per room. For the Indian population the figure is 0.88 persons per room and for the West Indian 1.01 per room. The chances of a West Indian family sharing a dwelling are seven times that of an English family. Only 14 per cent of the white population live in houses where there are more than five persons in the house, as compared with 53 per cent of the black population. Only 2 per cent of the white population

Tehran 1973: Peter Walker with the Shah of Iran at his summer palace, during trade agreement negotiations (*Paris News Agency*)

Hushang Ansary, Iranian Minister of Finance and Economics, with Peter Walker and his family on their Worcestershire farm in 1973 (*Berrows Newspapers*)

Peter Walker and colleagues at a weekend meeting of ministers of Trade and Industry in Devon, October 1973.
From left to right: Cranley Onslow M.P., Lord Limerick, Richard Luce M.P.,

Michael Heseltine M.P., Sir Geoffrey Howe M.P., Lord Drumalbyn, Peter Walker M.P., Tony Berry M.P., Chris Chataway M.P., Peter Emery M.P., Tony Boardman M.P., and Tony Grant M.P.

Sir Alec Douglas-Home as Foreign Secretary with Peter Walker in Luxembourg at a meeting of the Council of Ministers, 1973

Edward Heath and Peter Walker in Worcestershire, 1974 (*Birmingham Post & Mail*)

are officially overcrowded – with 1.5 or more people to a room – by contrast with 20 per cent of the coloured population.

As a result of the Labour government's changes in the Rent Act of 1974, changes that were genuinely intended to try to stop the exploitation of poor housing conditions, the problem of poor housing has become the problem of no housing. Statistics show that local authorities have been unable to cope with this problem.

The question of housing is basic to solving the problem of the immigrants. It is a sphere in which they are given very little real guidance or help. Frequently they do not know how to get their names onto the appropriate local authority housing list. Once they have been given local authority housing they have no idea of the possibilities of obtaining transfers. They are not aware of their rights under the Rent Acts, nor of the availability of rent allowances and rent rebates. There is in London a new class system in council houses, and the coloured population is being very much concentrated into the worst class areas. The voluntary housing movement, which has immense scope for tackling this problem, has made relatively few inroads into it. Coloured people themselves should be encouraged to take on the responsibilities of their own enterprise and activities. The availability of house improvement grants and the possibility of obtaining 100 per cent mortgages on houses to be improved are once again matters about which the majority of the coloured population remains totally ignorant.

There are only approximately 120,000 West Indian households in the United Kingdom. A substantial number of these will already have perfectly adequate housing. Some West Indians have good local authority accommodation, others will have become owner occupiers, still others will have obtained perfectly good rented accommodation. But according to the best surveys it is probable that two-thirds of the West Indian population need better housing than they have at the present time. The problem is therefore one of bringing housing aid to 80,000 West Indian families. These families are concentrated in a number of London boroughs and in Birmingham.

Both Birmingham and London have available to them housing accommodation outside London, as a result of the policy of new towns and overspill towns. Positive efforts should be made to ensure that West Indians are aware of the opportunities to move to other areas where housing is available. In each of those districts where there is a substantial concentration of West Indians a housing advisory centre must be created. And it must not be a centre that waits for people to call but one that has the task of doing a positive survey of the district concerned. It must survey West Indian housing conditions and offer advice to each family as to how best to improve its housing situation. It would advise some to take advantage of house improvement grants and 100 per cent mortgages to obtain housing of their own. It would see that every West Indian family knows about rent rebates and rent allowances, their rights of security of tenure and their rights under the various Rent Acts. It would make sure that West Indian families are properly placed on the local authority housing list.

If we carried out a scheme whereby all local authority housing was conveyed to the tenant we would be able to provide West Indian families with a far greater choice of housing. They would have available to them low-priced houses with a 100 per cent mortgage and an appropriate mortgage rebate scheme. Within a year we would know the scale of the problem, and within five years, with relatively little diversion of existing resources, we could see that the West Indian population was tolerably housed. That in itself would do a great deal to relieve a genuine inequality of opportunity.

The provision of good educational and training programmes and a much greater diversity of job opportunities is also central to solving the problems of immigrants. This is particularly important in view of the number of young coloured people in proportion to the size of their population. The 1971 census showed that whereas 24 per cent of the total population were under the age of fifteen, for the coloured population the figure was 39 per cent. There is a very considerable difference between the birth rate of the coloured community and that of the British community as a whole. Nationally 8.21 per cent of women between the ages of sixteen and forty-five have children each year, but for West Indians this figure is 11.5 per cent and for the Indian and Pakistan populations it is 17.8 per cent.

For some time young West Indians have suffered from a high level of unemployment. The 1971 survey showed that 8.1 per cent of those between the ages of sixteen and twenty in the U.K. as a whole were unemployed, whereas for the West Indian population the figure was 16.2 per cent. This figure also indicated that the official unemployment figures of the time grossly underestimated the unemployment of young West Indians. Many young West Indians fail to sign on at the local employment exchange. Doubtless this is partly because so many West Indians play truant in their last years at school, and having got out of the system they never return. They tend to become homeless and live off the proceeds of petty crime. In reality young West Indians receive a very inferior education, have very little motivation and no skills, and get no careers guidance.

West Indians have suffered from the increasing unemployment more than any other group. Unemployment doubled between 1973 and the beginning of 1976, but for the West Indian population it increased at a far faster rate. Between February 1974 and February 1976, according to official figures, it increased from 4,598 to 16,534. Remembering that the 1971 survey showed that the official figures underestimated unemployment among West Indians by as much as 50 per cent, it is likely that by February 1976 the real figure was 25,000 West Indians unemployed. This means that something like one West Indian household in five has an unemployed member. In some localities it means that amongst the young, the sixteen to twenty age group, there is up to 40 per cent unemployment. It is this massive unemployment rate amongst the young coloured population that has resulted in so many of the problems of crime and upheaval in the American cities.

A survey was done to show the increasing problems that West Indians have in obtaining employment and the discrimination against them. Taking a group of school-leavers of the same educational attainment, it showed that after six months 14 per cent of the black school-leavers were still unemployed, whereas only 5 per cent of the whites were without jobs. Seventy-five per cent of the white school-leavers found employment within a week; it took two months for the same proportion of blacks to find jobs. The black school-leavers primarily found manual work. Virtually all the professional white collar jobs went to whites. The black school-leavers were turned down for jobs three times as frequently as the whites, and whereas 70 per cent of the whites confessed themselves satisfied with the jobs they had obtained, only 50 per cent of the blacks expressed similar satisfaction. Fifteen months after leaving school 3.5 per cent of the whites were still unemployed as against 8.5 per cent of the blacks. Twelve per cent of the whites had been dismissed from their original jobs but 19 per cent of the blacks. There is no lack of desire to obtain better jobs. It is interesting that in the same category 17 per cent of the blacks went on to higher education whereas only 14 per cent of the whites did.

The very fact that the coloured population is concentrated in the inner city areas is another reason why they do not enjoy much diversity of job opportunity. There are considerable discrepancies between the job composition in inner city areas and that in the outer areas. In London only 8 per cent in the inner city areas have management jobs as compared with 20 per cent in the outer areas.

As we have seen, there are areas in the inner cities of our major conurbations where unemployment rates are considerably higher than in many districts of the development areas, and yet these areas have obtained none of the financial incentives of the benefits of I.D.C. (Industrial Development Certificate) control. If we are going to tackle unemployment amongst young coloureds we must have a postive job creation programme within our inner cities. This will of course benefit both whites and coloureds, but as coloured people are very much concentrated in these localities it will be an important measure in eliminating the high unemployment amongst them in particular.

In areas of Brixton and the inner city areas of Birmingham unemployment amongst West Indian adolescents is now between 30 per cent and 45 per cent. Given the opportunity of work and better housing a very substantial number of West Indians would be willing to move. There are various obstacles to such movement. They are unaware of the opportunities, such as in the new towns and development areas. They do not know how to go about enquiring about job opportunities in other areas, and are afraid of moving without work being definitely available. There is also the cost, and here there has been a failure to advise coloured people as to how they could go about buying houses. There are frequent examples of them being exploited by estate agents and failing to find the cheapest form of financing. Finally there is the very considerable problem that with many families the number of children makes it difficult to obtain suitable new housing. If these problems could be tackled more positively it would substantially ease the fierce competition for the few jobs that are available in inner city areas.

We have operating in Britain the general improvement areas, the priority neighbourhood scheme, the housing action areas, the educational priority areas, the urban aid programme, the job creation programme, the youth employment scheme and the community industry scheme, and yet all of them are failing to reach those in need of help. The coloured community itself does not know how to attract aid to its districts. Poor people are living in decaying houses that they cannot keep up, and the decay is therefore accelerating. In the absence of articulate spokesmen help is going to arrive too late. It will only arrive as in Watts, Los Angeles, when rioting occurs, the system of law breaks down and the ravages of fire sweep the area. I visited Watts the day after the rioting and saw the debris and the rubbish and the smoke still coming from buildings that had been destroyed. On every street corner groups of despondent and despairing blacks witnessed the destruction that had come to their community. It was only then that the commercial might of California recognized that it had to take positive action and organize not only the rebuilding of Watts but also the provision of better housing and jobs. This should not be the only way that action can be provoked.

We must see that considerable priority is given to education and re-training, and to making sure that literacy and numeracy reaches the coloured population. Training programmes could ensure that far more blacks acquired skills. Redevelopment programmes should be examined to see that they are not destroying job opportunities.

It is important to draw attention to the pre-school period. We have health visitors and social service visitors but at present little is done in terms of education during the pre-school period. The job could be combined very successfully with the health and social visiting that already takes place. With proper training, advice could be given to mothers about how best to foster their children's education at this vital age.

A number of surveys carried out to date have tended to concentrate on showing that immigrant children in English schools are largely to be found in the lower streams and do less well academically than English pupils, rather than highlighting those children who succeed in the education system in the face of many difficulties. Many immigrants come from demanding home backgrounds and are highly motivated. V. P. Houghton conducted a series of intelligence tests on West Indian and English children of the same age and found that there was no significant difference in the test scores between two matched groups of West Indian and English pupils, both from deprived backgrounds. In a thesis entitled 'Achievement of School Job Aspirations' J. H. Taylor shows that the scholastic achievement of Asian pupils at a sample of secondary schools was greater than that of the English children on all but one of the measures used, although 42 per cent had not come to England until after the age of thirteen. Fifty-three per cent of the young Asians continued beyond the statutory leaving age compared with 23 per cent of the English boys. Although a high proportion of English pupils went to selective schools almost two-thirds of them left with no certificate compared to only one in ten Asians. When interviewed the proportion still in full-time education amounted to 4 per cent of the Asian and 7 per cent of the English sample. Both groups hoped to stay in full-time education until they had got 'A' levels. When measuring aspirations Taylor found that the majority of Asians wanted a professional career. The English sample were less ambitious. Interviewed two years later Taylor found that although performance was disappointing the Asians were still pursuing their studies, even if it meant retaking 'A' and 'O' levels and readjusting their sights to other institutions of higher education.

Looking for reasons for the superiority of the Asian school children, Taylor found that there was more positive support among the parents for the children staying on at school: 66 per cent of Asian parents as opposed to only 34 per cent of English parents wished their children to stay on. In attempting to assess the social and economic class of the parents in his school sample, Taylor found that a higher proportion of Asian parents owned their own homes and were self-employed. He concludes that Asians are far more ambitious for their children than English people. He also advances the theory that two cultural traditions of the Punjabis are partly responsible for the strong motivation of some Asian children, their respect for education and their distinctive character of tenacity and enterprise.

Linda Dove in *New Society* in April 1975 found that among fifteen- and sixteen-year-olds at three London comprehensive schools, West Indian, Asian and Cypriot children set a higher value on the school than their white counterparts, and more white Britons than immigrants were eager to leave school as soon as possible, without taking examinations. Only a small proportion of any minority groups wanted to leave school as soon as possible. More than 50 per cent of West Indians and Cypriots intended to take 'O' levels, as did 25 per cent of the Asians. Two-thirds of these were aiming to take 'A' levels. The girls were not especially eager to leave school early. Miss Dove writes that her findings demolish one common myth: these young school-leavers did not fit the stereotype of the lazy good-for-nothing immigrant.

Also in *New Society* in April 1975, an article entitled 'Racial Discrimination: No Room at the Top', Ballard and Holden found that some young blacks were making good progress educationally and that increasing numbers were going on to study at university. The real difficulty begins when they compete for higher-paid jobs with higher status. They took twenty Asian graduates and matched them with white counterparts who had the same qualifications and class backgrounds. The samples differed in colour only, but while most white job applicants were successful at every stage, most black applicants were rejected. The general conclusion was that black applicants were discriminated against in the process of seeking a job. Coloured graduates had many fewer offers – half of them had none at all – while many students could choose which job to take.

We have in our society a minority who are currently suffering from a range of deprivations because they are recent immigrants to Britain and because they are coloured. Many of them are amongst the worst educated and the worst housed, they suffer the worst levels of unemployment and, when in employment, they tend to be the worst paid. They are concentrated in urban areas where, prior to their immigration, there already existed a range of similar problems for the white inhabitants. The problem of the coloured immigrant has not just aggravated that already existing urban problem but has added a new dimension to it. For Britain there are only three available options.

The first is to show total racial intolerance and to demand the deportation of all the coloured immigrants who have come here over the past twenty years in an attempt to create an all-white Britain. Such a policy would be totally devoid of moral justification. It would deservedly bring the standing of Britain to an all-time low, and create an impossible relationship with all the countries of Africa and Asia. It would create a mass of human hardship and degradation and add to the world's racial friction on a frightening scale. It would do a great deal to undermine the very stability of the world itself. The first option therefore is inconceivable unless Britain falls into the hands of an embittered and lunatic dictator.

The second option is to continue with a system whereby the law opposes racial discrimination but in practice it continues and the coloured population becomes increasingly noted for poverty, unemployment, bad housing, crime and eventually deep resentment. This is the course that has been pursued, be it innocently, by past British governments. They have failed to tackle with any success the problem of multi-deprivation in the coloured community. In the last three years unemployment has increased substantially among coloured immigrants, housing conditions have deteriorated, and crime, particularly in West Indian areas, has substantially increased. To allow this trend to continue much further will result in immense friction, riots and bloodshed. This second option is a very dangerous course for us to pursue. When the riots and bloodshed actually take place doubtless governments and local authorities will react and far more effort will be made to solve the problems. By then the effort will be more costly and the requirements will be far greater, and we will have only ourselves to blame for the years in which we failed to tackle a problem that was clearly apparent.

The third option is to accept as an historic fact that the immigrants are here, and to look upon this as an opportunity to give a lead to the world in showing how a nation can successfully create genuine racial harmony. We must use the productive and economic abilities of our new immigrant population to expand the British economy. We must show, from the success of our relationships with immigrants from both Africa and Asia, that on an international scale we can establish a similar relationship with African and Asian countries, most of which will be of immense economic and strategic importance in the decades that lie ahead. The British government should embark upon a vigorous programme for removing their deprivations and genuinely helping the coloured population to develop and apply their talents to the full. How much better we were at tackling the Ugandan Asian problem than we have been in dealing with other problems of immigration.

Altogether 26,000 Ugandan Asians came to Britain as the result of one particular crisis. Because it was an immediate crisis governments, local authorities and voluntary organizations, churches and others, worked together as a team to receive new immigrants in a reasonable and civilized way. Immigrants were given advice on education, housing, social welfare and job opportunities. They were even given assistance in starting new businesses on their own. They were dispersed to various parts of the country. The result was that this group of immigrants has created very few social problems and has not added to the overall problems of deprivation in the coloured community. If only we had received all the immigrants to this country in a similar way, the problems today would be very different. We have now to make amends for the fact that these other immigrants were allowed to come in devoid of advice or help, and we have to see that they and their children are now belatedly made welcome and given the means to become full and active citizens of the United Kingdom.

We must examine positively those communities where immigrants are concentrated, for where they are well dispersed they have tended to be absorbed into the local communities. Under my proposals in the previous chapter, these areas would be specially designated as priority areas. Each such district would have a task force to find out by door-to-door enquiry the extent of the problems in education, housing, employment and health and social service requirements. There would need to be a co-ordination of the existing services to see what currently existed, to measure the gap that needed to be filled, and to ensure that the resources were provided to fill that gap. There is no reason why our present surplus of trained teachers, many of them unemployed, could not provide the educational facilities that are needed to counter the language difficulties of the coloured population. Education is one sphere where we have the resources available and the help needed is relatively little.

To relieve the problem of housing we can turn to the available methods of dispersing people to other communities where housing is currently available, and we must consider the programme that will be needed to modernize and re-equip the existing houses in immigrant areas, a programme that will itself provide many job opportunities. There must be a crash programme whereby careers advice is made available to all members of the immigrant community, together with improved training facilities. The Industry Act should be utilized to encourage the creation of new industries in immigrant areas, preferably businesses started by entrepreneurs from the coloured community itself. There is no reason why an imaginative five-year programme should not be put into operation, by the end of which we would have achieved standards of housing, education, training, and employment that are equal to those of the white population.

Eventually something similar to this will have to be done. The question is whether it will be done before or after racial relations have deteriorated, hatred has built up in the hearts of young coloured people, and hostility has been created by the white community's resentment of the crime and the property damage that will have been blamed on the coloured community. Britain's present problem is manageable, and Britain has the resources to manage it. All we need is the will and a Christian sense of duty to see that we succeed.

CHAPTER IX

The Liberation of the Permanent Tenantry

IN Great Britain 5,615,000 families live in council houses. Nearly one family in three is a council tenant. A higher proportion of the population are tenants of a public authority than even in some of the communist countries of Eastern Europe. In 1975 I advocated that the council housing stock of this country should be transferred to the existing tenants. The immediate reaction was that this was a wild suggestion and that it would be unfair both to those who were not council house tenants, and who would have to buy their own houses, and to those waiting for council houses. Both of these objections lack validity.

When I first launched the idea I received 7,000 letters. Five thousand were from council tenants, all of whom were strongly in favour of my proposals. This one could expect, because they were the people who would clearly benefit. But what was interesting about these letters that poured in from council estates all over the country was not the desire to obtain a cheap bargain but the genuine feeling of frustration and injustice people had as a result of being council tenants. They objected to the way the houses were painted colours not of their choice but chosen by local officials. They objected to being part of a housing system in which they knew their rents would be forever increasing. Those who had been in the same council house for decades were able to point out that a house that had cost the council but a few hundred pounds in the 1930s had resulted in them paying thousands of pounds worth of rent over subsequent years.

There was almost a feeling that somebody had started a liberation movement. I was particularly impressed by the large numbers of ex-service men who wrote to me saying that when they returned from the war, married and needing accommodation, the only option open was a council tenancy, because the Labour government of 1945–50 had decided to concentrate all of their housing programme on council houses and build virtually no houses for owner occupation. From then onwards they were trapped. By the time they had paid their rent there was not enough surplus from their income to save towards purchasing a house, and they were never able to become owner-occupiers.

Two thousand of the letters were from owner-occupiers, and nearly all of these pleaded that it would be unfair when they had struggled to buy their houses that others should receive theirs practically as a gift from the state. These people did not understand that they had in any case paid for these council houses out of their taxes and rates and that, because of the way we administer our council financing, they were destined to continue paying a substantial subsidy to maintain a system that was as unsatisfactory from their own point of view as it was from the viewpoint of the 5,615,000 families who lived in council houses. Steadily I argued the case and dealt with the detailed criticism.

Naturally, it is important to overcome the feelings of jealousy and resentment that are aroused by such headlines as 'Walker wishes to give away council houses'. I have never, of course, proposed that council houses should be given away to all existing tenants. I have merely suggested a scheme whereby ownership would be transferred to all such tenants immediately, but depending upon the length of time they had been tenants they would have further repayments to make which would be in the form of mortgage repayments for the balance of the years. On vesting date, therefore, all council tenants would become the owners of their houses, with all the responsibilities and rights of ownership, but all but 8 per cent of them would continue to make payments at the level of their existing rents for varying lengths of time. Some of the leading newspapers and journals that examined the scheme have come out in favour of it, as has Frank Field of the Child Poverty Action Group. Mr Field is a person dedicated to improving social conditions in this country. His advocacy of schemes to eliminate poverty has resulted in wide support for them, across party lines. All this has resulted in political forces to the left as well as the right examining the scheme more objectively.

I remain convinced that the enfranchisement of a third of the population to a position of owner occupation could be one of the most important, advantageous and exciting social reforms that we have seen this century. We have taxed and charged rates on the wealthy in order that local authorities and housing managers should own a large stock of houses in which one-third of our people are to remain perpetual tenants. Most of these houses have already been paid for and therefore no additional income or taxation is required for their purchase. There is, of course, a very substantial debt repayment that is currently the responsibility of local authorities. But council house rents, do not, in fact, make any contribution towards these vast debt redemptions and interest payments.

To carry out my proposal would mean that for the first time we would provide a third of the population with a substantial stake in this country. One-third of the country, amongst whom are many of the poorer families, would suddenly be in possession of an asset probably worth between £5,000 and £12,000. An asset that they would be able to leave to their children, so giving them a better chance in life, an asset that they could themselves enhance, and which they could at last paint and decorate in colours of their own choice and not colours specified by some official. They would be free to let empty accommodation within the house to friends and other families, which would immediately end much of the under-occupation on British council estates. With individual ownership the conformist atmosphere on council estates would disappear, and we would cease to have our cities divided between council house estates and owner-occupied estates. I would recommend that those families who had been council tenants for thirty years or more should make no further payments of any description. Those who had been tenants for less than thirty years would continue to make payments at the present rent levels for what remained of those thirty years. They would become the owners and the remaining repayments would be treated as mortgage repayments. By this measure we would have succeeded in obtaining a transfer of wealth on a scale which would be meaningful to all families and we would have eliminated the vast expenditure on housing administration which burdens our local authorities. We would have eliminated the need for rent rebates and social security payments for council house rents and we would have removed one of the worst forms of social divisiveness still existing in Britain.

Let us look at the disadvantages of that one family in three whose destiny it is to be a perpetual council house tenant. Unlike the owner-occupier, they obtain no benefit from the increasing value of the house they occupy as inflation progresses. They have no freedom to use their house in the way that they wish and they have no substantial bequest to leave to their children. They have no incentive to improve their property, and in many parts of the country a considerable amount of vandalism takes place on council estates. Such vandalism would end quickly if it was directed not against public property but against property owned by individuals.

The council tenant is not able to move elsewhere if there is a better prospect of employment in another part of the country. The council tenant living in London who finds a new and exciting opportunity available to him in Birmingham has no possibility of taking advantage of that opportunity. There is no way for him to obtain a transfer to a council house in Birmingham. The prospect for such tenants is years of steadily rising rents with no permanent benefit to themselves or their families.

Let us look at the facts and figures of housing finance in Great Britain. From this we will see very clearly how under the current system the present owner-occupier obtains no benefit whatsoever from the council tenant continuing to pay rent. In the year 1975–6 the total income from rebated rents for the 5,615,000 council houses in Great Britain was £923 million. The cost of supervision, management and rent collection was £244 million. The cost of repairs and maintenance was £377 million. Hence after repairs and supervision the net receipt from council house rents was £302 million. But providing social security payments to council house tenants to enable them to meet their rent cost £380 million, so there was in fact a net deficit of £78 million. It will be seen from this that not one penny was contributed to the servicing and redemption of the massive debt owed by local authorities for capital expenditure on council houses.

For Great Britain as a whole debt redemption and interest in that same year amounted to £1,622 million. The whole of this sum, plus the £78 million deficit I have already mentioned, must be paid by the ratepayer and the taxpayer. In reality the figures given above fail to show the true size of the deficit for 1975–6, for the figures are based on 1974 prices, and whereas the rent figure will be correct because it is fixed by statute, it is almost certain that the cost of supervision, management, repairs and maintenance was substantially higher.

The prospects for the years ahead are that with inflation of wages and salaries the cost of supervision and management will rise substantially. The rising costs of both building materials and labour will result in a continuing rise in the amount attributable to repairs and maintenance, and these costs will perhaps rise more sharply as the existing housing stock gets older. Rents (after rebates) will certainly increase, but for political reasons it is unlikely that they will increase as fast as the increasing cost of supervision, management, repairs, and maintenance. And to the degree that they do increase, the social security payments and rent rebates to council house tenants will increase substantially too. Thus we do not carry out this system of permanent tenantry so that the tenants can steadily pay sufficient rent to service the capital cost of their houses.

If ownership were transferred to the tenant there would no longer be any need for the supervision and management of the housing stock, and repairs and maintenance would become the responsibility of the new owners. Nor would so much money be needed for social security payments. For the balance of the thirty years some social security payments would be needed for those who could not afford the mortgage repayments, but it would be a diminishing amount and would start off being substantially lower than the figure of £380 million that applies at the present time. Hence the owner-occupier would have to pay less in taxes and less in rates than he does at present.

Let us now examine the system that would operate as a result of my reform. Eight per cent of council house tenants have been tenants for thirty years or more. For these there would be no further repayments. Ten per cent of existing council tenants would have to make repayments for up to ten years. These would be the ones who have occupied their houses for twenty years. Twenty-four per cent of tenants would pay a mortgage repayment equivalent to their present rent for between ten and twenty years; 24 per cent for twenty to twenty-five years; 34 per cent for twenty-five years to thirty years. These last would be those who have only become council tenants during the last five years. The income paid in the form of mortgage repayments would be approximately £850 million per year at the commencement of my scheme, steadily diminishing over the next thirty years. At the end of ten years the income would have dropped to £757 million and, at the end of twenty years to £535 million. But this would be a net income with only two deductions from it. It would be my intention to stop collection by the local authorities themselves and to make an administrative arrangement with the building societies whereby the mortgage payments were made to an appropriate local building society office. The arrangement would be either that for a period of time the building society office could retain and utilize the monies in consideration of the cost of collection (the interest from the money meeting the cost of collection), or alternatively they could charge a collection fee. From enquiries I have worked out that the cost of that collection fee would be less than 5 per cent of the amount paid; working on this figure the total collection cost would amount to £43 million. Supplementary benefit payments to council tenants in respect of their rents would cease when tenants acquired their houses. The cost of these payments would fall at the outset to £350 million, and at the end of ten years, if there were no increases in the incomes of those receiving social security payments, it would have dropped to £313 million, and to £220 million in twenty years.

Instead of the existing deficit of £78 million, therefore, one would start off with a surplus of receipts of £457 million, and this would be £406 million in ten years and £228 million in twenty years, compared with what would almost certainly have been considerable increases in the deficit if we had continued with the existing system. The difference between the two systems can be set out as follows:

Present council house finance:

Rebated rents	£923 million
Less	
Supervision and management	£244 million
Repairs and maintenance	£377 million
Less	
Social security	£380 million
Net revenue	−£78 million

Council house finance under the scheme to transfer the houses to the tenants:

	Outset	After 10 years	After 20 years
Mortgage repayment	£850m	£757m	£535m
Less			
Collection fee to building societies	£43m	£38m	£27m

Less			
Supplementary benefit	£350m	£313m	£220m
Net revenue	£457m	£406m	£288m

The very substantial debt redemption and interest charges currently the responsibility of local authorities would obviously have to be borne by central government. In practice under the Rate Support Grant most of this is already paid for by central government. Under the present system, as I have clearly illustrated, council house rents make no contribution whatsoever towards the debt servicing and redemption, so there would be no additional burden. Under my scheme there would be a net contribution in the form of mortgage repayments to this, so the overall position would be improved as far as the taxpayer and ratepayer were concerned. In addition to this, the situation would not get worse through the building of further council houses. At the present time the enormous additional capital cost of providing 150,000 new council houses increases the burden each year.

Local authorities have to build to Parker Morris standards. Recently the Liverpool District Council discovered that the current cost of building a three-bedroomed semi-detached house to Parker Morris standards in Liverpool was estimated at £16,000 per unit. By building 150,000 council houses at the current cost of £16,000 per unit, therefore, we are adding £2,400 million to our total capital indebtedness. At current borrowing rates this means committing ourselves to an additional £300 million interest servicing a year plus a capital redemption cost of a further £40 million per year over sixty years.

Under my alternative scheme the capital cost would be substantially lower, and the contribution from the new owner-occupier substantially larger, so the total burden upon the taxpayer would be greatly reduced.

What are the objections to such a scheme? The objection most strongly put is that it is unfair to those who have struggled to buy a home of their own. But is it unfair? Let us consider two families who moved into a three-bedroomed semi-detached house in 1950. The family who moved into the owner-occupied semi-detached house would have paid £2,000 for it. If they could have obtained £200 for the deposit they would have had a mortgage of £1,800 to repay over twenty-five years. In the course of their twenty-five-year mortgage the total payments, including capital, interest and the original deposit, would have been £3,030. Assuming they were paying the standard rate of income tax they would have obtained £480 in income tax rebate upon the interest payments. The net cash payments of the family who decided to buy a house in 1950 would then have been £2,750. Compare this with the position of the family who moved into the council house. To start with their rent for a new house would probably have been in the region of £2 a week. It would have risen steadily in the twenty-five years from 1950 to 1975, probably reaching a rent of something like £5.50 per week in 1975. The total rent they would have paid would probably amount to £3,850.

Of these two families the council tenant would have paid more than £1,000 more than the owner-occupier. But in 1975 the owner-occupier would have completed the purchase of his house. The family would have no further payments to make. They would possess an asset worth about £12,000. They would therefore have made a profit of £9,250, and so long as inflation continues would be likely to make enhanced profits in future.

Look now at the position of the council tenant. His prospect is to continue paying rent for the rest of his life, almost certainly at ever-increasing levels. (In 1976 alone his rent will probably have gone up by between 75p and £1.) He is now paying more than £300 a year in rent payments, so has already paid nearly double the original cost of the house. He owns no asset of any description and gets no benefit from the effects of inflation on the value of his house. If we are judging fairness, there can be no doubt how unfair this system has been towards the council tenant. It is true that somebody starting to buy a house today will initially be paying far more in mortgage repayments than his equivalent in a council house will be paying in rent, but that was also true in 1950. Inflation gradually reduces the burden of mortgage repayments, whereas rents are raised to keep pace with it. In any case what would be the point in the owner-occupier feeling aggrieved at the transfer of council houses to their tenants if the present system requires an unnecessary additional subsidy to council tenants out of his rates and taxes? House owners should not allow any feelings of jealousy to prevent them supporting such a scheme. If they do they will have to pay for the satisfaction of their jealous instincts.

A further question is naturally asked. What about those on the waiting list? If you transfer the ownership of all existing council houses to their tenants there will be some who are hoping to obtain a council house who will be frustrated in their hopes. In fact most of them now have to wait for new council houses to be built. Under my scheme they would be rehoused much more quickly. A housing agency would be set up with the power to purchase for them a house in the cheaper range, probably an older council house which had come up for sale. They would be provided with a 100 per cent mortgage, with a mortgage rebate scheme, if they could not afford the repayments. As their income improved or their liabilities got less they would pay more towards their housing. They would benefit from improvements they made to the house or from any inflationary effects on house prices. This would be a cheaper way of providing houses for those with low incomes than the building of new council houses.

If my scheme was put into operation it is likely that plenty of council houses would come up for sale, for some people would decide to take advantage of being able to sell their council house and obtain some capital and move elsewhere using the proceeds of the sale as a deposit on a new house. At a guess most semi-detached council houses would probably fetch £7,500–£8,000 if sold on the open market. Pre-war council houses would come on the market at £4,000 or £5,000, and would provide a new source of low-cost housing for the person on a low income. It has been seen from the Liverpool example that the current cost of building a new semi-detached council house in Liverpool is £16,000. I believe plenty of Liverpool council houses would come on the market at £7,500 or £8,000, thus halving the cost of providing housing for those on the waiting list.

Not only would we halve the cost but we would have a system of housing finance whereby families would contribute towards the cost of their houses in accordance with their means. We would not have the situation that we now have in my own constituency of Longbridge, British Leyland workers earning £70 or £80 per week and enjoying highly subsidized council rents, with ratepayers and taxpayers with far lower incomes than themselves bearing the cost. Such families would, if they came for a council house under my scheme, be given a 100 per cent mortgage with a rebate scheme. The whole system of financing would be operated on a twenty-five-year (or at most on a thirty-year) basis, and not spread over sixty years. The effect of this would be a far smaller burden of interest payments than under existing housing finance schemes. It would also mean that the speed with which houses could be provided would be substantially increased, because the housing agency would have available to them a choice from amongst 85 per cent of the housing stock, which would then be in the hands of owner-occupiers.

It may be that in certain localities, for specific reasons, perhaps because of an extension of industry, a local authority would decide to arrange for a building contractor to put up a number of low-cost houses in order to meet an immediate shortage. These would be operated under the mortgage rebate scheme and not on a council house rent scheme, as would previously have been the case, and it would still be a far cheaper way of providing such homes as the families concerned would be making their maximum contribution towards the housing cost, and would have a responsibility for the repairs and maintenance of their homes. The local authority would not be involved in the collection of rents, or in the administration of rebates.

It is argued that local authorities administer housing as a social service. The truth is, of course, that for the majority of people housing is not a social service, nor should it be. They are perfectly able to repair and maintain their houses themselves and are similarly able to make a substantial contribution towards the cost of their houses. We have disastrously tried to turn the provision of housing into a social service, with incredibly unnecessary and very high costs. The state should still have the function of seeing that houses are provided for the aged and for the handicapped, but this is only a minute proportion of the total public housing sector. With the local authority relieved of its general duties it could concentrate far more on specific issues, such as the housing of the disabled and aged.

It is only because my scheme is such a radical one and unhappy human instincts of jealousy enter people's calculations that the major political parties have been unwilling to accept it. The social and economic benefits of the scheme are such that I am confident it will be implemented.

The next task of government should be to open a major drive for house improvement. It is cheaper and more economical to conserve and modernize the existing housing stock than to build afresh. It is also the best method of tackling the problem of inadequate housing in terms of human happiness and contentment. People do not wish to lose their neighbours and their friends, their local shopkeepers, their local pub and their local football team in major programmes of urban renewal. The provision of a modern bathroom and modern kitchen is what they primarily require.

My predecessor, Anthony Greenwood, passed legislation to make it easy for people to obtain generous improvement grants – a good measure, in my opinion. He did, however, make the mistake that many politicians and governments make: having passed the legislation he considered that all he then needed to do was sit back and wait for the public to take advantage of the provisions.

In practice only a small section of the public ever know the details of the legislation passed through Parliament, and if it is legislation that is meant to bring people benefits the government has a duty to bring to their attention the manner in which the benefits can be obtained.

In 1970 Julian Amery, as Minister of Housing, and I launched a nationwide campaign to step up the improvement of old houses in Britain. We wrote individually to the mayors of towns with large stocks of old houses and urged them to join in a campaign with us. We arranged for film vans to tour the streets, for leaflets to be distributed, and for numerous ministerial visits to be made. The campaign was a success and made an even greater impact on Britain's housing than the famous Harold Macmillan campaign to build 300,000 houses a year.

In 1970 64,000 council houses and 116,000 private homes were improved, a total of 170,000 houses. As a result of our campaign in 1973 we improved a total of 453,000 houses – 193,000 council houses and 260,000 owner-occupied houses.

Of my many criticisms of the present government few are stronger than my criticism of the way they have allowed the momentum of that campaign to be lost. The number of houses improved has dwindled month by month, and in 1976 they improved less than a third of the number of houses that were improved in 1973.

How incredible it it that with 250,000 construction workers unemployed, and so many families in Britain without a bathroom, modern kitchen, hot water or inside toilet, the socialist government should fail so dramatically.

The campaign for house improvements must in future be based upon a proper system of priorities. We should adopt a sliding scale of grants, starting with a substantial grant of 90 per cent for the provision of basic and essential services such as bathroom, inside toilet, hot water and kitchen in those homes devoid of them, and for homes designated by the local authority as being in a dangerous state of disrepair.

According to the last survey there were 1,244,000 unfit houses in Britain, of which nearly 900,000 had no inside toilet, no bathroom, no washbasins and no hot water. It is these houses that will have the priority under my 90 per cent scheme. As in the past we have succeeded in modernizing 450,000 houses a year, a three-year programme could improve the $1\frac{1}{4}$ million most inadequate homes. There are a further 1,600,000 houses which, apart from the lack of one or more of these basic amenities, are described as fit houses, so in a six-year programme the entire problem of homes without basic amenities could be eliminated.

A second level of grants at a rate of 75 per cent should be provided to district councils that have a high percentage of houses built before 1914 of low rateable value. This would concentrate aid upon the industrial towns where terraced houses were built in such numbers in the nineteenth and early part of the twentieth centuries. It is in these districts that housing problems are primarily concentrated.

Nearly one-third of our housing stock, over six million houses, was built before 1914. The majority of houses without the basic amenities fall within this third, so something like half of them would be dealt with under my priority 90 per cent programme. In addition a substantial number of these houses are owned by the higher income groups, so are already well maintained. There are, however, quite a number that fall into neither of these two categories and for which special priority should be given. For all other houses the traditional 50 per cent improvement grant would be available.

The higher grants would be available for only a limited period of time so as to give both individuals and local authorities a real incentive to act quickly. This would result in a considerable reduction in unemployment in the construction industry. The improvement grant is a very useful instrument for taking up slack in the construction industry and a vital one for raising housing standards. The tradition of either famine or feast for the construction industry has proved to be an expensive and damaging one.

Improvement grants would also help solve the problem of the private rented sector, which accounts for 16 per cent of housing in this country and in the main provides the worst 16 per cent. It is the area of the worst housing deprivation. For decades rents have been inadequate to meet the cost of repairs, maintenance and modernization. Frequently the tenant is more wealthy than the landlord. My improvement grant proposals would make it far easier for these properties to be improved, and it would be right for the rents to be adjusted to meet the enhanced value of the home after the improvement had taken place. There would then be a real incentive for a landlord to put in a bathroom, for example, if he was going to receive a 90 per cent grant for putting it in, and obtain a rent calculated on the cost, having provided only 10 per cent of that cost. Nor would the improvements be in any way detrimental to the tenant, because if he had sufficient income to meet the increased rent he would be only too pleased to have a bathroom at last, and if he could not afford the additional rent, rent rebates and rent allowances would make up the difference.

There is a strong argument for all future housing in the rented sector being free of rent control, because it would mean a substantial increase in rented accommodation, but so long as one major political party with a chance of gaining power promises it will reintroduce the restrictions there can be no increase in the supply. Nobody is going to provide a flat at a cost of £10,000 in the knowledge that whenever a Labour government comes to power the rent will be reduced. Both landlord and tenant are trapped in the existing rented sector. The landlord cannot dispose of his property because there is no market for purchasing such properties. The tenant cannot obtain improvements to his home because the landlord cannot afford it. We should work out a formula whereby if a landlord was willing to sell rented accommodation to his present tenant on the basis of a stipulated multiple of his present controlled rent, then a 100 per cent mortgage would be made available to the tenant and a mortgage rebate scheme would operate if his income was low. There would then be a substantial transfer of rented accommodation to the existing tenants, giving them the incentive to improve and maintain the buildings themselves. I see no other practical way of improving the quality of housing in the private rented sector, and sadly, until there can be all-party agreement, I see no way of expanding the sector. The one possibility which could well develop with all-party agreement would be some form of non-profit-making housing co-operative through the housing societies and housing associations, which could offer rented accommodation at genuine economic rents.

If by 1982 we have transferred the ownership of council houses to the tenants, allowed a good number of private landlords and tenants to extract themselves from their present impossible situation, completed a substantial house improvement campaign concentrating on homes without basic amenities and pre-1914 houses in industrial areas, and removed and rehoused those families living in homes currently defined as slums, we will have totally transformed the housing scene in Britain, largely eradicated homelessness, and created the best housing conditions in Western Europe.

CHAPTER
X
Positive Planning

THERE are few in this country who would want to abolish the important powers of local authorities and central government to control land use. The hideous results of the failure to have land use planning in many parts of the United States illustrate the considerable advantages of a positive planning policy.

We have made many mistakes in the pursuance of such a policy, but nothing like the mistakes that would have been made had free market forces been allowed to operate. The enjoyment of our national parks, the important impact of green belt policies and the way beautiful districts of England such as the Cotswolds have demanded that local facing materials be used on new buildings, are but a few of the benefits that Britain has enjoyed as a result of having positive planning policies.

There are criticisms of the present system of planning, however. One fully justified criticism is that long delays take place in providing planning approval for perfectly desirable developments. A problem easily tackled. The majority of planning decisions are taken by the planning authorities themselves. 2-3 per cent go to appeal and of those 75 per cent are settled by inspectors without direct reference to the minister responsible. Only 25 per cent are actually referred to the minister after a public enquiry before a planning inspector. It is important to see that there is an adequate supply of planning inspectors. When I was Secretary of State for the Environment I discovered there was an increasing time lag in dealing with planning appeals, and I found that one of the reasons for this was that there had been a drop in the number of planning inspectors. The department was reluctant to embark upon a recruiting campaign; they argued that such men were difficult to find, and many of them were selected from within the

Civil Service. Nevertheless they were persuaded to advertise, and we had a good many applications, from which there were many potential recruits. We were able to increase the number of inspectors from 150 to 215, which greatly reduced the time taken making planning decisions. Since then the position has been allowed to slip again. It must be the duty of government to see that the public enquiry system operates efficiently and speedily.

The foundation of our planning should be the regional planning strategy. I inherited the first of these strategies, the Southeast Planning Strategy, from my predecessors within a few days of coming to office. In 1970 it was feared that there would be a substantial increase in the population of the south-east between 1970 and the end of the century. The strategy therefore tried to decide how communications, homes, social amenities, offices and factories would need to be located to cope with the variations in population that could take place, so that even if there was a huge increase in population it would be dealt with so as to preserve the quality of the environment. Our worst fears of the population explosion have not been fulfilled, and rather than an increase in population a very substantial reduction may take place. That too will demand an examination of the effects of a contraction of population on land use. In the post-war period the new town has made an important impact upon the planning strategies of the south-east. It was decided sensibly that better conditions could be provided by building on either a green field site or a site adjoining a small existing town than by allowing the urban sprawl of Greater London to increase.

It is right to pursue a very vigorous green belt policy, and during the period that I was at the Department of the Environment I not only designated many new areas of green belt but also put very tight planning controls on any development in the existing green belt. The containment of urban sprawl is important both to the cities that are contained by it and to the preservation of beautiful stretches of British countryside.

I regret that governments since the early 1970s have not pursued the theme of regional planning strategies as vigorously as they should. Each region has steadily developed a planning strategy, however, and we now have completed strategies for all the regions other than the northern region. We should see that these are reviewed periodically and that all planning decisions are made within the context of the regional planning strategy. This would mean that those who wished to develop private housing could look at the regional planning strategy, discover areas designated for future housing development and apply for planning permission within those areas with the knowledge that their application would probably succeed. However, if they applied to build houses in areas designated for rural amenities and other uses, then the odds would be very heavily against their application succeeding. Land prices stabilize when sensible regional planning caters for all anticipated demands.

The regional planning strategy is prepared by the regional economic planning council and the local planning authorities and is eventually approved by the Department of the Environment, a combination of industrial, commercial and political institutions. It is surely this combination that should decide upon the future areas of development within the country.

There are a number of important areas of planning which should be matters for government policy, one of which is the development of the out-of-town shopping centre. As Secretary of State for the Environment, I insisted that all applications for out-of-town shopping centres were to be considered by myself. I turned down every application I received because I came to the conclusion that such developments would do considerable damage to existing town centres.

The United States of America has made a tragic mistake in allowing the prolific development of out-of-town shopping centres. It is true that they provide pleasant facilities for those in the suburbs and those that are mobile, but they have resulted in the death of the town centre. This has important social implications. Because of the reduction in demand, the few shops that remain in the city centres provide a worse range of goods at higher prices. Hence not only do the poor in the inner cities have the lowest incomes but they also have the most expensive shops. Many of the cultural activities centred on the theatre and the cinema cannot be supported because few of the residents of the town need to come into the city centre itself. The community as a whole do not meet as they did when they shared the one shopping centre in the middle of their town.

Governments should pursue a positive conservation policy in order to retain buildings of elegance or buildings with an important cultural or social function. I was very concerned at the way property developers were obtaining planning permission to build on sites previously occupied by London theatres. The London theatre can only provide its present service to the public because most of the actual theatre buildings were put up many years ago. It is almost impossible to build a new London theatre and run it economically. The new National Theatre cost £16 million and needs another £3 million spent on it. The theatre brings immense advantages to London: it attracts tourists and provides cultural facilities for Londoners themselves. I decided to use my powers to list the more important of these theatres. One day I went through all the theatres of London and decided that I would immediately list ten of them. This means that it would be very difficult for a property developer to obtain planning permission to redevelop these sites. This was surely a use of the powers of government to the benefit of the nation and an action that will be appreciated by generations to come.

We should also act positively to take advantage of the new transportation possibilities that the motorway has created. In 1972 I announced a road building programme that would have been completed by the early 1980s. It provided a bypass of motorway standard for every major conurbation in Britain. That programme will not now be completed until the end of the 1980s.

This capital investment should have been used to the full. We need to see that warehousing and distribution centres are no longer located in the centres of our towns and cities but are moved to the motorway system. I took powers under the Highways Act to purchase land near to motorway intersections for the purpose of creating warehousing and distribution facilities.

I am sorry that those powers have not been used by governments. I hope they will be. Using heavy lorries causes immense damage in our towns and cities. It would make sense to allow the heavy lorries to operate throughout the motorway system and for the loads to be broken down at depots strategically placed within that system. We could then reap the economic benefits of the heavy lorry without suffering the considerable environmental disadvantages of its use.

Congestion would diminish within our towns and city centres. At present a lorry makes a journey to the centre of a city to deliver goods to the warehouse; the goods are then redistributed to other parts of the city or to outside the city, resulting in another lorry journey to and from the warehouse. If warehouses were situated on motorways it would mean that distribution into the city could take place from that point on the motorway perimeter nearest to where the goods had to be delivered. Distribution to other places would not involve the city centre at all. There should be a positive attempt by local and central government to see that over the next ten years warehouses move from our city centres to the motorway system. This would also make available important and useful sites within our city centres for housing, commercial development and recreational facilities.

In replanning our cities we must respect the rights, freedoms, desires and tastes of the individual. We do not want urban areas where each citizen is merely an official record at the town hall, regimented from the cradle to the grave – or, rather, from the municipal ante-natal clinic to the county crematorium.

The areas of blight and disrepair are increasing. So are the despair of the homeless; the difficulties of the disabled; the noise and ugliness; the pollution of the air. In these conditions city life increasingly aggravates the worst in man instead of stimulating the best. It is this trend that brings more crime, more drug addiction and more cynicism. It is our task to see that our cities are reborn. Good planning and good housing are fundamental to that rebirth.

Unfortunately, there is a tendency for the public to wish to retain all that exists and to oppose all that is new. New motorway proposals always attract opposition, as do proposals for new reservoirs, while a railway closure is equally strongly oposed.

I was tempted when I was Secretary of State for the Environment to publish schemes for closing motorways and drying up reservoirs, and to announce the building of new railways through lovely stretches of countryside. A series of announcements such as these would certainly have made the public recognize the advantages of motorways and reservoirs and would have shown that railways intrude upon the country just as much as motorways.

Motorways have already brought peace to villages they have bypassed, given towns the civilized amenity of the pedestrian shopping precinct, and allowed countless thousands from our towns to enjoy coast and countryside never previously available to them. The reservoir which was cursed when its building was inaugurated has often become a recreational amenity of considerable beauty. I regret that with 250,000 construction workers unemployed we are foolish enough to delay further our road and water industry investment programmes.

CHAPTER
XI

Temporary Expedients or Permanent Solutions?

THE basic weakness of our present society is that by its nature our party and parliamentary system encourages the use of the temporary expedient at the expense of the long-term solution. Temporary expedients in politics, like drugs, gradually weaken the body politic until the expedients themselves bring about collapse.

The timescale of a parliamentary democracy is in itself a discouragement to those who wish to apply long-term solutions. In the post-war period the average life of a Parliament has been three years, four months. A major piece of legislation takes at least a year to prepare and a year to go through Parliament, and it is probably another year before it starts to be implemented. The moment of implementation is normally the moment of most discontent and probably coincides with a general election. If, on the other hand, an election takes place prior to implementation the political parties will offer the more attractive short-term expedients than the long-term solution in order to attract additional votes. There is a tendency for the electorate to believe the politician who states that no major or uncomfortable change is necessary rather than the politician who presents the unattractive reality of the situation.

During my three and a half years as a minister I made six major decisions that I knew would be immediately unpopular but that were essential for the future of the country.

Within a few weeks of becoming the Minister for Local Government in 1970 I announced to a Conservative conference that it was my intention to go ahead quickly with local government reform. I opened my speech with the words, 'Only once in each century will there be a politician fool enough to embark upon the reform of local government. I have decided to volunteer myself for that sacrifice this century. For there is no way in which one can reform local government that will be praised and applauded. For all those against change will be vocal, and after local government is reformed all future mishaps for at least a decade to come will be blamed upon the reform of local government.'

I cannot complain therefore of the large volume of criticism that has followed the reform of local government. I can, however, complain of its inaccuracies, and I do defend not just the decision to reform local government for the first time in almost a hundred years but also the principles I applied in making that reform.

To listen to the current critics, one would imagine that the great mass of the people and the politicians and those interested in local government had defended the existing system. It is worth recalling the events that led to local government reform.

On 3 February 1970 the then Labour government published its White Paper stating that it was absurd to continue with 124 county councils and over 1,000 district councils and that it was their intention to follow the principles of the Maud Report on Local Government Reform, which advocated the abolition of all existing local authorities and their replacement by fifty-eight large unitary authorities and three metropolitan areas: Birmingham, Liverpool and Manchester. After consultation the Labour government announced that it was going to have fifty-one unitary authorities and five metropolitan areas. Mr Crosland, speaking in the House on 18 February 1970, said, 'When we held our consultation on the Commission's Report there was no serious argument for keeping things as they are.'

Those who complain about the remoteness of local government following reform should remember that the two-tier system I brought in is far less remote from people than that advocated by the Labour government, and certainly far less remote than that advocated by the Liberal Party, whose central proposal was that the major power should be with provincial governments covering even greater areas than Labour's unitary authorities.

When I published my proposals almost the entire press approved of the reform. The only major critics were the *Economist* and the *Evening Standard*, together with the Labour Party, all of whom wanted more drastic reform – the creation of the large, all-powerful, unitary county councils. As to the Conservative Parliamentary Party, which now contains many critics of local government reform, one can read through the debates on the White Paper and the Bill itself to find virtually no criticism of principle. The few critics that there were, only demanded that more power be given to the bottom tier than I was willing to give. No Liberal spoke on the White Paper debate and no vote was taken against the White Paper.

What of the complaint that rates have soared as a result of the massive bureaucracies that were created by local government reform? The facts are available. We can compare the size of local government administrative staff in England and Wales in the year before reform and the year after it. We can also compare the change in the size of the administrative staff in the rest of the country with that in the Greater London area, where reform had taken place years previously so that any increases in staff could no longer be seen as a direct result of reform. In the relevant year administrative staff in London increased by 9.9 per cent while in the rest of England and Wales – which had been reorganized – the increase was less than half that figure, 4.7 per cent. There are also allegations that the reforms caused a massive inflation of local government salaries, but administrative salaries in London went up by 19.1 per cent and in the reorganized areas by only 14.3 per cent.

My successor, Mr Geoffrey Rippon, who was responsible during the period of the transition, very sensibly arranged for the whole salary structure to be referred to the Pay Board. Alas, the incoming Labour government abolished the Pay Board and put no instrument in its place to check upon the payment of local government salaries. Even without this safeguard, however, it can be seen that salaries in the administrative area of local government rose broadly in line with those of the country as a whole.

In the case of many senior grades there were substantial reductions in salary costs. The number of chief executives declined from 1,307 to 421, and the number of senior officers, whose salaries come under the Joint Negotiating Committee, was reduced from 3,129 to 1,913, giving a reduction in salary costs of more than £5 million.

It is of course fair to argue that the reform I advocated should have resulted in a reduction of staff, so there should have been no increase at all. That certainly was what I expected. If one takes account of extra tasks placed upon local government during the year in question there was a reduction of staff of 4.6 per cent, a reduction from 298,644 to 284,915. However, 27,800 extra posts were required to meet additional duties placed upon local government by central government during that year and by factors such as the replacement of outside contracting for professional services by smaller authorities.

It is new government legislation and circulars from government departments that have caused the increases in staff. When I became Secretary of State for the Environment I was annoyed to find that major departments sent out circulars to local authorities urging them to make greater provision in some field, while the ministers of those same departments joined in a general chorus of complaint at increases in local government expenditure. I made the suggestion that all circulars going to local authorities should first be shown to the Department of the Environment, as the department responsible for local government. The cost of the circular, if it was sent, could then be brought to the attention of the Cabinet, and the Cabinet could be made aware of the implications that these circulars had both for manpower levels and for public expenditure levels. My suggestion was rejected because the Treasury considered that this was their function and that it was not for one major spending department such as mine to scrutinize the actions of other major spending departments. Alas, the Treasury never put any control upon the issue of such circulars nor did they ever contain estimates of their own cost in terms of money or management.

I believe that the number of staff could have been cut far more than the real reduction of 4.6 per cent that took place. And doubtless there have been cases of individual people being paid more than was necessary.

Apart from inflating salary costs and swelling bureaucracies, the next most popular charge is that extravagant new buildings have been put up for the new authorities. In my own county of Hereford and Worcester there has been an immense outcry over the building of a new county headquarters, the need for which has been entirely blamed on local government reform. The truth, of course, is that Worcestershire County Council had decided to have a new county headquarters prior to reform, and so had Herefordshire County Council. As a result of the reforms we have one new county headquarters instead of two, but there is no doubt that for decades to come the blame for the entire cost of the new headquarters will be placed upon local government reform.

Certainly the building of the new headquarters was in no way related to any increase in staff due to local government reform.

The total number of administrative staff prior to reorganization was 3,212 and a year later it was 3,167, so there has been a decrease.

The savings I had hoped for as a result of local government reform are the responsibility of those councillors who are now in power in our local authorities. One of the disappointments of the reform was that new people did not come into local government, in spite of my personal attempts to persuade industry, trade unions and professional bodies to encourage more of their able members to take on these important tasks.

In many local authorities the same councillors were elected as prior to reform, and they were understandably reluctant to remove officials they had known over the years. Certainly if these officials had been removed it would have been right to treat them generously, and this would have been one temporary cost of local government reform. Our elected councillors should carefully examine all potential areas of staff savings and see to it that early retirement and other methods are used to reduce the existing staffing of the administrative part of local government. If, however, this is to succeed, government departments must stop sending out circulars urging local authorities to take on yet more tasks at even greater expense.

One thing I am very confident of is that although local government reform has been blamed for the whole of the massive inflation of the past three years, had such reform not taken place there would today be a whole range of small authorities in a position of collapse, totally incapable of meeting the huge inflation of this period. I am also certain that as the years go by a whole range of local government services will be of a higher quality as a result of local government reform. There is a natural tendency for services to improve to the level of the best of the previous authorities rather than be lowered to that of the worst. But doubtless we will continue for at least twenty years to give all credit for the benefits of reform to the councillors and to blame the difficulties of local government on local government reform.

I am proud to say that this reform was carried out with total integrity. Local government reform provided a unique opportunity to gerrymander the boundaries of the new local authorities so as to give my own party a considerable political advantage in a number of key localities. Many zealous party officials, Members of Parliament and local authority leaders made suggestions to me as to where the boundaries should sensibly be drawn for our political advantage. I rejected all such advice and every boundary was drawn in accordance with what made good sense for local government, irrespective of party advantage.

When later I read the Crossman Diaries and learned the degree to which both boundaries and election dates were gerrymandered when he had similar responsibilities to myself, I recognized the sharp contrast between our two approaches. I have suffered political unpopularity within my own party for having failed to take their political advice. I feel, however, that the integrity of government has been increased by my determination not to be in any way involved in such gerrymandering.

My second unpopular decision, which I took in the face of massive local authority mistrust, was the decision to reorganize Britain's water industry. When I made that decision I could in no way have predicted the years of low rainfall and drought that have followed, but without my reorganization the adverse effects of the drought years would have been far greater. There has been considerable switching of water supplies within the regional water authorities that would have been very difficult to organize in the fragmented authorities that existed previously.

In a review of the water industry in England and Wales in July 1976 the National Water Council states:

> The Council has no hesitation in saying that the 1973 reorganisation has shown itself to provide a viable and successful structure for the industry. The concept of multi-purpose regional authorities based on river basins is robust and well judged in relation to the essential needs of water management. The vigour and resourcefulness with which the present extraordinary drought is being dealt are convincing testimony to this.

The water crisis with which I was confronted was potentially far deeper and more far-reaching than the present one. I was told that the water industry I inherited in June 1970 was such that by the early 1980s one-third of the Midlands would be unemployed because of its inability to provide water to meet the industrial needs of the Midlands.

For an entire century we had had a system of organizing our water supplies that had allowed massive pollution of our rivers and wastage of our water resources and had totally failed to make the capital investments that were desperately needed. It is difficult to think of a water system more lunatic than one in which a small water authority upstream could pursue sewerage policies that polluted the whole of the river system, with all the adverse effects upon a multitude of authorities further downstream. The only practical course was to organize our water industry on the basis of rivers, and then to provide the capital investment that was needed to avert a water crisis throughout the 1980s and 1990s. There would never be great enthusiasm for reorganizing water and there would always be entrenched hostility from the multitude who enjoyed positions of power in minor water and sewerage authorities throughout the country.

Once again it was certain that in future public criticism of the water industry would place all blame upon water reorganization. The steep increase in water costs necessary to pay for the new investment programmes would be attributed not to these investment programmes but to the reorganization of water.

The Labour Party in opposition opposed the reorganization and made speeches about the importance of preserving local authority boundaries for water and local democratic influence. But once reorganization had been achieved, this was one long-term solution they could not reverse, especially as the water crisis had heightened in the interim years. The Labour government's White Paper totally vindicated my reorganization proposals. But although the proposals have been vindicated the political propaganda will not stop. Even ministers who know the facts continue to blame rising water costs on Tory reorganization.

When in June 1970 I reached the conclusion that the organization of water on a river basin basis was the only possible answer to the water crisis, I was told by both my permanent secretary and by the deputy secretary in charge of that section of the Department of the Environment that, in their judgement, there was no possibility of my persuading a Cabinet, a political party or Parliament to accept such a radical, although logical, solution. It is a sad reflection upon democracy that civil servants of thirty years' experience should conclude that Parliament would be incapable of accepting a logical solution to a major problem because of all the vested political interests opposing any major change.

The third major and unpopular decision I took was to reform housing finance. For decades past the whole of the housing subsidy system had been concentrated on bricks and mortar and not people. Irrespective of their income and their wealth, council tenants paid rents heavily subsidized by both taxpayers and ratepayers. In many local authorities tenants on low incomes and in impoverished circumstances obtained no greater subsidy than those who could well have afforded to buy a house of their own.

Four out of ten local authorities had no form of rent rebate scheme at all, and of the six out of ten authorities that did many provided a totally inadequate scheme. The Labour government had urged local authorities to use their subsidy to provide rent rebates, but the majority of local authorities still had no form of rent rebate schemes. I decided, therefore, to concentrate government help into two spheres: subsidizing those people who really needed help and accelerating the slum clearance programme.

I well recall, a few days prior to announcing the details of my Bill, having lunch with Dick Crossman in his capacity as editor of the *New Statesman*. He asked me what the broad outlines of the Bill were to be. When I told him he expressed considerable surprise and said, 'Surely no Tory Cabinet has agreed to that.' When I told him that all was agreed he said, 'But this is the most socialist housing measure this century – a measure I would have been delighted to introduce but I had no hope of persuading my colleagues to do anything so radical.'

It was radical. By extending my rent rebate schemes to the private sector, where at that time 1,300,000 families were concentrated, as well as providing rent rebates in the public sector, which housed nearly 30 per cent of the families in the country, I created a situation where for the first time in British history no family could say they were badly housed because they were unable to afford the rent.

My measure did mean, however, that those who could afford it would over the years pay a far more economic rent than they had paid to date. Fair rents would be fixed for all by an independent tribunal, and people would move towards this fair rent by rent increases of 50 pence per year. These increases were payable, of course, only by those who could afford it: for those who could not the rent increases would be met by an increase in their rent rebates.

My Bill also provided for more help to be given to those local authorities with the worst housing problems and less help to others. The Inner London boroughs, Liverpool and the inner areas of Birmingham benefited greatly by this measure, at the expense of more prosperous areas without any real housing need.

I introduced subsidies for slum clearance which meant there

could be no financial reasons for not clearing all the existing slums in Britain within ten years. Previously financial help had only been given provided that when the slums were cleared rehousing took place on the same site. The result of this was that when, as frequently happened, small businesses and factories were involved in a potential slum clearance local authorities suffered from a considerable financial disincentive. Under my new scheme 75 per cent subsidy was provided and it was left to the local authority to decide where best the people should be rehoused. If we had continued at the previous rate it would have taken twenty-five years to clear the existing slums, and of course by that time many more would have been created.

It was a just measure, though a radical one, a measure destined to eliminate some of the worst hardship in housing. How incredible it is that the then socialist Spokesman on Housing, Mr Anthony Crosland, described it as 'The most reactionary and socially divisive measure which is likely to be introduced in the lifetime of this Parliament'. He, like all other Labour M.P.s, sought to obtain political advantage from the fact that those council house tenants who could afford it would be facing rent increases of 50 pence a year. They immediately pledged themselves to repeal the measure. The moment they came to power they stopped all further increases in rents, but two years later they not only started the increases again but in order to make up the lost ground allowed increases of as much as treble those allowed under my measure. They retained the rebate schemes. They retained the slum clearance subsidy. They, in fact, retained almost the whole of the measure, having previously exploited it for political ends and then disrupted its progress in order to gain some additional votes on the council estates. As always in a democracy the millions of people who benefited from the rent rebates, the rent allowances and the slum clearance drive remained silent. Those who paid the 50 pence rent increases were more vocal, and the political atmosphere created was one of hostility towards what was beyond doubt a genuinely reforming measure.

I also persuaded the Cabinet to agree to build the Third London Airport at Maplin. The Roskill Committee had recommended Cublington. In my judgement this would have been a disastrous decision from the environmental point of view. It would have have ruined the Vale of Aylesbury, and created considerable noise problems. The Maplin site had the advantage of taking up no land, since the proposal was to create land from the sea for the location of the airport. It would have meant that much of the noise was over the sea and not over people's houses, and it gave us the opportunity of building at the same time an important deep sea port. It had one further and very important advantage. It would have brought more prosperity to the east of London, and would have helped make the job opportunities on the east side of London more equal with those on the west side.

Locating a major airport anywhere tends to be unpopular with those living near the new site, and there will also be general unpopularity from the public who feel they will have to foot the bill for a new massive development. The incoming Labour government went for the temporary expedient and announced that in their judgement there was no immediate need for a new runway so there would be no Third London Airport in the foreseeable future.

This decision is a classic example of the temporary expedient proving to be a long-term disaster. The decision first of all means that those who already suffer from the noise of Heathrow, Gatwick, Luton and Stansted are destined to have substantially increased noise problems for several decades to come.

The decision will also mean that by 1980 Britain will have the worst airport facilities in Europe, with serious congestion and delays at most of the existing airports. By the mid-1980s it will probably mean that many aeroplanes that wish to come to Britain will be unable to do so at those times of the year when traffic is at a peak.

By 1990 (it must be remembered that it takes at least ten years from the moment you agree to build a new airport to its total completion) meeting the projected demands on airport facilities will have created massive problems. Thirty-eight thousand more people will have to be employed at Heathrow, both on the airport itself and in all the sundry services that have to surround an airport, and this will mean an 80,000 increase in population in that locality. The figure for Gatwick during the same period will be 33,000 additionally employed and 65,000 additional population, and for Stansted 38,000 additionally employed and an increase of 78,000 in the population.

The cost in terms of congestion, new housing, new roads, new schools and new local authority facilities will be gigantic – added to which all four locations are in areas of high employment, so these demands will put an incredible strain upon an already difficult labour market.

There is no doubt that within the next five years a British government will have to decide to build a Third London Airport. There is little doubt that the site chosen will be Maplin. Nor is there any doubt that the cost of building the airport will be astronomically higher after the seven-year delay than it would have been had the project now been well on its way to completion. For much of the south-east there will be unnecessary noise, unnecessary congestion and an unnecessary strain upon local facilities and labour resources.

My fifth major decision was to proceed with the negotiations with the French for the building of the Channel Tunnel. My successor, Geoffrey Rippon, announced the government decision to proceed with the tunnel after the negotiations had been successfully completed by John Peyton. The tunnel would have linked the railway system of Britain with that of Western Europe. It was a unique opportunity to bring a new lease of life to Britain's railway system. It would have created important long-haul facilities to every part of the continent and created exciting major new inter-city routes for passengers. It would have been an important project for the construction industry, and would doubtless have resulted in future international tunnelling projects being more readily available to the British construction firms that had been involved. The cost would have been less than the additional capital costs that will now be required for ship port facilities and roads that will have to take the traffic that would otherwise have gone by rail. Had the tunnel been built, railway freight equivalent to 250,000 lorry loads would have gone by rail in 1980 and the equivalent of 500,000 lorry loads by 1990. That means that 1,500 lorries a day will be cramming the roads of the south-east to take advantage of the various port facilities and ferry services that will need to be provided.

Had we proceeded with the Channel Tunnel and with Maplin, the total cost by 1980 would have been about £150 million per year, a minute fraction of our gross national product, for which we would have had the permanent benefits of a railway linked with Europe, the best airport facilities in Europe, and an important new deep sea port. Instead we will have a dwindling railway system, a congested and noisy south-east, the worst airport facilities in Europe and no new deep sea port. It is inconceivable that the French, the Germans, the Americans or the Japanese would have failed to complete such potentially rewarding projects as these. It certainly reflects upon the low morale of Britain that we missed these opportunities. We will come to regret our decisions to do nothing.

Finally, I announced the much needed modernization of the steel industry. As we have seen, the 1964-70 Labour government had avoided the decision to modernize because of the unpopularity the inevitable redundancies in steel would have caused them. Prior to the 1974 election, motivated by short-term constituency interests, the Labour Party pledged themselves to halt the modernization programme if they were elected. This they did, with continuing disastrous results for the British steel industry.

All of these six proposals resulted from a genuine assessment of the medium- and long-term priorities of policy in those spheres for which my departments were responsible.

I have, I suppose, the privilege of being the only minister to have been responsible for both the two largest departments in Whitehall. I believe it is right to have one department responsible for the whole range of environmental policies because of the close inter-action between planning, housing, transportation and local government. Likewise it seems a nonsense to have separate departments responsible for trade, energy and industry when all three are so totally inter-related.

The argument against such departments is that they are too large for any one person to manage. This is true, but they are not too large for one person to lead; what is essential is that these departments should be operated by ministers working as a genuine team.

In the few months prior to the creation of the Department of the Environment I was the Minister of Housing and Local Government with four ministers working under me. I was totally new to Whitehall, never having been a junior minister. My only experience of government was that of being P.P.S. to Selwyn Lloyd when Sir Alec Douglas-Home, on becoming Prime Minister, brought him back into the Cabinet as the Leader of the House of Commons.

I was very fortunate after only two years in Parliament to be asked by such a distinguished parliamentarian to take on this task. Some months after he had been so wrongly sacked by Harold Macmillan, when the economy was responding well to the unpopular measures that he had taken, I made a speech which was reported in a number of newspapers stating that it was time some tribute was given to the man responsible for these successes, Mr Selwyn Lloyd. When I made that speech I did not know him personally and had virtually never spoken to him. He wrote me a nice letter thanking me for my generous remarks and I believe it was because of this that he decided to choose this new young member to be his P.P.S.

Selwyn Lloyd taught me a great deal from his wealth of experience. Few men in British history have occupied so many of the high offices of state – Foreign Secretary, Chancellor of the Exchequer, and Minister of Defence – and few men who have held such offices have remained so totally without conceit, arrogance or bitterness over any of the mishaps of the past. He was let down by the Americans at Suez and yet took a great deal of personal trouble to visit Foster Dulles a few days before his death, to the immense delight of Foster Dulles himself. He was badly treated by Harold Macmillan, but in spite of my very close association with him as his P.P.S. I never once heard him say anything against the man who had so quickly and ruthlessly dismissed him from the Cabinet. He became an excellent Speaker of the House of Commons. He is a most popular godfather to my six-year-old son, and has remained over the fourteen years since we first came together a constant friend, whose judgement and advice I greatly value. And I am not alone in valuing this advice. Certainly he has throughout that same period of time remained a close political friend of Sir Alec Douglas-Home.

When I was asked by Sir Alec to join the front bench in 1964 I experienced a moment of real anxiety. I was told by Selwyn Lloyd, with whom I shared an office in the House of Commons, that the Leader of the Party wished to see me in his room at three o'clock as he was very annoyed at the speech I had made that weekend. I could think of nothing I had said in my speech that could have offended him, and I questioned the stern-looking Selwyn Lloyd as to what had caused offence. 'Alec will make it perfectly clear,' he said, 'at three o'clock.' It was therefore with some fear and trepidation, and also eager to defend myself, that I entered Sir Alec's room. He immediately said that he wanted me to join the front bench as Spokesman on Economic and Financial Affairs under Ted Heath as Shadow Chancellor. It was typical of a whole range of practical jokes carried out on myself and my family by Selwyn Lloyd over the fourteen years of our association, and one which ended in great relief on the part of a rather anxious twenty-eight-year-old backbencher.

The Leader of the House has no department, so despite my experience as P.P.S. to the Leader of the House I did not know the normal relationship between civil servant and minister. On my first day I requested that in future all the ministers working with me should meet in my office at nine each morning so that we could inform each other of what was going on and benefit from each other's views on any issue that was confronting any section of the department.

I was surprised when the ministers assembled in my room the next morning to see that they were accompanied by the head of my private office with a notebook. I told him I wished to meet the ministers alone, to which he replied, 'Ministers never meet alone. You must have a civil servant present to record any decisions that are made.' I told him that my ministers would be meeting alone with me. I explained that we might well want to discuss political matters not affecting the Civil Service, and that any decisions we made would, of course, be conveyed to the department in the usual way. He said that the permanent secretary would be very unhappy at such an arrangement. I told him I regretted the unhappiness but it would continue. The permanent secretary, Sir Matthew Stevenson, a very distinguished civil servant, who taught me a great deal and helped me immensely in my early months as a minister, then came himself to express his disapproval and suggested it would create the impression that I did not trust the Civil Service. I said that this was not my intention but I did want to meet my ministers alone to discuss political strategy. Naturally if any decision came from those meetings they would be transmitted to the department, and if the department had any opposition to the decisions we made we would want to consider their views immediately.

For several days the permanent secretary continued to express his unhappiness, but the argument ended when I said I would be willing to have a civil servant present for such meetings on condition that he guaranteed that there would never be a meeting of civil servants without a minister present!

I was a minister for three and a half years, with eight ministers under me at the Department of the Environment and nine at the Department of Trade and Industry. I met these ministers every morning, and eventually the Civil Service came to recognize that these meetings were of immense value in speeding up decision-taking within the department. Instead of memoranda slowly coming up from parliamentary secretaries to ministers and then to the Secretary of State, agreement could be obtained verbally from the Secretary of State on a whole host of matters each morning. It also meant that all ministers knew what was going on throughout the department. We were a united team both within the parliamentary party and in our relationship to the country, and the strategy of the department was one that all the ministers contributed to.

In recent times here has been criticism of the quality of the Conservative Parliamentary Party. I considered the ministers who were with me in those two departments were of extremely high quality.

In the Department of the Environment were John Peyton and Julian Amery, both politicians of considerable experience and character and with an admirable independence of mind. I think in recent years Julian Amery has been one of the most under-utilized of our politicians. He has lived and breathed politics from the day he was born, and probably has greater experience of the realities of international affairs and international personalities than any living parliamentarian.

Amongst my junior ministers at that department was Michael Heseltine, a politician of considerable ability and energy who possesses the important quality of originality in his approach to practical political problems. Eldon Griffiths and Paul Channon were also part of the team. They are both politicians who have obtained considerable experience at a young age and who will make a significant impact upon the British political scene in the years ahead.

Graham Page is one of Parliament's institutions; with the vigilant eye of the skilled lawyer, he has assiduously watched the power of the executives. Finally, we were fortunate at the Department of the Environment to have completing the team both a lord and a clergyman in Lord Sandford. Our early morning meetings of ministers became known as morning prayers, and it was therefore appropriate that we should have a clergyman present.

Michael Heseltine had moved to the Department of Trade and Industry before I went there, and a number of actions he took, particularly in his dealings with the nationalized industries, will have saved the taxpayer many millions of pounds.

Three other ministers working under me at that department were Christopher Chataway, Tom Boardman and Geoffrey Howe. I very much regret that both Christopher Chataway and Tom Boardman have left the political scene – though in the case of Tom Boardman the absence will only be temporary. With Peter Emery, Tom Boardman bore the brunt of the severe energy crisis of 1973; both carried out this work with immense distinction and obtained very little credit for it. Without their work the staggering achievements of production within the three-day week and the avoidance of petrol rationing would not have been possible.

Whatever else Geoffrey Howe does in politics, certainly his achievement at the Department of Trade and Industry in devising and steering through important consumer legislation will have a lasting effect upon the quality of life in Britain. In this task he showed that intense application for which he is noted. One could speculate as to how political events might have changed if I had asked for Margaret Thatcher to join me at the Department of Trade and Industry instead of Sir Geoffrey Howe.

One Sunday morning in November 1972 I was telephoned by the Prime Minister to say that he wanted me to move from the Department of the Environment and become the Secretary of State for Trade and Industry. He asked me whether I would prefer Margaret Thatcher or Geoffrey Howe to become the Minister for Trade and Consumer Affairs in the department. It was a difficult choice. I liked them both. They would both have strengthened the department considerably. They would both have been creative and congenial colleagues. I decided on Geoffrey primarily because unlike Margaret he had never before headed a department and would not therefore be disappointed at no longer leading a department of his own.

Since Margaret Thatcher removed me from the Shadow Cabinet it is natural that the media should have looked for animosity and acrimony between us. As it does not exist, they have at times imagined it. Our careers followed a remarkably parallel course until Margaret became the party leader. We both fought our first two elections as Conservative candidate for Dartford. When Margaret joined the Shadow Cabinet not only was it an appointment I had advocated but she was to take my place as Shadow Spokesman on Transport while I moved on to Housing and Local Government. We both joined the Cabinet together and were virtually always in agreement. The educational aspects of my local government reform were directly inspired by her suggestions in her capacity as Secretary of State for Education. She was an enthusiastic supporter of my housing finance reforms, and I was a keen supporter of the policies she vigorously and successfully pursued of improving nursery and primary education and retaining our best grammar schools.

Since she became leader, we have been in contact on a number of important issues and always in a constructive and congenial way. Any woman who has a degree in chemistry, is a qualified barrister, has fought numerous successful election campaigns, has become a Cabinet Minister, is happily married and has successfully brought up twins deserves admiration.

I regret to say that after our defeat in 1974 there was a growing and genuine difference in view between Keith Joseph and Margaret Thatcher on one side and Ted Heath, myself and the majority of the Shadow Cabinet on the other. It was a difference devoid of personal hostility. Ironically, it was only four years previously at the time of the election of the new leader that Keith Joseph had telephoned me to say that Margaret would be voting for Ted. I recall the incident well because there had been some doubt as to which way she would vote and Keith had agreed to contact her to discover her final intentions. Had she voted against Ted Heath it would have been the first time we had differed on a major political decision.

It was courageous of her to take up the challenge to Ted Heath when Keith Joseph decided not to stand against him, and having been successful I think she was right to replace me in her Shadow Cabinet with men like Angus Maude, Airey Neave and John Biffen, who at that time appeared to share the approach of Keith Joseph to economic policy.

Having by 1974 spent all but two of my thirteen years in Parliament as either the parliamentary private secretary to a senior Cabinet Minister or on the front bench, I have welcomed the freedom and the time to rethink, travel and meditate that her action has given me.

At a junior level in the Department of Trade and Industry, Tony Grant and Cranley Onslow made a considerable impact on our total strategy. Both are politicians who will, when they become better known to the public, make a real contribution to our political life. The final member of the team was Lord Limerick, whose considerable commercial expertise and knowledge were an immense help in our many international negotiations.

When I contemplate the quality of the fifteen ministers who were with me during those three and a half years I am certainly not depressed about the future quality of the Conservative Party.

And I think we would all agree that if we did achieve some major reforms during that period it was because we never concentrated upon the temporary expedient at the expense of the long-term strategy. At regular intervals we would go away together for three days to discuss longer-term strategy of the department. We were all determined that we would thrash out such a strategy, pursue it, and when necessary defend it, rather than, as so often happens, becomes bogged down in the mass of detailed decision-taking that the day-to-day administration of departments requires. My regret is that already a number of the more important decisions we made have been rescinded, and that we were not given a longer period at the Department of Trade and Industry to complete the restructuring of the British economy that was and still is so desperately needed.

Looking back upon the Conservative government of 1970-4, one of my regrets is that we did not as a Cabinet find the time to stand back from the day-to-day pressures and talk over the long-term strategy we wished to pursue. We would all have benefited if periodically we could have spent two or three days together discussing the longer-term objectives, as my colleagues and I did within the two departments for which I was responsible. It was a talented Cabinet, with stimulating intellects such as those of Lord Hailsham and Keith Joseph, and men of considerable political experience such as Alec Douglas-Home and Peter Carrington, and all, in my judgement, were people of integrity whose shared objective was to revive our nation's fortunes. From time to time the Prime Minister arranged meetings on a Friday at Chequers at which the Cabinet was supposed to discuss long-term forecasts prepared by the Think Tank. These meetings served relatively little purpose, however, as there was never time to develop a dialogue in depth. By the time the Cabinet had arrived at Chequers and enjoyed a welcoming cup of coffee and the Think Tank had presented its paper there was very little time for discussion before lunch. After lunch the discussion was fairly short because normally Cabinet ministers had to leave by 4 p.m. for various speaking engagements throughout the country.

At our departmental weekends we were engrossed in discussion for most of the waking hours of the two and a half days we were together, simply talking through the major problems facing one department. The three or four hours of discussion that took place at the Chequers meetings on the major long-term problems of the nation were obviously totally inadequate.

Because we did thrash out a longer-term strategy at the Department of the Environment we were able to embark upon reforms and policies that, had we been allowed to continue them, would have transformed the British environment within a decade. Working on the principle that the first priority must be given to the worst environments, we would within ten years have removed all existing slums, improved older houses, cleared all scheduled derelict land, substantially improved the quality of the water in all our major river systems, made smokeless zones in those remaining industrial areas where smoke and grime still worked to create a perpetual ugliness and dirtiness, and completed a motorway system which would have confined the bulk of heavier traffic to the motorways, thus substantially easing a great deal of urban congestion. Alas, that department now drifts on, making totally fragmented decisions with no clear long-term objectives in mind.

At the Department of Trade and Industry, had we been given ten years to pursue the long-term strategy we had agreed upon, Britain would have ended that decade with one of the most modern steel industries in the world, an off-shore oil industry that would have entered into important partnerships in those many parts of the world where off-shore operations are developing, a much more efficient mechanism for international marketing, and an economy benefiting from a considerable volume of new investment and closely inter-linked with a number of the new growth economies in South America, the Middle East, and Africa. Alas, the Department of Trade and Industry is no more. Four separate departments operate with seemingly no co-ordination, and the bigger visions important to British commerce are way beyond the responsibilities or grasp of any of the four minor departments that have been created.

Britain's present powerless position demands a political approach that will concentrate upon the bigger and wider opportunities for recovery. Our failure to see some of the difficult issues in recent years has contributed substantially to Britain's relative decline compared with other industrial nations. It is important that we should record and recognize our failures in foresight in recent years. We did not foresee the potential effects of an energy crisis and the dangers of the world becoming dependent upon Middle East oil supplies. We did not foresee the increase in crime and the new social problems that would result from greater affluence, nor the disastrous long-term effects on the environment of industrial growth created by industries devoid of social and environmental responsibilities. We did not foresee the impact of education upon attitudes, demands and discontent, nor the immense dangers to an urban society of failing to remove the barriers of race.

We are failing now to foresee the impact on the availability of raw materials and the world's environment that the future expansion of the giant economies of the United States, Japan, and Western Europe will have, combining as they will from now onwards with the new industrialized countries of the Middle East, Africa, and South America.

We will continue to fail on issues as big as these unless we have a quality of political leadership that can for a period persuade the country to concentrate upon the long-term solution and disregard the damaging, temporary expedient.

CHAPTER
XII
The Ascent of Britain

THE oil crisis which followed in the aftermath of the Yom Kippur War fundamentally altered the prospects for both the British and the world economy. For Britain, it imposed the immediate necessity of a fall in the standard of living. Was this fall to be achieved by a policy of deflation leading to unemployment, or would the good sense of the British people ensure a voluntary limitation to collective bargaining, thereby preserving full employment? This was the question posed by Edward Heath when the oil crisis hit Britain. He was the first British politician to understand that the crisis fundamentally altered most of the assumptions upon which economic planning had been based. The effects on the world economy were equally important. By quadrupling the price of oil in a little over a year, the OPEC countries have effected an instantaneous redistribution of the world's weath on a scale unsurpassed in history. By 1980 this one measure will have created for them surpluses probably amounting to £100,000 billion. This has created an enormous increase in the velocity of international money.

The breakdown of the Bretton Woods settlement, the emergence of the petro-dollar, and the growth of the Euro-dollar market – in which a virtually unregulated £150,000 million worth of Euro-dollars surges throughout the world, affecting the balance of payments and the level of inflation in all the countries through which the Euro-dollar travels – had already increased the velocity of international money. This had led to a far greater instability throughout the Western world. Major European countries like Italy had had to be provided with £8,000 million to save them from insolvency. Within a few months American unemployment had soared, creating all the social problems associated with a 40–60 per cent unemployment rate among the young black population.

These new velocities of international money bring with them an intricate problem of inflation that cannot be dealt with by any of the traditional fiscal or monetary methods. Potential enemies such as the Soviet Union are discovering that they can not only pervert raw material markets but also cause damage and destruction by interfering in the capital markets of the West. This only serves to reinforce the conclusion that inter-dependence is essential, which means that British domestic policy and foreign policy must be considered together.

These dramatic social and economic changes are accompanied by the very real potential danger of a change in the balance of power between the Western democracies and the communist world. The retention of a balance of power must be given the highest priority. A balance of terror is better than the terror of imbalance.

Unfortunately, however, the balance has turned against the West over the past decade.

During 1976 alone the Soviet Union will have brought into service over 200 new generation inter-continental ballistic missiles, a variety of other missiles, 1,000 combat aircraft, 700 helicopters, 3,000 tanks, 4,000 personnel carriers, 10 nuclear submarines and a number of major surface ships, including a new 40,000-ton aircraft carrier. And yet with all these facts known to the West the voices of appeasement are as strong today as they were in the worst period of the 1930s.

The decision by the present Labour government to reduce defence expenditure by £4,700 million over the next ten years has proved totally acceptable to the British electorate. This sort of acceptance is always a danger for Western democracies in any period remote from a previous war. In the 1930s Neville Chamberlain enhanced his popularity by going to Germany and coming back with a piece of paper – a piece of paper that so quickly proved to be meaningless. In the 1970s President Nixon considered that a mission to Moscow and a return to America waving a similar meaningless piece of paper would assist in increasing his popularity following Watergate.

The whole record of East–West negotiations on disarmament is a record of a disastrous softening in the West. On every issue the Soviets negotiate to preserve disparities where they favour the forces of communism and to eradicate them where they are of advantage to the Western democracies. The perpetual pleas of optimism on the part of the West provide finance ministers and chancellors with a constant excuse for reducing expenditure. In the Soviet Union, however, one nuclear submarine is produced every month. In seas once dominated by the Royal Navy or allied navies the Soviet Union is creating a naval strength that exceeds the combined allied naval forces. On the vital routes providing our oil and many of our most basic raw materials Soviet naval activity has quadrupled in six years. Soviet spy ships are constantly photographing Britain's vital North Sea oil installations. The Soviet Union is investing millions of pounds in a new port in the Indian Ocean. The British, under pressure from the Left, are abandoning their facilities at Simonstown.

In ten short years of history the strong defences of the West have been dangerously eroded compared with those of the Soviet Union. In 1964 the United States had four times as many intercontinental ballistic missiles as the Soviet Union. Ten years later the Soviet Union had half as many again as the United States. In 1964 the United States had more than three times as many submarine-launched ballistic missiles as the Soviet Union. By 1974 the Soviet Union had many more than the United States. In the same ten years the United States reduced the number of men under arms by half a million and Britain by 80,000. The Soviet Union increased the number by 125,000. The West constantly cuts back on its investment for research into new weapons. The Soviet Union increases its investment year by year in order to enhance the effectiveness of its offensive weapons.

The Soviet Union is increasing its current expenditure on civil defence and has so dispersed its industrial might that a major nuclear attack would only destroy a small proportion both of its population and of its industrial strength. Every Soviet citizen has to undergo civil defence training every year. A massive organization of men and materials is constantly maintained. Expenditure this year alone will be £300 million. This is in sharp contrast to the British situation, where our voluntary and auxiliary services have been reduced from 600,000 to 67,000 over fifteen years and where police forces are frequently under establishment.

But we are not even aware of the very real threat much closer to home. The British people should wake up to the fact that the Soviet Union has in recent years built up an enormous military presence on our northern flank, at the Soviet military base at Murmansk to the north of Norway. They now have ground forces of 25,000 men there and the maritime ability to move these men swiftly to parts of Scandinavia and northern Europe. They have no less than 320 aircraft stationed there, and, most frightening of all, a naval strength of 60 major surface vessels and 175 submarines, the majority of them being nuclear submarines. It is probably the case that there is hardly a major port in Britain or in the whole of Western Europe that is not constantly covered by a nuclear submarine. Such a force could quickly destroy the whole of our North Sea oil installations. Nobody can argue that this is the type of force one would place at Murmansk for purely defensive reasons. It is but another indication of the terrifying Soviet military build-up.

The West should also be alarmed at the Soviet Union's massive injection of armaments into the Middle East, and at its ever-increasing military presence in a host of African countries. The West should be aware of the way the Soviet Union has encouraged guerrillas and revolutionaries in continent after continent.

But the Soviet threat is not one confined to other countries. The British Communist Party itself aims to disrupt British industry and has had considerable success in doing so. When the miners opposed – and opposed successfully – the Conservative government at the beginning of 1974, Boris Ponamarev, head of the International Department of the Central Committee of the Communist Party of the Soviet Union, stated in Brussels two months later at a conference on Western European communist parties: 'As the Communists predicted, the strike movement is increasingly taking on the form of direct struggle with the State monopolistic system and with the government's policies. The national upsurge of the workers' movement in Britain brought down the Conservative Government. A large role is played by the trade unions, whose militancy has noticeably increased.'

Mr Gormley himself has made it clear that Mr Ramelson, the Communist Party's industrial organizer, successfully interfered in negotiations carried out by the union to obtain a productivity deal. Mr Ramelson has been seen in the offices of the National Union of Mineworkers in the company of Mr McGahey, Mr McLean and Mr Whelan, immediately prior to executive meetings.

It was Mr Ramelson who stated, after the productivity deal was ruined: 'I want to congratulate the Yorkshire miners on the active role they played alongside miners in other coalfields in rejecting the reactionary productivity deal attempted to be shoved down their throats by some right-wing leaders in order to shore up the social contract.' To the present government that productivity agreement was essential. Indeed only a mild and temperate winter enabled the government to recover from its failure to obtain it.

I was the first Conservative Cabinet Minister to visit Moscow when, in my capacity as Secretary of State for Trade and Industry, I went to negotiate a new trade and scientific agreement with the Soviet Union.

When the Conservatives came to power in 1970 the Prime Minister and Sir Alec Douglas-Home took the decision to expel 111 Soviet spies and return them to the Soviet Union. This action created a situation in which the Soviet Union spent the next two years castigating Britain as being the worst of the imperialist powers. We had our daily mention in Pravda. We were referred to in all the appropriate releases of leading Soviet politicians. The Soviets soon discovered, however, that this harder line impeded their progress rather than assisted it, and that in the atmosphere of détente, continuing hostility towards Britain would be a disadvantage.

They then embarked on a new diplomacy. More visits to Britain by the ballet; more invitations to leading British personalities, including members of the Royal Family, to visit the Soviet Union; and the political invitation to welcome a Tory Cabinet Minister to Moscow. I was flown there in a Soviet aeroplane. I was greeted with champagne and caviar at the airport and provided with a large sumptuous suite with the heaviest, ugliest Victorian furniture I had ever seen. The negotiations were made easy – every concession I demanded was granted – but like so many concessions in trade agreements they were of little importance if there was no ultimate decision to purchase British goods.

I had the opportunity of meeting a number of Soviet ministers, and spent a fascinating one and a half hours with Mr Kosygin, a man with considerable personal charm, a sense of humour, and a very good grasp of the detail of Soviet economic development.

We met at the Kremlin and enjoyed a provocative discussion on whether the ideas of Disraeli or Karl Marx had proved to be more successful. Mr Kosygin then endeavoured to interest me in the prospect of providing the Soviet Union with long-term credit facilities and technical aid for the development of Soviet raw material resources, in return for which we would have a share of those raw materials. This was the idea that he and the Soviet government had so readily sold to the United States. After its initial enthusiasm the United States was soon to discover that there was little joy to be had in pouring money into developing the Soviet economy when the fruits of those investments would always of necessity be at the dictate of the then ruling generation of Soviet politicians. The astronomic development plans agreed between Nixon and Breshnev will never come to fruition.

My visit to Moscow and my talks with Soviet ministers convinced me that the Soviet Union had as its leadership a self-perpetuating clique of politicians free from the controls of a democratic electorate, men of immense ability and ambition, men with the traditional imperialistic ambition that has been the hallmark of Russian history, with an economic and social dogma which gives them a doctrinaire passion to dominate the world.

The dramatic change that has taken place in Soviet strategy over the past decade is that it has become a worldwide strategy. The seas of the south Atlantic, the Indian Ocean and the Mediterranean are now dominated by the Soviet naval presence. Southern Africa, Malaysia and the industrial West are increasingly the current battlegrounds of Soviet political and economic strategies.

The question of how private enterprise survives in such an unstable era is, then, closely related to the question of the stability of Britain in foreign affairs. Our prosperity depends, as it has always done, upon our relationship to the wider economic units to which we belong. How then are we to deal with these new problems? For Britain the solution must be seen in a European context. And certainly a Britain diminishing its contribution to the Western Alliance and with its nuclear deterrent becoming ever more out of date will be devoid of influence in the creation of a strategy to defend the West.

The reality of the modern world is that there are four major powers and one potentially great power. The four major powers are the United States, the Soviet Union, China and Japan. The potentially great power is the European Community. If Europe turns this potential into reality then five major power groups will contain within them nearly half the world's population, nearly two-thirds of the world's trade, and three-quarters of the world's wealth.

The European Community has two-thirds of the national income of America and twice that of the Soviet Union. It is responsible for one-third of the world's trade. It has two million men under arms and contains within it two nuclear powers. The Community possesses the strength in terms of money, markets and military might to exercise, together with the other four great powers, great influence for good in the world, and to establish mutually beneficial relationships with the oil-producing nations and with the independent nations of other continents.

It should be the prime purpose of British foreign and defence policy to strengthen the Community, and to see that it develops a collective approach to the economic and military dangers of the future, a unity that involves both industrial and military decisions. We must move towards a common European defence policy and a common European foreign policy. This means that Britain must play an active role in building European unity and developing a political structure appropriate to a united Europe. It is no good dragging one's feet, as the present Labour government has done in the interests of insular socialism. Such insularity poses as great a threat to Britain as the pacifists and disarmers did in the 1930s. Wise political leadership consists, then as now, in alerting the British people to the dangers involved and showing how they can be met.

At present France is not a member of NATO, and some non-Community countries are. Within the Community countries there is a failure to agree upon rationalized training systems and procurement programmes. The result could well be that NATO develops into an organization that proves immensely costly in meeting any minor challenges and inadequate to meet a major challenge.

Europe must agree upon a major world strategy, including a sensible and close alignment with the United States and a rational and mutually beneficial relationship with the oil-producing countries of the Middle East. It is vital that we should achieve these objectives. For under existing or changing Soviet leadership the potential domination of the whole of Europe by the Soviet Union is a considerable danger.

One help to the West is the hostility towards the Soviet Union of communist China. It is impossible to predict the direction of Chinese foreign policy in the decade ahead. There will be a major generation change in the leadership of China. When I visited China in 1973 to negotiate a new trade agreement and to open the British Trade Fair, China was still governed by that remarkable group of men who had undertaken the Long March in 1935.

Chairman Mao and Prime Minister Chou En-Lai were the two dominant voices. Indeed beyond their voices and that of Chairman Mao's wife it was difficult to calculate the currents of Chinese political thought.

In my discussions with our own ambassador and members of the diplomatic corps who had been in Peking for many years past I gathered that the one thing they had in common was an inability to penetrate the inner councils of the Communist Party. Changes of ministers and changes of policy always came as a surprise to the Western diplomat. It is this that makes it so difficult to be certain of the future political, economic and military views of China. Under the old leadership their hostility to the Soviet Union was limitless and their desire to be friendly towards the West as a protection against the Soviet Union became the very foundation of their world diplomacy. In terms of the balance of power it must be right for the West to encourage this and to establish the closest and most friendly relations with China.

Whatever one's views on the nature of communism, the Chinese regime has probably brought to China more happiness for the individual citizen than has been achieved for centuries past. At last China is free from internal wars. Every family is clothed and housed, millions no longer perish in uncontrolled floods, and everybody has a job of work to do. Education and health facilities are available to all upon an unprecedented scale. In the talks I had with Chou En-Lai there was little doubt about his own pride in what his form of communism had achieved in China and his confidence about what would be achieved in the century ahead. It is an immense advantage for the Chinese that their timescale is so much longer than their Western counterparts. Perhaps as a result of this they see world problems on a clearer strategic scale than many in the West. My talks with Chou En-Lai took place at a time when both America and Western Europe were expressing increasing anxiety at the scale of Japan's trade surpluses and demands were increased for action to be taken against Japanese exports. Chou En-Lai pleaded with me to have no part in economic measures that would be hostile to Japan. When I asked why he felt so strongly that this would be a mistake he shrugged and said,

> Nobody has more reason to be hostile towards Japan than I have, and no country has a greater ingrained hostility towards Japan than China, but in these coming years we will be

friendly towards Japan. We will encourage their economy. We will join with them in developing our oil. We will purchase their goods and allow them to participate in the expansion of our economy. For if we, and far more important you, neglect Japan, Japan can only turn towards the Soviet Union. And if the Soviet Union ever joined forces with Japan the rest of the world would stand no chance at all.

He explained to me the readiness of the Chinese people for war with the Soviet Union, the extent of their underground shelters and their food and water stores, and his confidence that any invading Soviet army would eventually be engulfed by the Chinese people. China was indeed fortunate in having a man of the calibre of Chou En-Lai, with strength of character, intellectual ability and administrative skill, to see it through the post-war decades. We do not know the qualities of the generations about to take power, but for the foreseeable future the only sensible policy for the West is to increase and improve its relations with China.

We need a new strategy in politics which will first of all comprehend the conditions that actually exist and not pretend they are just an extension of the conditions we have known in the past. Because the problems are international the strategy too will have to be based upon international solutions.

We need to agree with our allies of the West, the United States, Japan, and Western Europe, a common attitude towards the multinational corporation, so as to see that the parliamentary democracies have the overall control of their economies that is necessary and that major economic policies cannot be determined by boards of directors responsible only to shareholders. This is not to discourage multinational corporations, which have already played an immense part in improving living standards, but we must see that large corporations cannot play off one friendly nation against another, or move their manufacturing potential or currency flows without adequate consultation with governments.

We need to develop a European approach to the whole question of the use and recycling of raw materials. It costs more to recycle raw materials than to acquire them direct. The result is a diminishing source of raw materials, an increase in demand, and eventual disaster. Recycling must start now, but it will never start without an international agreement, for otherwise those nations that recycled would have higher costs than those that did not.

We must agree upon a programme of monetary reform that recognizes that in the present-day world there should be a fair relationship between the costs of manufacturers and the costs of primary products. An era of leapfrogging would be disastrous because of the inflation it would create. We must end the pretence by the manufacturing countries that they possess all the skills in monetary policy and will therefore lay down the policy. We must recognize the sophistication of the primary producers and the realism of their demands.

We urgently need a monetary system based upon a genuine assessment of each nation's wealth. It will involve an agreement as to the magnitude and valuation of mineral resources. It will require an agreed international index of manufacturing investment. It will require a totally new machinery and a new realistic approach.

The European nations must agree upon a rational policy for the stockpiling of surpluses, using them to assist in the elimination of world poverty and also to bring greater stability to world markets. Unless such surpluses and stocks are created, the opportunities for the Soviet Union to disrupt world markets will be immense. Unless such sensible stockpiling takes place there will continue to be irreparable wastages of valuable world resources.

One of the most typical aspects of our rapidly changing world has been the energy problem. Governments in all countries have had to face the effects of uncertainty and instability in the patterns of energy use. This is not a recent phenomenon; it is simply that the events of 1973–4 focused attention on an existing problem.

Despite dire warnings, the world does not suffer from a physical shortage of energy at the present time. This does not mean, of course, that we should be profligate in our use of what are limited reserves of fossil fuels. The difficulties stem not from scarcity but from the fact that energy reserves are rarely in the country that needs to use them. The U.K., for example, imports over half of the energy supply needed to sustain her industry and trade. Consequently changes in prices have unforeseeable and dramatic effects.

The instability of the energy market is further compounded by the competition between already existing fuels as well as by the huge potential for developing new ways of creating energy. From 1960–74, a space of only fourteen years, solid fuels declined from providing 52 per cent of total world energy to 19 per cent, while oil rose from 41 to 54 per cent.

Such rapid changes will continue, but the direction of change is much less predictable. It is in this field perhaps more than any other, that the U.K. has great permanent advantages. Her vast reserves of coal, gas and oil are much greater than those of any other country in the E.E.C. With today's high oil prices and the once again increasing demand for petroleum products, this country has assets of great worth. And we can guarantee domestic supplies of energy for decades to come.

Despite this useful assurance, we cannot be secure from future rapid change. Oil prices may fail to rise as fast as the costs of development and extraction of off-shore resources. New sources of cheap energy may compete with Britain's existing fuels. Complacency and ignorance of changes in technology are ever-present dangers. Our natural resources below the North Sea will give us considerable short-term strength, but it may ebb away as fast as it came.

A few of the possible trends in energy utilization are already apparent. The technology exists to produce electricity from tidal and solar energy. Use of such potential sources does not entail diminution of future reserves, for the sources are renewable and the energy virtually costless once the necessary capital equipment has been installed. The development of the technology for nuclear fission is within sight, an innovation with almost limitless applications over a wide spread of the modern economy. So, despite our present position, it would be wrong not to invest heavily in research into new energy technology to ensure that Britain remains at the boundaries of science in this field, ready to use knowledge for her own good and the good of the whole world. Only in this way will we be able to keep up with the speed of change in this vital sphere of modern life.

Britain is fortunate to have discovered substantial oil deposits at a time when the world faced its first energy crisis. The value of our North Sea oil reserves could be between £200,000 million and £350,000 million. We must consider carefully how to take advantage of this incredibly valuable new asset.

If an industrial firm was heavily in debt to the bank, desperately needed new plant and machinery and a new factory extension, and discovered under its floor boards a valuable raw material that the firm itself used and in sufficient quantity to satisfy its demand for decades to come, it is probable that the firm would decide to sell off a substantial amount of the newly discovered raw material and so pay off the bank and make the desired improvements.

The British economy is in an identical position to such a firm in that it is heavily in debt and its industrial capacity is in desperate need of substantial modernization.

We are at present borrowing substantial sums against the potential of our North Sea asset. This could be a dangerous strategy to pursue. If other forms of energy replaced oil, or savings in oil consumption and the discovery of new oil resources combined to bring down the price of oil, we could find ourselves with a diminishing asset from which we had received relatively little benefit and upon which we had borrowed heavily.

The country is getting the wrong perspective on the financial advantages of North Sea oil if we are to continue with the present arrangements.

The Labour government have announced that they anticipate that the total revenue from royalties, the Petroleum Revenue Tax and Corporation Tax in the four years ending in December 1980 will be £5.5 billion. It is interesting to compare this figure with the cost of servicing the government's debts during that same period of four years, which will amount to £28.6 billion. The government's total revenues, therefore, between now and the end of 1980 will only meet less than one-fifth of their debt servicing cost. As to the period thereafter, when North Sea oil is fully on stream, they are anticipating an income of about £3.5 billion per year. During that period there is no doubt that the cost of the government's debt servicing will be at least £8 billion per year and probably by then the public sector wage bill alone will exceed £30 billion per year.

We should consider disposing of a substantial proportion of this asset in order to reduce our indebtedness and finance major modernization programmes.

If Britain is to remain an industrial power we need to invest large sums of money in the basic ingredients of economic progress. The steel industry needs an investment of £6,500 million. We should be investing far more in nuclear energy. Vast investments are needed to guarantee our future water supplies. Our balance of payments would greatly benefit from a substantial injection of capital into British agriculture. Our machine tool industry and many sections of our engineering industry are in desperate need of modernization.

It must also be in our interests to reduce the nation's indebtedness. In the Labour government's first three financial years they will have plunged us into debt to the extent of £30 billion. By 1980 the debt servicing will work out at £15 per week for every family of four in the country. For every family of four the Labour government will have borrowed £2,500 in three years. There is a massive overseas borrowing as a result of nationalized industries and local authorities having been encouraged to borrow from abroad so as to bring some momentary advantage to the balance of payments. The total burden is too heavy. North Sea oil provides a unique opportunity for substantially reducing it.

Such a decision would have the added advantage of facilitating the creation of a European Community energy policy. Our Community partners have virtually no oil resources and would be only too willing to pay considerable sums to obtain a share in Britain's off-shore oil, which would give them an important insurance policy against any future disruption in Middle East oil supplies.

The disposal of one-third of our oil resources would still leave us with very large resources of oil. It would be vital, however, that the money realized should be properly used. It should not be used to enable us in the immediate future to enjoy levels of consumption which are as yet beyond our means.

As a nation we are heavily in debt, we are suffering from inefficiencies in management, and from over-manning and restrictive practices, and we have failed to dominate any of the major world markets. We are now confronted with perhaps our last opportunity for revival.

We must follow a new international strategy based upon the realities of a fast-transforming world. We must create a new industrial society where technology benefits man and does not dominate him; where partnership replaces strife. We must create a stronger alliance with our Western allies to protect our freedoms and our heritage. From new economic strength we must seek a new quality of urban life that brings man enjoyment in place of anguish and anxiety.

It is essential if democracy is to survive that we have leaders who will be realistic in facing the existing problems, new and dramatic as they are, and statesmen who can foresee the problems that are emerging.

There are already serious commentators saying that democracy will not survive. History shows us that any form of totalitarian regime is very soon found to be less compassionate and less tolerant than a democracy. If we are going to continue obtaining the benefits of the compassion and tolerance of democracy we must be willing to follow those political leaders who are willing to provide long-term solutions and recognize the necessity of short-term discomforts. Milner defines patriotism as pride in a nation which does its best to provide everyone with the opportunities which their birthright demands. Political leaders must tell people the truth so that we can create such a nation. This, and nothing less, is the task of political leadership in modern Britain. We must achieve the ascent of Britain.

Index

Abs, Herr, head of Deutsche Bank, 85
Acland, Sir Richard, 11
Adult education, 49
Agriculture, need for capital, 213
Alexander the Great, 62
American War of Independence, 15, 16
Amery, Julian, 14, 36–7, 173, 196
Amery, Leo, 14, 36
Ansary, Hushang, Iranian Minister of Economics, 105–8, 110
Appeasement, 203
Area management, 144–5
Asians in Britain, 159; owner-occupiers, 152; intelligence tests on children, 158
A.S.L.E.F. (Associated Society of Locomotive Engineers and Firemen), 52
Attitude surveys, 77
Attlee, Mrs (Lady Attlee), 8
Australia, 114

Balance of payments, 213, 214
Balfour Commission on Trade and Industry (1929), 44–5
Ballots, secret postal or factory, 69–70
Barber, Anthony (Lord Barber), 55, 108–9
Beeching, Dr (Lord Beeching), 28
Belgium, works councils, 76
Benn, Anthony Wedgwood, 79, 92, 93, 99
Benthamite rationalism, 35
Biffen, John, 198
Birmingham, 189; study of deprived district, 129; children in care, 131; mental illness, 131; crime rate, 131; changes of schools, 138; slum areas, 147; West Indian families, 153;
unemployment among West Indians, 56
Boardman, Tom, 196–7
Boyle, Sir Edward (Lord Boyle of Handsworth), 55
Brasilia, 116
Brazil, 115–19; balance of payments deficit, 115; resources of power and agriculture, 116; oil industry, 117–18; growth of economy, 118; chance of British participation, 118; investment expenditure, 118; British exports, 119
Brazilian Oil Company, 116
Breshnev, L. I., 207
Bretton Woods settlement, 202
Briginshaw, R. W. (Lord Briginshaw), 56
British Council of Churches, report on coloured population, 147–9
British Leyland, 71, 87–9, 96, 109, 171
British Rail, 96–7
British Steel Corporation, 92; modernization plans, 89–90, 92–3
Brixton, 147, 149; unemployment among young West Indians, 156
Bullock Committee, 48, 72
Bureaucracy, and public housing, 30–1
Burke, Edmund, 14–17, 36, 39; founder of modern British Conservatism, 14, 17; attack on arrogance of 'private reason', 14–15; defends American colonists, 15, 16; attacks French Revolution, 15, 17; views on reform, 16; first modern political thinker, 17; importance to present-day Conservatives, 17

Callaghan, James, 92
Callard, Sir Jack, 87

Canada, 114
Capital Gains Tax, 57
Capitalism, 20, 23, 24, 29, 30, 80; socialist criticism, 23; in the 1930s, 26; and planning, 28; and human relationships, 31
Cardiff, demonstration of steel workers, 92
Carey, Sir Peter, 108
Carr, Robert (Lord Carr of Hadley), 53, 55
Carrington, Lord, 199
C.B.I. (Confederation of British Industry), 77
Chamberlain, Joseph, 36–9; reformer and Imperialist, 36; contrasted with Salisbury, 37; social and economic reform, 37, 38; tariff reform, 37–8
Chamberlain, (Sir) Austen, 36
Chamberlain, Neville, 9, 39, 203
Channel Tunnel, 53, 192–3
Channon, Paul, 196
Chataway, Christopher, 196; missions to Japan and Germany, 123
Chequers, 60, 199
Cheshire Regiment, 43
Chicago, population changes, 125–6
Child Poverty Action Group, 164
China, 104, 207–10; hostility to Soviet, 208–10; friendliness towards Japan, 209–10; need for improved relations with West, 210
Chou En-Lai, 208–9
Christianity and coloured communities, 147
Churchill, (Sir) Winston, 9, 10, 12, 63, 124; wartime speeches, 7–10; Romanes Lectures (1930), 81; suggests Parliament of Industry, 81; on the West Indies, 150
Cities: dominance of, 124; sprawl, 125, 178; deterioration of inner cities, 125–7; deprived areas, 127–32, 156; job opportunities, 132–8, 156
City of London, 18, 45, 46, 86–7, 120
Coal industry, 96; *see also* Miners
Coal Industry Bill (1972), 64–5
Cobden, Richard, 39
Coloured communities, 147–62; elements of disorder, 148–9; population figures, 151; housing conditions, 152, 153; overcrowding, 152–3; unemployment, 159, 160; crime, 160; *see also* Immigrants *and* West Indians in Britain

Commissariat General au Plan (C.G.P.), 102, 104
Common Market, *see* E.E.C.
Commonwealth Party, 11
Communism, 203, 205, 209; British Communist Party, 205
Company law reform, 69–71
Conservation policy, 179
Conservative Party and Conservatism, 9–11, 14, 15, 17, 25, 27, 29, 36, 37, 58–9, 89, 98, 127, 206; defeat (1945), 12; central principle, 16; reforming nature, 16; and private enterprise, 18–20; and redistribution of wealth, 20; in industrial society, 34; concept of responsibility, 35; imperialism and nationalism, 36; Joseph Chamberlain's policies, 38–9; and trade unions, 53, 63; prices and incomes policy; 53, 54, 67, 68; lack of relationships with industry, 85; and 'Operation Eyesore', 136; and housing, 140, 173; and immigrants, 152; and local government reform, 183; quality of party, 196, 198; Government of 1970–74, 199
Co-operative ownership, 78–9
Co-operative Societies, 79
Corporation Tax, 57
Cotswolds, 177
Council houses: proposal to transfer them to existing tenants, 163–72, 175; housing finance, 166–9; cost of supervision and management, 166–7; cost of repairs and maintenance, 166–7; income from rents, 166; deficit, 166; social security payments, 166, 167; capital cost, 169; position of owner-occupiers, 169–70; position of council tenants, 170; waiting lists, 170–1; sale of council houses, 171; building of low-cost houses, 172
Cousins, Frank, 51
Cousins, John, 51–2
Crime prevention, 138
Crosland, Anthony, 183, 190
Crossman, Richard and Crossman Diaries, 14, 187, 189
Cublington, proposed for Third London Airport, 190
Cypriot children, intelligence tests, 158

Davies, John, 98
Day care project, 143
Defence expenditure, 11, 12, 203
Denationalization, 91, 94

Denmark: works councils, 76; joins E.E.C., 114
Depressed areas, 61–2; *see also* Development areas
Deprived people, 142–3
Deutsche Bank, 85
Development areas, 156
Devolution, 101
Disraeli, Benjamin (Earl of Beaconsfield), 12, 31–9, 206; 'One and Two Nations', 32–4; Conservatism in an industrial society, 34; founder of modern Conservative Party, 34; and decline of the Tory Party, 34–5; support for extension of franchise, 35; his 1874–80 ministry and social reform, 35; foreign policy, 35–6
Douglas-Home, Sir Alec, 54, 57, 58, 193, 194, 199, 206
Dove, Linda, 152
Dulles, Foster, 194
Durham County Council, 137

East India Bill, Burke's speech on, 16
Ebbw Vale, 92
Economist, 183
Eden, Sir Anthony (Earl of Avon), 59
E.E.C., 25, 114, 121; and worker participation, 72, 75; Britain's membership, 114, 120; potential power, 207–8; Britain's need to strengthen it, 204; need for energy policy, 213–14
EFTA, 114
Egalitarianism, 19
Elizabeth II, Queen, 107
Elizabeth the Queen Mother, Queen, 10
Emery, Peter, 197
Employee directors, 78
Employee participation, 69, 71–80, 84, 98; employers' attitude, 72; German experience, 72–6; supervisory boards, 73–7; works councils, 74–6, 78, 79; trustee councils, 78; co-operative ownership, 78–9; compulsory departmental meetings, 79; unquoted companies, 79–80
Energy problem, 211–14; instability of market, 211; competition between fuels, 211–12; British reserves, 212; policy for E.E.C., 213–14
Enlightenment, the, 15
E.P.A. (Educational Priority Area) report, 137–8

Euro-dollar market, 202
European Community, *see* E.E.C.
Evening Standard, 183
Exports: government and export strategy, 104–5; information service, 110–11; products sold below price, 111–12; meetings with businessmen, 112–13; need to strengthen commercial posts abroad, 113

Feather, Victor (Lord Feather), 52, 60
Feudal societies, 19, 22, 35
Field, Frank, 164
Finance Act (1965), 57–8
Finance Houses Association, 86
Finniston, Sir Monty, 92
Foot, Michael, 93
France, 90, 115, 124, 208; fall of (1940), 9; recovery, 18; profit-sharing, 76; supervisory boards, 76; Civil Service and industry, 85; increase in steel-making capacity, 94; partnership with Iran, 110; top level interest in Iran, 119; and Channel Tunnel, 192; *see also* French Plan system
Free collective bargaining, 55, 66–8
Free enterprise, 12, 18, 23, 94; moral legitimacy, 19; and self-interest, 21–2; defence of, 29; *see also* Private enterprise
Free trade, 39
French Plan system, 101–4; seven Plans, 102; C.G.P., 102, 104; reconstruction, 102; emphasis on industrialization, 102; sixth plan and growth industries, 102; seventh plan and social environment, 103; possibility of introduction into Britain, 103–4
French Revolution, 15, 17
Friedman, Milton, 21

Gatt (General Agreement on Trade and Tariffs), 88; Tokyo talks (1973), 82, 83
Gatwick airport, 191
General Election, 1945, 10–12
George III, King, 15
George VI, King, 10
Germany, 45, 203; technical education, 44; *see also* Western Germany
Gilmour, Ian, 54
Giscard d'Estaing, Valéry, 82–3; and profit-sharing, 83

Glasgow: changing population, 124; children in care, 131; slum areas, 147
'Glorious Revolution' (1688), 15
Goodhead, Mr, teacher and librarian, 11, 31
Gormley, Joe, 65, 205
Grant, Tony, 198
Green belt, 177, 178
Greene, Sid, 52-3
Greenwood, Anthony (Lord Greenwood of Rossendale), 173
Griffiths, Eldon, 196
Growth, economic, 25, 28, 29; rate of, 20, 28

Hailsham, Lord, *see* Hogg, Quintin
Hallmarks, distribution of equity to employees, 83
Healey, Denis, 133
Heath, Edward, 54, 55, 57-63, 107, 109, 194, 197-9, 202, 206; and trade unions, 55-7, 60, 63-80; and 1965 Finance Act, 57-8; technique of combative questioning, 58; as leader of Conservative Party, 59; patriotism, 59, 60; internationalism, 59, 62; President of Oxford Union, 59; hostility to Munich, 59; sailing and music, 60, 63; at Chequers and 10 Downing Street, 60; and depressed areas, 61-2; international impact, 62-3; Godkin Lectures (1967), 63
Heathrow airport, 191
Herberts, machine tool manufacturers, 109
Hereford and Worcester, new county headquarters, 185
Heseltine, Michael, 196
Highways Act, 180
Hitler, Adolf, 10, 11
H.M.V. factory, Hayes, 7, 40
Hogg, Quintin (Lord Hailsham), 61, 199
Home Guard, 9-10
Houghton, V. P., 157
Housing, 30-1, 94, 132, 137-8, 140-2, 163-76; variations in costs, 141; rented accommodation, 141; failure to maintain standards, 142; need for variety, 142; bad areas, 147; voluntary movement, 153; improvement grants, 153, 154, 173-5; housing finance in Britain, 166-9, 188-90; extension of rent rebates, 189; subsidies for slum clearance, 190; house improvement, 172-5, 200; successful campaign, 173; momentum lost under Labour Government, 173; system of priorities, 173-4; sliding scale of grants, 173-4; figures of unfit houses, 174; private rented houses, 174-5; increase of rents, 175; rent control, 175; transfer of rented accommodation, 175
Howe, Sir Geoffrey, 88, 196, 197

I.C.I. and the government, 87
Immigrants: English teaching for children, 138; contribution to Britain, 150-1; register of relatives proposed, 152; intelligence tests of children, 157-9; options for dealing with problems, 159-60; need to use immigrants' abilities, 160; proposals for positive action, 161; *see also* Coloured communities *and* West Indians in Britain
Imperial preference, 39
Import Duties Bill (Act) (1932), 39
Incomes policy, 54-7, 63-4, 68, 69
Indians in Britain, 154; *see also* Asians
Industrial assembly, proposal for, 69
Industrial democracy, 71, 76, 77
Industrial Development Advisory Board, 99
Industrial development certificates (I.D.C.), 134, 156
Industrial investment, 30, 100; plans, 89, 99; international index, 211
Industrial relations, 40-2, 53, 55, 67, 84
Industrial Relations Act, 53, 70
Industrial Revolution, 98, 125
Industry Act, 90, 98, 99, 161
Inequalities of income and wealth, 19-21; and demand for devolution, 101
Inequality of opportunity, 22, 46-7
Inflation, 28, 29, 55, 67, 93, 166-7, 170, 203; wage inflation, 68, 69
Intelligence tests on immigrant and English children, 157-9
Inter-continental ballistic missiles, 203, 204
International monetary system and oil revenues, 107, 202-3
Iran, 105-10, 117-19; biennial Anglo-Iranian trade talks, 105; development programme, 106; boost for Anglo-Iranian trade, 106;

Iran—*continued*
   investment projects discussed in
      Persepolis, 106; proposals for
      collaboration with Britain, 109–10;
      proposals by Labour government,
      110; partnership with other powers,
      110; balance of payments deficit,
      115; investment programme, 117,
      118; oil resources, 117; British
      exports, 118–19
Iran, H.I.M. the Shah of, 106–10;
   meeting with him in Persepolis,
   106–7; enthusiasm for new
   relationship with Britain, 106–7; his
   co-operation, 107; meeting with him
   at St Moritz, 108–10; and proposals
   for industrial and economic
   collaboration, 109–10, 114
I.R.C. (Industrial Reorganization
   Corporation), 54
Italy: works councils, 76; aid to, 202

Japan, 90, 114, 115, 123, 192, 207;
   rise of, 18, 40, 86; merchant houses
   and the government, 85–6; export
   of British Leylands cars to, 88;
   increase in steelmaking capacity,
   94; partnership with Iran, 110;
   exports to Iran, Venezuela and
   Brazil, 119; and investment in
   Britain, 121, 122; capital exports,
   122; conurbations, 124, 125; future
   expansion, 201; and China, 209–10
Jarrow hunger marchers, 67
Job opportunities in inner cities,
   132–40, 156; plans for renewal, 133;
   need for training facilities, 133, 137;
   school preparation for work, 133,
   137; industrial development
   certificates, 134; government's job
   creation programme, 134;
   redevelopment, 134; small business
   advisory services, 134–5; 'Operation
   Eyesore', 135–7; control of pollution,
   136; distribution of population, 137;
   local government finance, 138;
   crime prevention, 138; better school
   buildings, 137; local enterprise
   development, 139–40
John Lewis Partnership, 79
Jones, Jack, 52
Joseph, Sir Keith, 198, 199

Kapital, Das (Marx), 11
Kennedy, President John F., 126

Kennedy, Senator Robert F., 126–7
Keynes, John Maynard (Lord Keynes),
   and Keynesian policies, 24, 27, 39
King, Coretta Scott, 149
King, Martin Luther, 149
King's Royal Rifle Corps, 43
Kosygin, A. N., 206

Labour Party and Labour
   Governments, 11, 25, 29, 51, 67, 68,
   90, 92–3, 110, 173, 189; and
   unemployment, 26; and the miners'
   strike, 57; and trade unions, 63,
   80–1; and inflation, 93; and the steel
   industry, 92–4, 193; loan from
   U.S.A., 113; relations with Iran,
   119; and deprived areas in cities,
   127; and housing, 140; 1974 Rent
   Acts, 153; and council houses, 164,
   190; and rent control, 175; White
   Paper on local government reform
   (1970), 183; abolition of Pay Board,
   184; opposition to water
   reorganization, 188; and Third
   London Airport, 191; reduction of
   defence expenditure, 203; and
   E.E.C., 208; borrowings, 213
Laissez-faire, 14, 25, 26, 28, 39
Lambeth, inner city study on, 129,
   133, 141; projects, 143–4; flying
   squad principle, 144, 145
Land use and land use planning, *see*
   Planning
Latymer Upper School, 10, 31
Lewisham, 149
Liberal Party, 11, 34–7, 183
Limerick, Earl of, 198
Literacy, standard of, 46–9
Liverpool, 189; study of deprived
   district, 129–30, 144; children in
   care, 131; mental illness, 131; crime
   rate, 131; area management, 144;
   slum areas, 147; cost of building
   council houses, 169, 171
Lloyd George, David (Earl Lloyd
   George), 11
Lloyd, Selwyn (Lord Selwyn-Lloyd),
   193–4
Lloyd's of London, 45–6
Local Enterprise Development Unit
   (Northern Ireland), 139–40
Local government finance, 137–8, 171
Local government reform, 182–7;
   Labour Government's plans, 183;
   two-tier system, 183; increase in
   rates, 184; salary structure, 184;

220

Local government reform—*continued*
increases in staff, 184–6; integrity
of decisions on boundaries, 186–7
Local information post project, 143
Location of industry, 98
London: changing population, 124,
137, 142; study of deprived district,
129, 133, 141; children in care, 131;
mental illness, 131; crime figures,
131; illiteracy, 132; West Indian
families, 153; Greater London
sprawl, 178; conservation of theatres,
179–80
Luton airport, 191
Luxembourg, works councils, 76

MacDonald, Ramsay, 25
Machine tool industry, 213
Macleod, Iain, 30, 54–5
Macmillan, Harold, 24–8, 36, 39,
193, 194; and planning, 27, 28;
and Keynesian policies, 27; and
government intervention, 28;
experiences of Stockton-on-Tees,
41–2; and housing, 140, 173
Macmillan, Maurice, 140
Mao Tse-Tung, 208
Maplin site for Third London Airport,
190–3
Martins, Governor of São Paulo, 116
Marx, Karl, and Marxism, 11, 14–15,
19, 36, 38, 206
Maud Report on Local Government
Reform, 183
Maude, Angus, 198
Maudling, Reginald, 55, 58–9
Melchett, Lord, 92
Middle Way, The (Macmillan), 24, 42
Milner, Viscount, 38; definition of
patriotism, 13, 215
Miner (N.U.M. official magazine),
64–5
Miners: and pay policy, 63–4; and
Coal Industry Bill (1972), 64–5;
strike (1974), 57, 58, 63, 64, 66
Monetary reform, 211
Monypenny and Buckle's life of
Disraeli, 31
Motor corporations and the
government, 87–9
Motorways, 180–1, 200
Multinational companies, 120, 210
Multi-service project, 143
Multi-space project, 143
Municipal and General Workers'
Union, 50

Murmansk, 204–5

NALGO (National Association of
Local Government Officials), 50
National Bus Company, 96
National Coal Board, 64, 65
National Economic Development
Council (Neddy), 26, 28, 81
National Incomes Commission, 28
National parks, 51, 177
National Plan (1965), 103
National Theatre, 180
National Union of Mineworkers
(N.U.M.), 57, 63–5, 96, 205
National Union of Railwaymen, 52
National Water Council, 187
Nationalization, 11, 12, 18, 26, 31,
79, 80, 85, 90–8; of steel, 92
Nationalized industries, 90; chairmen,
90–1; proposal to make employees
future owners, 95–8; borrowings
from abroad, 213
NATO, 208
Nazis, the, 10
Neave, Airey, 198
New Society, 158, 159
New Statesman, 189
New towns, 137, 153, 178
New York: transformation of
population, 124; crime, 139
New Zealand, 114
Nigeria, 114, 115, 117; investment
programme, 117, 118; oil resources,
117; British exports, 118
1954 (Orwell), 142
Nixon, President Richard M., 126,
203, 207
Noise pollution in factories, 136
North Sea: assets, 123, 212, 213, 214;
revenue from assets, 213; Soviet
threat to installations, 204, 205
Northolt aerodrome, 9
Nuclear energy, 118, 213

O'Brien, Conor Cruise, 17
O'Brien, Sir Leslie (Lord O'Brien of
Lothbury), 86
O.E.C.D (Organization for Economic
Co-operation and Development),
117–19
Oil, 116–18, 200, 202, 212–14; OPEC
countries and oil revenues, 107–8,
202; embargoes in 1973, 108; oil
obtained from Iran, 108–9; Soviet
spy ships, 204
Old age pensions, 38

Oldham, study of urban problems, 129
Oliveira, General Araken de, 116
'One Nation' theme, 32
Onslow, Cranley, 198
OPEC and OPEC countries, 104, 117; and oil revenues, 107-8, 202
Open University, 45, 49
'Operation Eyesore', 135-7
Organization of Unquoted Companies, 80
Orwell, George, 12, 142
Out-of-town shopping centres, 179
Overspill towns, 153
Oxford by-election (1938), 59

Page, Graham, 196
Pakistanis in Britain, 154; *see also* Asians
Palmerston, Viscount, 35
Parker Morris standards, 169
Patriotism, 12-13
Paulinelli, Alysson, Brazilian Minister of Agriculture, 116
Pay Board, 54, 184
Peel, Sir Robert, 20, 35, 37
Perez, Alfonso, 117
Perez, Carlos Andrés, President of Venezuela, 116
Perez, Guerrero, 117
Peterlee and Aycliffe New Town, 61-2
Petrie, Sir Charles, 39
Petro-dollars, 202
Peyton, John, 52, 192, 196
Phase III pay policy, 63
Pitt, William, 62
Planning, 27, 28, 101-4, 177-81; agreements, 89-90; approval, 173; appeals, 177; inspectors, 177-8; public enquiry system, 177, 178; regional strategy, 178-9; new towns 178; green belt, 178; conservation policy, 179; London theatres, 179-80
Plowden Report, 28
Pollution, 132, 136; of rivers, 137-8
Ponamarev, Boris, 205
Popper, Sir Karl, 24
Population: drift, 98; changes in cities, 124
Port Talbot, steel development plans, 93-4
Poverty, elimination of, 18, 19, 21, 23
Pravda, 206
Price mechanism, 24
Prices and incomes policy, 54-5
Prices Commission, 54

Private enterprise, 18, 19, 24; *see also* Free enterprise
Profit-sharing, 68, 82-4
Public libraries, 47-8; decline in borrowing, 47
Public sector of British economy, 18, 71; wages bill, 67, 68; borrowing requirements, 68
Puerto Ricans in New York, 124
Punjabis, 158

Racial discrimination, 22, 147, 159
Radicals and radicalism, 34, 37
Railways, 52-3; and Dr Beeching, 28; trade unions, 50, 52-3; and Channel Tunnel, 192
Ramelson, Bert, 205-6
Rate Support Grant, 145, 169
Rates, and local government reform, 184
Raw materials, use and recycling, 210
Reading and reading standards, 47-8
Redcar, steel development plans, 93-4
Redistribution of wealth, 30-1
Reflections on the Revolution in France, (Burke), 15, 16
Reform Bill (1867), 35
Regional policies, 98-101; creation of jobs, 98-100; building of new factories, 100; Exchequer flow, 100-1; political case, 101; need for development agencies, 122
Relativities Board, 63-4
Rent: allowances, 153, 154, 175, 190; control, 56, 175; rebates, 94, 153, 154, 166, 175, 189, 190; of council houses, 56, 166-9, 171, 190; fair rents fixed by tribunal, 189
Rent Act, 153, 154
Richardson, Gordon, 99
Rippon, Geoffrey, 184, 192
Rolls-Royce, 96
Roskill Committee on Third London Airport, 190
Rotherham, study of urban problems, 129
Royal Armoured Corps, 43
Russian Revolution, 15

Salisbury, Marquess of, 25; and Joseph Chamberlain, 36-7
Sampson, Anthony, 25
Sandford, Lord, 196
São Paulo, 116
Scanlon, Hugh, 56, 69
Second World War, 7-10

Selby coalfield, 66
Seligman, Madron and Nancy-Joan, 60
Selsdon Park meeting, 54
Shaw, George Bernard, 11
Sheppard, David, Bishop of Liverpool, 147–8
Shop stewards, 44, 45, 76, 92
Shotton, 92, 93
Simonsen, Mário, Brazilian Minister of Finance, 116
Simonstown, abandonment of British facilities, 204
Slag heaps, removal of, 65
Slum clearance, 200; subsidies, 189–90
Small business advisory services, 134–5
Smith, Adam, 29
Smith, T. Dan, 61
Smokeless zones, 200
Social Contract, 63
Social democrats, 29–30
Social security payments to strikers' families, 67–8
Socialism, 14, 19, 24, 29–31, 38, 94
South-east Planning Strategy, 178
South Harrow, 7, 11
Soviet bloc, 104
Soviet Union, 106, 107, 203–11; and capital markets of the West, 203; armaments, 203–5; naval strength, 204, 207; spy ships, 204; new port in Indian Ocean, 204; expenditure on civil defence, 204; dispersal of industry, 204; base at Murmansk, 204–5; in Middle East and Africa, 205; and British Communists, 205; hostility to Britain, 206; change of diplomacy, 206–7; attempted agreements with Britain and U.S.A., 206–7; worldwide strategy, 207; potential domination of Europe, 208; hostility of China, 208–10
Soya beans, 116
Spanish Civil War, 59
Stansted airport, 191
Steel industry, 89–94, 96, 200, 213; modernization plans, 89–90, 92–3; battle over modernization, 91–2, 193
Stevenson, Dennis, 61–2
Stevenson, Sir Matthew, 195
Stockton-on-Tees, 41–2
Stokes, Donald (Lord Stokes), 88
Suez Canal shares, purchase of, 35
Sunderland, study of urban problems, 128–9
Supervisory boards, 73–7
Surpluses, stock piling of, 211

Suspecting Glance, The, (O'Brien), 17
Switzerland, 80
Sybil (Disraeli), 32–4

Tariffs and tariff reform, 26, 37–9
Taxation, 22, 30, 85; local, 137
Taylor, A. J. P., 38
Technical education, 44
Television watching by children, 48
Thatcher, Margaret, 197–8
Think Tank, 199
Third London Airport, 190–2
Thomas Cook's, denationalized, 94
Three Choirs Festival, 60
Times, The, 86
Tokyo, population of, 124
Tory Party, under Disraeli, 32; *see also* Conservative Party
Trade unions, 35, 41, 50–3, 55–7, 60, 63; and unrestricted collective bargaining, 55; and secret postal or factory ballots, 69–70, 75; and multinational companies, 120; and inward investment, 122–3
Trades Union Congress (T.U.C.), 52, 58, 75
Traffic congestion, 132, 180
Training: of employees' representatives, 76; in inner cities, 133, 137
Transport and General Workers' Union, 50
Truancy, 132
Trustee councils, 78
'Two sides of industry' concept, 72

Ugandan Asians in Britain, 160–1
Unemployment, 23, 25–8, 30, 98, 133, 137, 159, 160, 202–3; among teachers, 47; regional differences, 99–100; among West Indians, 154–6
Union of Construction Workers and Allied Trades, 50
United States, 45, 85, 103, 146, 192, 207; productivity, 40; technical education, 44; partnership with Iran, 110; loan to Labour Government, 113; and Canada, 114; exports to Iran and Venezuela, 118–19; and investment in Britain, 122; deterioration of inner cities, 125–7, 137; young coloured unemployed, 155; lack of land use planning, 177; out-of-town shopping centres, 179; and Suez crisis, 194; future expansion, 201; unemployment, 202–3; growing

United States—*continued*
　disparity of strength with Soviet, 204; attempted agreement with Soviet, 207; alignment with Europe, 208; and Japan, 209

Vandalism on council estates, 166
Varley, Eric, 92
Venezuela, 115–19; development programme, 116–17; investment programme, 117, 118; oil resources, 117; British exports, 119
Victoria, Queen, 31
Vivian Grey (Disraeli), 32

Walker, Peter, education, 7, 31; and Second World War, 7–9; and 1945 election, 10–12; speaks at Conservative Party Conference, 14; encouraged by Leo Amery, 14; national service, 42–3; educational instructor, 43; Lloyd's insurance broker, 45–6; Minister for Housing and Local Government, 50; and trade union leaders, 50–3, 64; Secretary of state for Environment, 50, 52, 61, 65, 90, 128, 129, 172–9, 185, 193, 195–7, 200; and the railways, 52–3; and 1965 Finance Act, 57–8; Secretary of State for Trade and Industry, 45, 65, 72, 90, 109, 111, 129, 134, 195, 197–8, 200, 206; policies for coal industry, 64–6; and employee participation, 72–3; and Giscard d'Estaing, 82–3; relationship between Department and industry, 86–9; and Iran, 105–10, 115; meetings with the Shah, 106–10; and export drive, 110–12; Brazil and Venezuela, 115–16; plans for inner city areas, 128–9; 'Operation Eyesore', 135–7; proposals on council houses, 163–5; housing improvement campaign, 173; London theatres, 179–80; motorways, 180–1; local government reform, 182–7; water industry, 187–8; housing finance, 188–90; Third London Airport, 190–2; Channel Tunnel, 192–3; steel industry, 193; and Selwyn Lloyd, 193–4; ministerial colleagues, 195–9; visits to Moscow and China, 206–10

Walker, Sydney, father of Peter Walker: in H.M.V. factory, 7, 40–1; Conservative Party workers, 9, 10; in Home Guard, 10; keeps shop in Brentford, 41; active trade unionist, 41; deafness and dermatitis, 42

Warehousing near motorways, 180–1
Water industry, 213; reorganization, 187–8, 200
Watergate, 203
Watts, Los Angeles, rioting, 157
Western Germany, 90, 111–12, 115, 123, 192; recovery, 18; and employee participation, 72–8; illegality of closed shop, 73; law on strikes, 74; works councils, 74–5; compulsory arbitration in disputes, 74; industry and the banking system, 85; partnership with Iran, 110; and Brazilian nuclear energy programme, 118; exports to Brazil, 119

West Indians in Britain, 147, 151, 153–8, 160; need for housing advice, 154; need for educational and training programme, 154, 157; birth rate, 154; unemployment, 154–6; obstacles to moving, 156; pre-school period, 157; intelligence tests on children, 157–8; crime, 160

West Indies, 150
Wheat, 116
Wilson, (Sir) Harold, housing legislation, 141
Wood, Wilfred, 149–51
Works councils, 78, 79; in Germany, 74–6; and works assemblies, 75; elections, 75

Yom Kippur War, 202
Youth and community work, 145–6